BLOOD ON THE THISTLE

BLOOD ON THE THISTLE

*A Casebook of
20th Century
Scottish Murder*

DOUGLAS SKELTON

•

MAINSTREAM
PUBLISHING
EDINBURGH AND LONDON

First published in Great Britain 1992 by
MAINSTREAM PUBLISHING COMPANY (EDINBURGH) LTD
7 Albany Street
Edinburgh EH1 3UG

ISBN 1 85158 468 4 (paper)

A catalogue record for this book is available from the British Library

Typeset in Baskerville by
Falcon Typographic Art Ltd, Edinburgh
Printed in Great Britain by
Billings & Sons Ltd, Worcester

*To Margaret, who told me I could do it
and who put up with the nightmares*

From his brimstone bed at break of day,
A-walking the Devil is gone,
To visit his snug little farm the earth,
And see how his stock goes on.

The Devil's Thoughts,
Samuel Taylor Coleridge
and *Robert Southey*

Contents

Acknowledgements

to Martin Jones for his guidance

to Graham Turnbull for his help with a word processor with a mind of its own

to Katie Parry, Lea Browndie and Edward Murphy for their encouragement

to Sandra Lamb and John Mellors for the photographs

Acknowledgments

There are always a variety of sources for a book such as this – too many to list fully. The basics of each story were known to me, the details were furnished by a number of books, documents, magazines, newspapers and individuals.

The main published references are continued in the Bibliography, while much of the detail came from articles in a variety of newspapers including the Glasgow *Evening Times, Glasgow Herald, Daily Record* and the now defunct *Caledonian Mercury* and *Glasgow Courier.* The quotes from detectives and witnesses were those given to reporters at the time. Some names have been changed, others not mentioned at all, in a bid to protect the innocent, as they used to say in *Dragnet.*

Thanks are due to a number of people without whom this book would never have seen the light of day:

to Russell Kyle, Features Editor of the Glasgow *Evening Times,* for his invaluable advice;

to David Robertson, Assistant Picture Editor of the *Sunday Mail,* and Pat Baird, *Daily Record* and *Sunday Mail* Librarian, for their assistance with the pictures;

to Martin Jones for his guidance;

to Graham Turnbull for his help with a word processor with a mind of its own;

to Katie Parr, Lisa Brownlie and Edward Murphy for their encouragement;

to Stanley Leech and John Morton for the photography;

finally, thank God for Glasgow's Mitchell Library!

INTRODUCTION

One of the most commonly used murder weapons in Scotland is the short-bladed kitchen knife. This is because, eight times out of ten, the murderer is known to his or her victim – a husband, a wife, a father, a lover – and the murder itself is committed in the heat of the moment with the first weapon that comes to hand.

Unlike their fictional counterparts, real-life killers do not plot and plan their murders with military precision. Murder in real life is cheap and nasty and messy. It is a sordid and often bloody act committed out of madness, hate, fear and the most destructive emotion of all, jealousy.

For such a small country, Scotland has had more than its fair share of notable murders. In any one year there can be hundreds of killings, from the results of street fights and domestic squabbles to gangland slayings.

Death is the great leveller and murder sweeps across social barriers. No stratum of society is safe from it, although up until the early part of this century it was only of interest to the reading public if committed in the middle or upper classes. The lower ranks of society often fought and quarrelled among themselves, it was no doubt believed, and if they killed each other who really cared? Those unfortunate enough to live in the city's slumlands were deemed as 'non-persons' by the vast majority of their social 'betters' and so were ignored, even in tragedy. In their world death was cheap and murder was cheaper.

Had Madeleine Smith, who may or may not have poisoned her former lover in Glasgow in 1857, been the daughter of a street sweeper rather than a respected Glasgow architect, it is doubtful whether there would have been quite such a furore during and after the trial. Her sexual relationship with victim Pierre Emile L'Angelier was paraded before the court, her frank love letters outraging the delicate sensibilities of prim, proper but hypocritical Victorian society.

Miss Smith was found Not Proven by the Scottish court, as was Christina Gilmour, who in 1844 was accused of murdering her new husband, a moderately wealthy Paisley farmer. The case bore many similarities to the more famous Madeleine Smith story; in both cases arsenic was administered; the accused were attractive young women; and the alleged murderesses walked free.

The depredations of Burke and Hare, who murdered at least sixteen people in Edinburgh in the early nineteenth century, may also have passed forgotten but for the involvement of Dr Robert Knox, an esteemed surgeon who bought the fresh cadavers for dissection in his anatomy classes. That he was aware of his suppliers' business methods is by no means certain, but is a distinct possibility. However, he escaped subsequent punishment just the same. The working-class William Burke slowly choked to death at the end of a hangman's rope while his partner-in-crime, William Hare, turned King's Evidence and ended his days begging in the filthy streets of London after being blinded in a Midlands lime kiln.

But position in society was no guarantee of release, as Dr Edward Pritchard found when he was convicted of murdering his wife and mother-in-law by poisoning. He may also have burned a servant girl to death earlier, when she told him that she was pregnant – and he was the father. The doctor was hung in Glasgow on 28 July 1865 – the last man to be publicly executed in the city.

Poison is no longer fashionable though. This century has seen the rise in firearms and edged weapons as means of murder and as the class divisions became ever more blurred and indistinct, so the public interest in homicide – any homicide – grew. Murder by and of working-class folk, which before would only rate the briefest of mentions in newspapers, was now big news.

The interest in crime-related murder has also grown in recent years, probably through the much publicised activities of the American gangster during the twenties and thirties. At the beginning of the century there was very little so-called organised crime. Now newspapers are filled with reports of kneecappings, shotgunnings and stabbings all over the country, often seemingly connected to the fight to control the lucrative drug markets.

Sometimes, it seems as if the men who commit these crimes have seen too many gangster movies. Cars screech round corners while passengers pump bullets into a man walking in the street; members of rival gangs are executed with a shot to the back of the head; a hooded gunman walks into a busy pub and empties his gun at point-blank range at his target, then calmly walks out again. All of these scenarios could have been orchestrated by Francis Ford Coppolla but have actually taken place in Glasgow within the past ten years.

But there have also been killings related to so-called wars between rival taxi firms and owners of ice-cream vans. Disagreements between the latter climaxed in 1984 when six members of the Doyle family were burned to death in their Glasgow home. Two men were subsequently convicted of the murder but have consistently pleaded their innocence.

In the following pages you will find just a few of those men and women who have sprinkled blood on the thistle of Scotland in the past ninety years. They killed for a variety of reasons, out of greed, fear, anger, lust and hate. Some of the killers are dead now, others are free or are still in prison. The identity of one – the shadowy Bible John – is still a mystery.

And if there is such a place as Hell, then these people have ensured that one small corner will remain forever Scotland.

Douglas Skelton,
Glasgow,
November 1991.

Chapter One

THAT BASTARD
VERDICT

The Not Proven verdict is a curiosity of Scots Law. It is a hybrid, neither guilty nor innocent, prompting Sir Walter Scott to call it 'That Bastard Verdict' after witnessing the trial of Mary Elder in 1828, accused of poisoning her maidservant. Nevertheless, hybrid or no, the verdict can set the accused free without fear of punishment or a retrial.

As is well known, an accused person is presumed innocent until proven guilty. In other words, the Crown is expected to prove the guilt in a case – and the jury must be convinced of that guilt beyond the famous shadow of a doubt. There are times that the prosecution fails to convince the jury, although the fifteen good men and women may still not be sure of the accused's innocence. This is when the Not Proven verdict comes in – as good as an acquittal but still not a public declaration of innocence.

Cynics say that the verdict says to the accused: 'We know you did the crime, but can't prove it, so go away and don't do it again.' But public dissatisfaction with the verdict that criminologist William Roughead termed 'that indefensible and invidious finding' has often forced the accused to leave the country. Others have felt it necessary for one reason or another to change his or her name.

Whenever the controversial nature of the Not Proven verdict is debated, critics often point out that it allows killers to go free and perhaps to kill again. And the example they give of the verdict's fallibility is that of John Donald Merrett.

Born in New Zealand in 1908, the only son of a maritime engineer and the daughter of a wealthy family, John Donald Merrett was brought to Edinburgh at the age of eighteen to study at University.

Although a more than competent scholar with an affinity for languages, young Donnie, as he was known, was a wastrel, a womaniser and a spendthrift. Bertha, his widowed mother, had hoped that under her influence – not to mention her watchful eye – he would bend to his studies and make something of himself.

However, the youth was not interested in books and lectures and was soon cutting classes in favour of more carnal pursuits. He formed a relationship with a dancing instructress at the Dunedin Palais, squandering all his money on her. His doting mother, with more money than sense, gave him ten shillings a week pocket money – a tidy sum in the days when some people earned little more than that for a week's hard work.

He bought his ladyfriend presents and jewellery and together they lived a high life. Merrett soon discovered that ten shillings was not enough to keep him in the style to which he had grown accustomed and so he started to steal from his mother.

These thefts enabled him to buy two motorbikes, one of which had a sidecar for jaunts around the countryside with his girlfriend. But as time went on he found he could not steal enough cash from his mother to support his lifestyle. And so, like many another son before and since, his thoughts turned to murder.

It was on 17 March 1926 that he put his plan into motion. It was stunning in its simplicity and highly effective, for he would never be convicted of the crime.

He and his mother enjoyed their breakfast together as usual on that morning in the house at 31 Buckingham Terrace. Later, as the woman sat at her desk opening her mail and writing her own correspondence, the young man sat watching her from an armchair. He was supposedly reading a book, but his mind was fixed on murder.

Housekeeper Mrs Henrietta Sutherland was working in the kitchen when she heard the loud bang, the scream and the sound of something falling heavily to the floor. She straightened up from the fire she was lighting when John burst into the kitchen and said: 'Rita, my mother has shot herself.'

Together they rushed back to the sitting-room, where Mrs Merrett lay on the floor, blood streaming from her ear, the pistol still lying on the desk. The woman was alive but unconscious.

Mrs Merrett was rushed to Edinburgh's Royal Infirmary where she was placed in a locked and barred room – as an attempted suicide she was treated as a prisoner.

She died on 1 April of meningitis. But before she passed away Donald visited her, ever the faithful son, and kissed her fondly on the cheek. Then he dashed off to Dunedin Palais to take his girlfriend out for the afternoon.

Before she died she managed to give doctors an account of what had happened. She had been writing at her desk, she said, when she became aware of her son standing at her side. She said to him: 'Go away, Donald, and don't annoy me.'

Then, she said, there was a loud explosion and she did not remember anything else until she woke up in the hospital room. She was barely lucid as she made the statement but it was enough to force police to question young Donald.

Strangely enough, without knowing what his mother had said, he told the same story – only his version ended with him turning away from her, hearing the gun go off and then turning back just in time to see his mother slumping to the floor.

He also admitted that the gun was his, and that he had loaded it to shoot rabbits but his mother had confiscated it. He didn't see it again until the day his mother shot herself, he claimed. The investigating officers believed his story – particularly as they found letters on the woman's desk showing that she was overdrawn at the bank.

The housekeeper also gave confused statements, at first saying that the pistol was lying on the desk when she came rushing in, then saying she saw it fall out of the wounded woman's hand. However, police appeared to put the death down to suicide and John Donald Merrett thought he had managed to get away with it.

But, in November 1926, he was arrested for the murder and for forging her cheques to the sum of £457 to meet his increasing expenses. His trial began in February 1927 and almost immediately there was a difference of opinion between the prosecution and experts hired for the defence – and all over the subject of the dead woman's ear, which was produced in court as evidence.

The former, including Scotland's foremost forensic scientist Professor John Glaister, were of course convinced that the nature of Mrs Merrett's wounds pointed to murder; the latter, represented by the famous English pathologist Sir Bernard Spilsbury and firearms expert Robert Churchill, disagreed.

The gun used was a .25 calibre automatic and the bullet had travelled upwards, carving a furrow in the neck beneath and just in front of the woman's right ear. The two factions could not agree over the thorny problem of the powder burns – or rather the lack of them.

When a firearm is fired at close range, between two and eight inches, the propellant – in old ammunition black gunpowder, in

modern material it is based on nitrocellulose and nitroglycerine –
leaves tell-tale marks on the flesh of the victim and even on the hand
of the killer. There were no such burns on Mrs Merrett and so the
prosecution contended that the gun could not have been fired at
close range, as Donald Merrett claimed.

However, Sir Bernard Spilsbury argued that the blood flowing
from the wound could have washed away any trace of the burning.
Suicide, he said, was a possibility.

In his summing up, Craigie Aitchieson, KC for the defence,
described the prosecution's case as stale and attacked the investigating officers in the case, saying that their failure to obtain a
dying declaration from Mrs Merrett was a criminal neglect of 'a
most obvious and imperative duty'.

The Lord Justice-Clerk, Lord Alness, in his address to the jury
of nine men and six women said: 'Was the accused a consummate
actor as well as a villain . . . ? The accused kissed his mother in
the infirmary. Was it the kiss of a Judas?'

The conflicting views of the expert witnesses, the confused evidence of the housekeeper and the attempts by the defence to call
into question Mrs Merrett's state of mind on the day of the shooting
were enough to create sufficient doubt in the jury's mind for them
to return a Not Proven verdict on the murder charge. However,
Merrett's guilt on the forgery charge was clear and he was sentenced
to a year in prison.

On his release, Merrett decided to leave Scotland and went
to live with an old friend of his mother's, a Mrs Bonnar, who
lived in Hastings. She took him in, treated him with kindness –
and he promptly seduced her seventeen-year-old daughter, Isobel
Veronica, running off with her to Scotland, where they were married
in 1928.

By this time, Merrett had changed his name to Ronald Chesney
and was continuing his career as a fraudster. The cash he inherited
from his mother's estate did not last long and he and his wife travelled throughout the country, signing cheques which subsequently
bounced.

Eventually the law caught up with him in Newcastle and he
was given six months in Durham Jail. On his release, he inherited
£50,000 from his grandfather's estate, a tidy sum even now but
one which he promptly squandered on a large house and servants.
He also became a blackmailer and a smuggler and at the end of
the war, after serving in the Royal Naval Volunteer Reserve, he
managed to immerse himself in the murky black market of post-war
Germany.

After doing another term in prison for smuggling women's stockings into Britain, he found himself – as usual – in need of cash. Before he had gone to the continent, Merrett and his wife had set up a trust fund of over £8000, payable to whoever was the survivor. His wife Vera was living with her mother in Ealing; she had taken to calling herself Lady Menzies, in the house in Montpelier Road which they ran as an old folks home.

Merrett/Chesney wanted the money back. Right away. And so he turned again to murder.

He planned the murder carefully while in Germany. He would sneak back into England using a false passport, murder his wife – being careful to make it look like an accident – and then return to Germany. No one would suspect him, he would be able to claim the money and be free to marry his latest girlfriend, thirty-two-year-old blonde Sonia Winnickes.

But his luck was running out. He managed to slip into the country undetected and then sneak into the Ealing house where, on Wednesday, 10 February, he got his forty-two-year-old wife drunk and then drowned her in the bath.

But then everything went wrong. His seventy-two-year-old mother-in-law surprised him as he was sneaking out and he was forced to kill her too. Snatching up a pewter mug, he lashed out viciously at her head, beating her senseless. Then he throttled her to death with her own stockings and wrapped the brutally battered body in a carpet before hiding it behind some wood in a storeroom. He had also taken the added precaution of winding a scarf around her head to prevent the blood from seeping through the carpet.

Vera's body was found by residents on Thursday after they broke down the bathroom door. Her mother was discovered after a search.

Police launched a murder hunt – and when they discovered that Mr Chesney was in fact Donald Merrett, they instantly put him at the top of their suspect list.

Merrett/Chesney, back in what he thought was the safety of Cologne, read about the full-scale search for him. He knew the game was up – he would not be so lucky to escape the noose a second time.

Or would he? On 16 February 1954 he made his way to a wood near the German city and there he placed the barrel of his Colt revolver in his mouth and pulled the trigger. When his body was found most of his face was blown away with only the lower part and traces of his greying brown beard being recognisable. Old scars on his hands aided identification.

The police had no doubt that he killed the two women in London. On examination, they found hairs and fibres on his clothes that linked him to the murder of Mrs Bonnar. However, in letters he had written just before he killed himself, Merrett denied any involvement in the murders. In a note to his girlfriend Sonia, he said: 'When you read this letter I will no longer be alive. I die with your face before my eyes.'

The subsequent inquest in London ruled that Merrett/Chesney was responsible for the deaths of his wife and her mother.

Merrett was buried in a small graveyard in Cologne. A Roman Catholic priest had refused to conduct a service and so the plain oak casket was placed in the graveyard's 'suicide corner'. Apart from cemetery officials, there were only four people at the funeral – a representative of the British Government, a photographer and two women in black.

One of the women was Gerda Schuller, who had claimed that Chesney had married her some years before. The other woman was a companion. A plain cross of brown oak would later be erected over the grave, at the insistence of Gerda Schuller, who also covered the grave with red carnations.

And so ended the remarkable criminal career of John Donald Merrett, alias Ronald Chesney. In his forty-six-year life he had squandered at least two fortunes, defrauded countless companies, been a blackmailer, a smuggler, a black marketeer and a bigamist.

And a triple murderer. Had he not been given the benefit of the doubt at his first murder trial, he would not have been freed to murder again.

It is one of the shames of 'that bastard verdict'.

Chapter Two

SUFFER THE LITTLE
CHILDREN

It was on an early evening in late November 1911 that the two boys were last seen alive. The sky was heavy with rain as the man walked between the two youngsters. The youngest held his hand as they stepped around the muddy puddles that dotted the wet, rutted surface of the road leading from the Midlothian town of Winchburgh, while a chill wind bit deeply into their bones.

The three of them, father and sons, disappeared into the fast approaching night, thunder rolling ominously around the heavens in the wake of the sparking lightning that died as swiftly as it was born.

It was just the sort of night that you would expect foul plots to be hatched and dark deeds to be carried out. And the darkest deed of all was about to be committed. For this man was about to murder his two children.

Patrick Higgins was a labourer whose wife had died the year before. He was in the habit of travelling around the Linlithgow area looking for work and was able to make enough money to keep himself moderately comfortable. But as time went on he increasingly found his two sons John and William a burden and something of a nuisance. At one time the authorities had taken the children from him, charged him with neglect, and placed them in the charge of a Broxburn woman. However, he had failed to keep up the maintenance payments and the big-hearted woman sent the two youngsters back into the care of a man who had no time for them.

On that night in November, Higgins walked into a pub in Winchburgh, soaked to the skin and out of breath. He was also alone. Miner James Daly, who had known the labourer since he was a boy, asked him where the children were.

'In a good home,' the man replied.

He had been on a train to Edinburgh with the lads, he explained, when he met two ladies of quality who had taken a liking to them. The women had expressed an interest in adopting the two boys. They had a nice large house in Edinburgh and the children would be well taken care of.

Higgins gave the boys to them, he said, got off at Ratho station and walked the four miles back to the Winchburgh pub. Daly asked where the women lived, but Higgins said that he had not taken their address, although they had his if they needed to contact him. There was no need to worry about the boys, he assured Daly. They were better off where they were. They were in a better place.

And so life carried on for the hard-drinking labourer. For a year and a half nothing more was heard of John and William Higgins. And no one asked any questions.

Over eighteen months later, on Sunday, 8 June 1913, ploughmen John Thomson and Thomas Duncan were working in the area around Hopetoun Quarry, long since disused and permanently flooded, when one of them saw something floating in the water. It could have been anything. A large piece of wood, perhaps. But as it floated closer they saw it had a vaguely human shape. A scarecrow, then?

But then they realised it was no scarecrow. What they had found floating in the muddy waters of this lonely place was a body. Plucking a large broken branch from the bank, the two men snagged the corpse and dragged it on to the land, where another shock awaited them.

For this was not one corpse, but two – young boys as far as they could tell, tied together by a piece of window cord that snapped as soon as they pulled them ashore. The little bodies were hideously decomposed but still retained their original shape, with what looked like white bone shining through the rotting flesh of their faces and arms. But as the men looked closer they realised that it was not bone they could see glowing in the early summer sun. They did not know what the spongy substance was – all they knew was that it turned their stomachs. The men ran from the grisly sight to fetch the police.

Uniformed officers, the county's procurator-fiscal, Deputy Chief Constable Robinson and police surgeon Dr Cross were among the first at the scene. At first glance they could tell that the children had been in the water for some time but anything further would have to wait for the post-mortem.

After a full examination of the area, the little corpses were taken to Linlithgow. The news of the chilling discovery soon spread throughout the area. Murder is an event in any town or village: in Winchburgh it was more than that. As the *Glasgow Herald* reported, it was the first such case in decades '. . . and nothing so painful and revolting a kind can be remembered as having happened before in the district'.

Meanwhile, the post-mortem was carried out by Professor Harvey Littlejohn with Dr Cross. The youngsters were in an advanced state of decomposition which made it difficult to ascertain the cause of death. From an examination of their teeth they estimated that the younger was three or four years of age, the older six or seven.

The spongy substance cleaving to the little bones which helped retain their human shape was the result of adipocere, or saponification, in which the body's natural fats solidify into a substance that is yellowy-white or grey in colour and of a wax-like consistency.

This condition occurs when a body has been immersed in water or kept in particularly damp conditions over a period of several months. The contact with the water causes a gradual chemical reaction which breaks the body fat into fatty acids and soap. It was this substance that kept the distinctly human shape of the bodies despite the putrefaction of the flesh.

It is rare to find a body in such a condition, even rarer for there to be two similar corpses in such an advanced state. Normally, adipocere is confined to the fatty areas like the thighs and buttocks, but on these two unfortunate youngsters it had extended throughout the entire body.

It had also preserved the contents of the stomach and on examination this showed that the boys had eaten a meal of Scotch broth about one hour before their death. The pathologists could also estimate that they had been immersed in water for almost two years, the remoteness of the disused quarry accounting for the length of time the corpses lay undiscovered.

Having identified the boys through barely visible laundry marks on their clothes, police were able to trace a woman who recalled giving John and William a bowl of soup on the day they disappeared.

On Monday, 9 June – the day after the boys were found – police arrested forty-year-old Patrick Higgins in his rooms in a model lodging house in Broxburn. And the following day, he appeared in Linlithgow court-house where a clerk read out the charge:

'Patrick Higgins, at present in custody, did between August 24 1911 and June 8 1913 at a disused quarry known as Hopetoun

Quarry in Abercorn Parish, Linlithgow, in which there was then a large quantity of water, assault John Higgins, aged about seven years, and William Higgins, aged about five years, his children, did tie them together with a cord, did throw them into the said quarry, and did leave them in the water and did murder them.'

The thick-set man showed no emotion as the charge was read out and remained impassive as he was remanded for trial in Edinburgh High Court and sent to Calton Jail.

The trial began on Thursday, 11 September 1913. Higgins pled Not Guilty to the charge of murder, lodging a special defence that at the time of the killings he was insane and not responsible for his actions.

His plea was based on a claim of epilepsy, which he alleged forced him to leave the army five years before. His counsel called witnesses to him having thrown epileptic fits. These included a quarryman, who testified that he had seen Higgins fall on his back and foam at the mouth several times, and a former police constable who, while on duty in Winchburgh, had seen Higgins in fits on two occasions. However, he did admit that he knew the man to be addicted to drink.

Higgins himself said that he had had no fits since his discharge from the army unless he had been drinking, but Professor Littlejohn, who had examined him in prison, said he could find no sign of epilepsy. There was no trace of mental unsoundness, he said, and in his opinion Higgins was sane.

But counsel for the defence was not to be stymied.

'Might epilepsy not be caused by overindulgence in drink?' he asked the expert witness.

'I think that the effects of overindulgence in drink are often mistaken for it,' replied the learned professor.

Dr Keay, medical attendant at Bangour Asylum said that Higgins was of average intelligence 'for a man of his class'. Like Professor Littlejohn, he could not find any trace of delusions, epilepsy or mental deterioration.

Higgins was found to be both mentally and physically healthy and gave clear and proper answers to questions put to him under examination by physicians. His memory was found to be quite good, except where it came to the events of that stormy night in November 1911.

Broxburn GP, Dr Kelso, testified that he had been approached by Higgins' mother shortly after the man returned from military service in India. She had asked the doctor to see if her son was 'right in the head'. She had awakened in the middle of the night on occasion to find him standing in the room waving a poker in a threatening manner. She said she had also seen him fall out of bed several times and take 'shaking fits'. However, she also had to admit that her son was 'imbibing freely' at this time.

Meanwhile, an Edinburgh doctor who had visited Higgins in Calton Jail said he had found marks of wounds on his head that could well have been caused during epileptic fits.

However, he also noticed that the prisoner did not show any of the depression or anxiety that was expected of a man charged with double child murder. In fact, he seemed to be indifferent, callous and did not fully realise the seriousness of his position.

The Lord Advocate had said that the murders were 'the act of a cold-blooded creature; but callousness, cold-bloodedness and deliberate cruelty were not insanity'.

It was this callousness that the Lord Justice-Clerk, Lord Johnston, touched on in his remarks to the jury. However, he said that the insensitivity did not lie with Higgins alone, but also lay with the parochial authorities who had shown no concern over the whereabouts of the missing boys in the two years since their disappearance.

Describing this as a 'scandal', he asked that the matter be brought before the local government board, saying that the authorities had a duty towards 'the paupers for whom they are responsible'.

Lord Johnston discussed the matter of insanity in his closing remarks. He believed that if a man was in a state of deterioration then he would grow progressively worse. If he was deteriorating two years ago then he would continue to deteriorate today.

The judge confessed that he could not comprehend how a man could be in such a state of mind that he did not understand the effects of his actions one day and yet be quite capable of understanding them two years later. However, he told the jury that even if they regarded Higgins as sane now, they had to consider if there was anything to suggest insanity on the night of the murder.

The jury took one hour and twenty-five minutes to reach a unanimous verdict of guilty. However, they recommended mercy owing to the length of time which had elapsed between the murders and the arrest, and the lack of expert medical evidence as to Higgins' mental state at the time.

Lord Johnston, though, was in no mood for mercy. After thanking the jury, he turned to Higgins and said: 'Patrick Higgins, it is with the greatest commiseration that I find myself called upon to pronounce sentence on you, and that commiseration, I assure you, is felt not only by myself but by the jury who have considered your case and, I have no doubt, by all others present in court.

'You have been convicted of a heinous crime against God, against Man and against nature and for such a crime there is only one penalty of the law. I trust that you will take it to heart during the time that remains to you and that you will repent of this act which you were led to commit and make your peace with the God that made you.'

And on that pious note, he placed the black cap on his head and formally pronounced sentence of death. Higgins heard his fate with the same calmness that he had shown since the day he was arrested, and as he was taken from the court to the cells below he turned and nodded to a friend in the public gallery.

He was to be only the sixth person to be hung in the city since the act of 1868 which abolished public executions. At 7 a.m. on Thursday, 2 October 1913, the Reverend Canon Stuart of St Mary's Cathedral and chaplain to the Roman Catholic prisoners in Calton Jail arrived in Higgins' cell and stayed with the condemned man until the appointed hour. During this time, Higgins made his confession, saying that drink and neglect of his religion had caused his downfall. The canon administered Holy Communion and Mass.

On the stroke of 8 a.m., the priest led Higgins the few steps from his cell to the small yard where the execution would take place. The scaffold itself was a temporary device over a well, the rope dangling from a beam above. The official witnesses included the prison governor, Dr Sydney Smith, representing the police surgeons, and Professor Harvey Littlejohn.

Higgins stepped on to the platform and English hangman John Ellis, brought in for the deed from Rochdale, and his assistant quickly pinioned his arms, pulled a white hood over his head and adjusted the rope.

Once again, the chaplain stepped forward and said: 'Into thy hands I commend this spirit.' And then Higgins cried out, his voice muffled by the hood: 'Lord, justly receive my spirit!'

The hangman then pulled the lever, the trap sprang open and Higgins's body snapped into the well. According to the official report, death was instantaneous. The body hung at the end of the rope for an hour, as prescribed by law, and was then cut down and buried inside the prison grounds.

Outside, a large crowd had gathered to see the black flag hoisted on the prison wall, the sign that the execution had been carried out.

They had begun to gather at 7 a.m., hundreds of people lining the cliffs which overlooked the prison, while on Calton Hill a fiddler played. At 8 a.m., the noise of the masses died down and all eyes turned to the prison wall where, three minutes later, the black flag was raised.

Gradually, the area cleared and the good people returned to their homes or went on to their jobs, satisfied that, with this judicial murder, suitable retribution had been paid by Higgins the child killer.

Hangman Ellis, who received a fee of £15 plus expenses for each Scottish execution, went on to hang Sir Roger Casement for treason in 1916. During his twenty-three-year career as a public hangman he carried out 203 executions in England, Scotland and Ireland and finally cut his own throat with a razor in 1932 after attacking his wife and daughter.

It was said that the guilt he felt in putting to death 203 people, some of whom should never have been executed in the first place, had been preying on his mind.

Assault of a child, whether sexual or violent, is the most heinous act an adult can ever commit. When that assault becomes murder, whether by accident or design, it is doubly horrifying.

As in the Higgins case, many child murders are committed by parents or relatives. Family tensions can reach boiling point and a child is an easy victim. Alcohol and drugs can also play their part.

Children can also fall victim to other children. As I write this, Glasgow newspapers are carrying the tale of a fifteen-year-old girl who has been charged with the stabbing of a sixteen-year-old schoolmate in the playground.

Another common source is the mysterious stranger who preys on the young, invariably for sexual reasons. All children are warned not to talk to strangers and never on any account accept sweets or lifts from them.

The most famous British case is surely the Moors murders, in which Glasgow-born Ian Brady and his Mancunian girlfriend Myra Hindley were convicted of torturing and killing at least three youngsters between 1963 and 1965. Doubt remains as to the true number of victims, but there have been suggestions that they may have been responsible for a total of eight murders.

In 1934, a young girl was found dead near her home in Aberdeen. At first the motive seemed to be sexual. However, as investigations progressed, police realised that the killer had deliberately faked the physical evidence. Whatever the reason, sex had nothing to do with it.

Shortly before 5 a.m. on Saturday, 21 April 1934, the body of eight-year-old Helen Priestly was found bundled in a sack lying in the lobby of her Aberdeen tenement home at 61 Urquhart Road. The child had been missing for fifteen hours, ever since her mother, Agnes, had sent her to a local shop on an errand during her school lunch break.

The young girl had been strangled and wounds around her vagina suggested that she had been sexually violated, or 'outraged' as the newspapers of the time so delicately put it.

The *Glasgow Herald* described it as the 'most brutal crime to have occurred in the north of Scotland for many years', and the murder and subsequent investigations aroused public opinion to fever pitch. Parents feared that there was a sex maniac on the loose who preyed on young children. All strangers were viewed with increasing suspicion, as was any man who lived on his own. The truth, though, lay somewhat closer to the girl's home.

Helen was last seen alive by a five-year-old, Jane Yule, in the street after she had left the shop. The eight-year-old appeared to be making her way home with her loaf of bread.

She did not make it. Somewhere in the 100 yards between the shop and the front door of her home she met her killer.

Later that afternoon, John Priestly, a painter and decorator, returned home to find his wife in an extremely anxious state. He first went to his daughter's school to see if Helen had just gone straight back. However, her teacher told him that the girl had not been seen all afternoon.

The police were alerted and a search party was organised at 7 p.m. that night. They combed the area all night in the pouring rain but there was no sign of the missing girl. By midnight the searchers decided to break up for the night and begin again at first light. Mr Priestly, however, refused to give up the search and continued alone.

Just after 2 a.m. he sat in the kitchen of friend Alexander Parker, who lived across the street at No. 60 Urquhart Road. Mr Parker and his wife gave the distraught father a cup of tea and suggested that he go home and get some rest. Eventually, John Priestly agreed and went home.

At 4.30 a.m. Mr Parker was going across to his friend's flat to help him begin the search again. In the street, he met another neighbour who was going to widen the search pattern by driving around the streets in his car. The two men talked for some time and then Mr Parker walked into the tenement close.

He found the sack almost immediately. Curious, he opened the top and looked inside, reeling back in shock when he saw the dead body of the child.

'I was stunned for a moment,' he said later, 'and don't know what I shouted. Mrs Priestly came running down the stairs, crying "Oh, my bairn, my bairn" and made to lift Helen into her arms, but I stopped her and assisted her upstairs to her house. I then summoned the police.'

The main clue in the case at that time was the sack itself. It was a canvas flour sack with the word 'Boss' printed on it in five-inch-high red letters. They discovered that it was supplied by the Lukena Milling Company of Atchison, Kansas, through their Canadian mills. It had been washed but still bore the faint blue Canadian customs stamp.

However, the bag was rare in Aberdeen. No direct consignment had been sent to the area, although it was thought that a broken quantity may have been received by a local merchant. There was also a small hole on the left corner near the top, as if it had been hung on a hook in a cupboard.

The sack material was dry, as were the dead girl's shoes, suggesting that she had been killed near her home. The fact that the sack was found in the tenement lobby only yards from her front door meant that the girl may have known her killer.

He may even have taken part in the search on Friday night, knowing that it would be disbanded in the early hours, giving him time to place the sack in the lobby at some time between 2 a.m. and 5 a.m. And, despite a false clue by a young boy who claimed he saw her being dragged down the street by a tramp, police felt that only someone who was known to her would have been able to approach her in the busy road at lunchtime on a Friday. Although tall for her age, the fair-haired girl was shy and not likely to talk to strangers. Police decided to focus their search on the immediate area.

Hundreds of people were interviewed within hours of the body being discovered. Officers searched coal cellars and outhouses as well as sheds, dog kennels and other buildings.

Grocers were questioned with regard to the sack. One tradesman in the city centre recalled 'a woman of the poorer classes' calling at his shop on Friday, the day the girl disappeared, asking for a sack. He took one from a bundle in his store and gave it to her. He could not remember if it had any determining marks.

Mothers took to escorting their children to and from school. A feeling of unease gripped the area and the child-slaying was the main topic of conversation when groups of adults gathered at street corners or at close mouths.

On Wednesday, Helen Priestly was buried in secret in a short and simple ceremony at Allenvale Cemetery. Neither the family nor the police wanted to risk any public scenes. Then, early the following morning, came the arrests.

Shortly after midnight, a police superintendent and police surgeon arrived at 61 Urquhart Drive and called at the flat above the Priestlys'. A hostile crowd gathered in the street and uniformed officers had to form a cordon to protect the man and woman who were brought out and placed in the back of a police van. A pathway had to be made to allow the van to leave Urquhart Road and make its way to Lodge Walk Police Headquarters.

However, news of the arrest had preceded them and the arresting officers found another crowd, about 2000 strong, waiting for them outside the police station in Castle Street.

On 4 May, a crowd gathered outside the police court, wrongly thinking that the accused would be appearing before a magistrate. When the doors opened a flood of people rushed in, looking for space in the public gallery.

However, they were in for a disappointment. The accused were to be charged in private in Aberdeen Sheriff Court. Hundreds of people milled about outside the building, hoping to catch a glimpse of the monsters who had murdered wee Helen Priestly, but they too were disappointed: the couple were smuggled into the court building surrounded by several policemen.

The accused were Alexander Donald and his wife Jeannie Ewen or Donald, both thirty-eight years. They were charged with assaulting Helen Wilson Robertson Priestly by seizing her, holding her, compressing her throat, cutting or stabbing her and murdering her. No plea or declaration was made and the couple were remanded for trial.

But on Monday, 11 June, barber Alexander Donald was freed, leaving his wife to face the murder charge alone. At the time of death determined by pathologists, he had been at work and police were satisfied that he knew nothing of the killing.

Helen Priestly had been murdered by her upstairs neighbour. But why? And how did she fake the signs of rape?

Jeannie Donald's trial began in the Edinburgh High Court of Justiciars on Monday, 16 July 1934. The indictment against her

28

now read that 'on August 20 1934 in the dwelling-house occupied by her husband, Alexander Donald, at 61 Urquhart Road, Aberdeen, she assaulted Helen Robertson Priestly, then aged eight years and six months, daughter of and resident with John Bain Priestly, of a separate dwelling-house at 61 Urquhart Road, inflicted serious injury upon her, compressed the girl's throat with her hands or did, in some other method, asphyxiate her and did murder her; and that she previously evinced malice and ill-will against the girl'.

Interestingly, there was now no mention of cutting or stabbing. Obviously, the prosecution now had a better idea how the wounds around the girl's sexual organs had been made.

The indictment also contained a list of 202 productions and 164 witnesses for the prosecution – none of which deterred Mrs Donald from pleading Not Guilty. Ultimately though, there would be no evidence called for the defence. Mrs Donald's only hope of escaping the gallows at this time was for her counsel to discredit the evidence of the prosecution, including the scientific evidence which would prove so important to the Crown case.

Throughout it all, Mrs Donald would remain silent, although she continued to express her innocence. Among the witnesses against her was her own daughter, who testified that a loaf found in her mother's home was not the type usually eaten by the family. It was, in fact, the french loaf bought by Helen Priestly on the day she died.

A shop assistant from the Co-operative bakery where both families shopped confirmed that she had never known Mrs Donald to buy such a loaf.

The court also heard that there was bad blood between Jeannie Donald and Mrs Priestly. John Priestly said that the families never spoke to each other unless to pass the time of day. He said that the wives were not on friendly terms, a dislike that stemmed from an old argument between neighbours in which Mrs Donald had refused to take part.

Mrs Priestly broke down in the witness box when she was asked to identify her daughter's clothing – and again when she was asked what she had seen in the sack on that Saturday morning.

The grieving mother confirmed that she and Mrs Donald did not get along and claimed that Helen had said that the upstairs neighbour had often 'looked after her' – glared at her in the street. Mrs Priestly said that the young girl did not seem to be upset by this treatment from the adult and had decided to ignore the woman.

George Munro, a slater, stated that he heard a scream coming from No. 61 on the afternoon that Helen vanished. He was working in the back court of No. 59 when he heard what he called 'a screech' at about 3 p.m.

Testimony was given by Mr Parker and others that on the morning the body was discovered every door in the close was knocked to arouse the tenants. Only the Donalds ignored the insistent banging at their door. Little Jeannie was in bed with her parents at the time, sleeping in the kitchen as many families did. She said that they heard the noise outside and the knocking, but neither her mum nor her dad made any move to get out of bed.

But as is often the case in a murder trial, it was the scientific evidence that would prove the most damaging. The court heard that police and forensic technicians ransacked the Donald flat from top to bottom, taking ashes from the fire, a quantity of hair found clinging to the leg of a chair, further samples of hair from a bucket under the sink and from one of Mrs Donald's brushes.

They also found what they believed to be bloodstains in a cupboard. However, further examination found this to be false – a point that defence counsel tried to make a great deal out of, but failed.

Professor John Glaister, of the Chair of Forensic Medicine at Glasgow University and something of an expert in the study of hair (see Chapter five) compared the various samples taken from the house with those taken from the head and clothes of the dead girl and from a brush used by the accused in prison.

He found that some of the strands taken from the ashes matched the accused, while others showed the same characteristics as the victim. The hair in the bucket was also similar in all respects to Helen Priestly's. And strands found in the sack bore 'a striking similarity' to Jeannie Donald's hair.

Things were looking bad for the woman. They would get worse. A strain of bacteria found on the girl's clothing matched that found on the washing cloth taken from the Donalds' kitchen. Dr Thomas Mackie of Edinburgh University's Bacteriological Department stated that the bacteria could have come from a common source.

Fibres similar to those found in the house were taken from the sack, while the mysterious hole in the top corner matched holes in other sacks hanging in the Donalds' cupboard.

The defence's trump card were the signs of rape found on the dead girl. Surely this pointed to the killer being male, they argued. But pathologists were adamant that these wounds had been inflicted artificially – possibly by a broom handle, a spoon or even a poker – to create the appearance of a sexual assault.

Lord Aitchison described the case as 'a crime of the utmost unspeakable cruelty and wickedness committed upon a young innocent child who had done no harm to anyone in the world'. He continued: 'There are some crimes which are committed in darkness and gloom. This was one. When this foul thing was done there were only two persons present – the murderer and the victim.'

Although the prosecution had built up a solid body of evidence pointing to Mrs Donald's guilt, no motive had been presented for the murder. Lord Aitchison pointed out that it was not necessary for the prosecution to provide such a motive.

'To your mind, to my mind, no motive could ever be adequate for taking the life of a child,' he said.

As the jury of ten men and five women retired to make their decision, counsel, public and pressmen drifted out into the corridors of the High Court. This is when the tension of any trial is at its height. All the evidence has been heard. All the pleading is over. Now it is up to the fifteen men and women sitting in a small room near the court to discuss, consider, sift and finally decide.

Eighteen minutes after the jury filed out, the bell rang in the public corridors to announce that they were ready to deliver their verdict. All pairs of eyes except one were on the jury as they walked back into the courtroom. Only Mrs Donald stared straight ahead as the foreman stood to announce their decision.

When the Guilty verdict was delivered, Jeannie Donald groaned and slumped in her seat, her head falling against the shoulder of the policeman sitting in the dock by her side. Her moan was so plaintive and so hopeless that many women in the courtroom, including a few on the jury, felt tears welling up in their own eyes.

Lord Aitchison also felt the emotion. While the verdict was being recorded he looked down at the benchtop as he vigorously cleaned and polished his glasses. It was the first time he had been called upon to pronounce the death sentence on any individual, let alone a woman, and it was clearly not a task he relished. However, the law was the law and justice had to be done.

Placing his spectacles carefully on his face, the judge looked directly at the accused, put the black cap on his head and formally announced the death sentence. Jeannie Donald was to be hung in Aberdeen on Monday, 13 August, the first female to be executed in Scotland since Susan Newell in Glasgow's Duke Street Prison in 1923. Like the Aberdeen woman, Mrs Newell had been convicted of child murder, in her case a thirteen-year-old male newspaper seller.

The hangman who dropped Mrs Newell was the aforementioned John Ellis. That execution and the earlier hanging of Edith

31

Thompson, found guilty along with lover Frederick Bywaters of murdering her husband in Ilford in 1922, contributed considerably to the mental deterioration that would lead him to commit suicide.

But Jeannie Donald was not to be on his conscience. On Friday, 3 August her lawyers lodged an appeal, expecting the due process of law to take at least two weeks. However, on Saturday, 4 August, Aberdeen's Lord Provost Mr Henry Alexander darted from his holiday home in Ballater to Craiginches Prison with a very important letter from the Secretary of State for Scotland.

In her small cell, Mrs Donald listened with outward calm as the Lord Provost read out the words she had long hoped to hear.

'With reference to the case of Jeannie Ewen or Donald now being under sentence of death in His Majesty's Prison, Aberdeen, I have to inform you that, after full consideration, I have felt justified in advising His Majesty to respite execution of the capital sentence with a view to its commital to penal servitude for life.'

Jeannie Donald thanked the Lord Provost and sank on to her bed in relief.

On 15 August, two days after she had been due to hang, she was transferred from Aberdeen to Duke Street Prison where she was to serve her sentence. Accompanied by two wardresses, she left Craiginches early in the morning and walked the mile through Aberdeen to the station where they caught the 6.45 a.m. train to Glasgow. All three women wore civilian clothes and no one recognised the woman who only a few short weeks before had been the object of fierce hatred from all quarters of the city.

Ten years later, Jeannie Donald walked out of Duke Street Prison a free woman. To this day, no one knows for certain why she killed the unfortunate Helen Priestly.

But there are theories. There are always theories. According to the post-mortem report, death was due to asphyxiation, apparently caused by compression of the neck. There were finger and thumb prints on the flesh around the throat. However, at least one medical examiner was of the opinion that Helen had choked on a piece of food.

The post-mortem also showed that the girl suffered from an enlargement of the thymus, a chest gland which grows until the child is about two years old and then should slowly shrink in size again. In Helen's case, the gland had not shrunk. Such an enlargement can place pressure on the heart and, according to some medical opinion, leave the child susceptible to sudden death if he or she receives a shock.

The most prevalent theory about the Donald case is that the woman thought Helen was playing a prank – perhaps chapping her door and running away. The woman hid in the lobby and, when the girl went by, leaped out.

The youngster collapsed in fright and the woman panicked, thinking she was dead. She might have dragged the unconscious girl into her house and simulated the signs of rape. The pain of the instrument being forced into her body may have made the still unconscious child vomit and choke. Once again, Jeannie Donald may have panicked as she heard the child gasping for air and to silence her wrapped her fingers around the girl's throat, leaving the tell-tale marks on the neck.

Chapter Three

AMBUSH

With certain notable exceptions, Scotland has been mercifully ignored by terrorists.

Certainly, there were those would-be political reformers of the 1970s, the Workers Party and the so-called Tartan Army. Both groups robbed banks in the early part of the decade with the latter also breaking into explosive stores and army bases to obtain weapons for their proposed insurrection. But there were no Scottish Angry or Red Brigades, no tartan Baader-Meinhoff.

Of course, there were riots during the early days of the trade union movement and when the Chartists were trying to make their views known, while in the years immediately prior to the First World War the suffragettes were particularly active in Scotland.

Between 1912 and 1914 the women's campaigners did not just chain themselves to railings to attract attention to their cause, they also turned to fire-raising, bombing and causing disturbances in public places. Their activities at this time included: trying to set fire to Shield Road Railway Station in Glasgow; putting a torch to Kelly House in Wemyss Bay; placing bombs in Glasgow's City Chambers, the Kibble Palace in the city's botanic gardens, in Belmont Church in Glasgow's West End and even in Burns' Cottage in Alloway!

However, these pale into insignificance by the acts of the IRA. While England has reeled under a succession of bombings and shootings, including the horrors of Guildford, Birmingham and the Harrods outrage, the terrorists have ignored the country north of the border, being content merely to use Glasgow as a supply base – a tradition which dates back to the twenties and thirties and continues until the present day. The most recent example was a massive arms cache found in a flat in Shawlands on the city's south side in 1984.

There was a time though when Scotland was a regular target for bombers, although not nearly as much as England.

34

On 20 January 1883, members of the Fenian Brotherhood – the forerunners of the IRA – tried to blow up Tradeston Gasworks, Buchanan Street Goods Station and Ruchill Canal Bridge. Two gasometers were also blown up at Dawsholm in 1890, injuring a number of people.

And in May 1921, bombers attempted to dynamite a series of telegraph poles outside Darnley in a bid to cut communications between the city, south-west Scotland and Ireland. The attempt failed: when the dust settled, the poles were still standing.

However, it was in the previous month that the Irish problem spread violently to Glasgow streets in an incident that would leave one police officer dead, another wounded and cause riots in the east end.

Glasgow's High Street was strangely quiet as the police van laboured up the steep hill towards the prison gates. It was a warm day in May and the drone of the Black Maria's engine seemed uncommonly loud as it pulled closer to the Drygate turning.

Anyone who did see the van making its way up the street paid little attention. Vehicles just like it made trips regularly from the city's various courts to the dark, brooding prison perched at the top of the hill.

But this one was different. In the cab, the driver and his three colleagues watched the road ahead carefully. Two of the men had been issued with pistols and they nervously gripped the butts of the weapons as they studied each alley mouth and every entrance to every building.

The police officers were expecting trouble. Locked in the back of the van were two prisoners, although there was nothing unusual about that. Both were being moved from the Central Police Court in St Andrew's Square to Duke Street Prison. And there was certainly nothing unusual about that. It happened every day.

One of the men was an insignificant little man charged with indecent assault. The other was a Commandant in the Sligo Branch of the Irish Republican Army. And he made the difference.

The prisoner was Frank J. Carty, alias Somers, wanted by the Irish police for jailbreaking: first from Sligo Jail in June 1920 and then again from Derry Prison in February 1921. He was also wanted for the theft of a revolver in Sligo during November 1920.

Carty had been arrested in Glasgow and had appeared in the Central Police Court before Stipendiary Neilson, who remanded him in custody until the following Saturday when he would be

35

taken back to Dublin. In the meantime he was to be held in Duke Street Prison, only ten minutes away from the court.

Carty and the other prisoner were placed in separate compartments in the back of the police van. They were each guarded by a police officer. The main rear doors were slammed shut and securely locked. Then the black van with its seven occupants set off on its journey up High Street towards the prison.

It was 12.10 p.m. on Wednesday, 4 May 1921. Death was only a few minutes away . . .

Inspector Robert Johnston was perched on the edge of the seat in the van's cabin, his left leg over the edge, his foot resting on the running-board. Beside him sat Detective Sergeant George Stirton and Detective Constable Murdoch McDonald. Both men were armed. They knew they were carrying a man who was an active member of the IRA. The man was certainly dangerous, but he was locked up safely in the rear of the van and unarmed.

His friends, though, were a different matter. The authorities had been warned that they were planning a rescue attempt at an unknown point along the van's route. They were somewhere out there in the streets and they would most certainly be armed.

The van driver, Constable Thomas Ross, slowed down as he neared the crest of the hill, at a section of High Street known as 'The Bells o' the Brae', in order to change gear before turning into the Drygate. The van swung into a man-made canyon, banked on the left by the Corporation Water Pumping Station and on the right by the steep walls of the prison. Directly behind those walls lay the prison's execution yard. Murder was about to be committed in the shadow of the gallows.

It was the perfect place for an ambush. There was no one to see what was about to happen and warn the approaching guards. Any witnesses would be further along the road and too busy taking cover to pay close attention.

The three groups of men rushed out into the street with guns blazing. They completely surrounded the van, one group bursting out of Rotten Row, another from the south-west corner of Cathedral Square, the third from the Cat's Close, a lane running off High Street.

Bullets slammed into the side of the vehicle. The windscreen exploded in a shower of glass, while steam hissed from the ruptured radiator.

Inspector Johnston was hit by one of the first shots, a bullet tearing off the side of his head. He tumbled from his seat but did not die immediately. He sprawled on the cobbled street before pulling himself briefly on to his hands and knees, blood streaming down his face, then collapsed between the tram lines. He did not move again.

Detective Sergeant Stirton leaped out after him. Standing over his superior's dead body, his own gun in his fist, he blasted at the ambushers as they closed in. Bullets whined through the air around him as he emptied his pistol into the throng.

He was joined in the street by Detective Constable MacDonald, who had also drawn his weapon and was firing at the IRA men. The unarmed Constable Ross, meanwhile, was struggling with the nearest attackers, kicking and gouging while doing his best to avoid stopping a bullet.

The attackers at the rear were struggling with the van's heavy doors. They forced the muzzle of a revolver into the lock and tried to blow it off. Amazingly, the lock held, although the bullets ricocheted around the interior of the mobile prison, forcing the four men inside to dive for cover.

Screaming with rage, Carty's would-be rescuers kicked and clawed at the metal, determined to pull the doors open. But still they held and the men finally realised they had been beaten. Later, it would be discovered that the doors had somehow jammed and it would take the combined efforts of a number of big strong Glasgow policemen with all the time in the world to force them open.

At the front of the van, Stirton and MacDonald were still engaged in a fierce gunfight. The sergeant raised his gun to fire another round when a bullet shattered his wrist. The pistol slipped from his nerveless fingers and clattered on to the cobbles. But still the policeman stood his ground, ignoring the blood pumping from his wounded arm and defiantly facing up to the gang.

However, they had had enough. By this time they knew they had failed in their attempt. The element of surprise had been lost and it would only be a matter of time before reinforcements arrived from the prison.

They began to pull back, splitting up again and disappearing into the warren of side streets.

As they dispersed, a woman who lived nearby ventured out of her front door and rushed to help D.S. Stirton. She told him she used to be a nurse and offered to treat his wound until help came.

'Don't mind me anymore, missus,' he said. 'Go and help my chum.' He nodded towards Inspector Johnston, who was lying in a pool of blood in the middle of the road.

Then D.S. Stirton, still ignoring his wound, ran off after a group of ten ambushers who had escaped along Rotten Row. However, loss of blood had greatly weakened him and he soon had to give up the chase.

Other members of the ambush party had rushed down the Drygate and into Cathedral Square, thrusting their guns into their pockets before they merged with the street traffic there and disappeared from sight. A few people who knew what had happened tried to stop them, but a grim look and a threatening word made them step back. These men had already been involved in the murder of one police officer and the attempted murder of others. They would not hesitate to gun down an innocent bystander.

The attack began and ended so suddenly – within three minutes – that most people did not realise what had happened until it was all over. But when they realised that the sound they were hearing was not that of a car exhaust backfiring, the pedestrians nearby ran for shelter in the nearest shops and houses.

Among those taking cover were some children on their way home from school at lunchtime. With the number of wild bullets filling the air, it is a wonder that no one was hurt (bullet holes made during the rescue attempt can still be seen in what is left of the prison wall in the Drygate).

Descriptions of the attackers were scant. In the confusion and excitement of the moment, no one – not even the policemen involved – had more than a glimpse of what was happening.

Constable Ross eventually managed to start up the van again and it limped into the prison yard. D.S. Stirton followed behind, still expecting a second attack, and as the huge prison gates closed behind him, he collapsed. He had lost a lot of blood but would later recover.

During the rest of the day, investigating officers slowly pieced together what evidence they had. Descriptions were taken from the people who had seen the IRA men rush into Cathedral Square after the attack. Two policemen patrolling the area around the prison had noticed a rather large body of men congregating in the square. At the time they had not thought much about it, as large groups of unemployed men were in the habit of meeting in Cathedral Square. But they gave what details they could.

Small pieces of the puzzle began to fall into place. The police rounded up the usual suspects that afternoon. Tip-offs were received, information was gathered.

Meanwhile, news of the attack spread throughout the city. Glaswegians were horrified that such acts of terrorism could be carried out so close to home. The incident was soon dubbed 'The Glasgow Atrocity' by newspapers.

The scene of the attack acted like a magnet to large crowds of people throughout the day. Shock began to give way to anger. Feelings were running high. Tension between Catholic and Protestant heightened and there was a growing awareness among the authorities that the violence might not be confined to the gun battle.

They were right.

Police investigations into the murder of their officer and the attack on the van centred on those areas of the city which housed the majority of Glasgow's Irish Catholic community.

In the mid-19th century, and particularly after the Irish Potato Famine reached its height in 1846, cities on the mainland like Liverpool and Glasgow were flooded by Irish immigrants too poor to make the longer trip to America.

They arrived in Glasgow in their thousands – a total of 43,000 in one four-month period from 1847 to 48. Penniless and destitute, they took work where they could find it and at any price. This did not endear them to the Glasgow working man who saw this source of cheap labour as a threat not only to his income, but also to his religion. Many of the immigrants were Roman Catholics, then a minority in the west of Scotland – there was not even an Archbishop in the city until 1878, when the Pope reinstated the office.

And so Glasgow saw its first signs of the antipathy between Catholic and Protestant. Ferociously bitter and often violent, signs of this hatred are evident to this day in Central Scotland and in some parts of the Highlands – witness the disdain the Protestant islanders of North Uist hold for the Catholics on South Uist, and vice versa.

In 1921, the Orange and the Green did not mix. Glasgow had Protestant areas and Catholic areas and neither the twain would meet – except on those occasions when the Protestant street gangs, like the Billy Boys from Bridgeton, and their Catholic counterparts, the Norman Conks from Norman Street, clashed bloodily.

It was this feeling of mistrust that sparked the unrest on that April night in 1921. The disturbances which followed the attack and subsequent arrests centred on Abercrombie Street, part of the Gallowgate. When police raided some of the flats and dragged a number of people off for questioning – as well as finding a number of firearms – news spread through the area like fire in a dry field. The fact that at least one of those taken for questioning was a priest only fanned the flames.

As well as several flats in the street, detectives visited the Chapel House attached to St Mary's Roman Catholic Church. Questions were asked, a search was made and two people were arrested, one of them a Father Patrick McCrery.

While the police were inside, word filtered out to the locals. When the officers came out of the building with their two charges, they were confronted by a large crowd, ready to turn ugly at the slightest provocation. Stones and a number of harsh words were thrown.

But when police dragged another five men out of their homes in the same street, the crowd demonstrated, in the words of one report of the time, 'their keen indignation'. The majority of the people voicing their complaints were innocent workers who saw the police as tools of the Protestant authorities. They mistrusted the police and believed fervently that a Catholic would never receive fair treatment from them – especially after an officer had been shot dead by IRA men.

However, the arresting officers managed to get away without any real injury. But as the afternoon wore into evening and the evening into night, the crowd grew steadily larger – and more unruly. Any policeman unfortunate to pass the street on patrol became the focus of the crowd's hate and bitterness. Some were lucky to escape with only a few bruises.

Eventually there were over 2000 angry people milling in the streets around the Gallowgate. As their mood grew more and more violent, it was obvious that they would not stop at hurling stones and screaming a few hoarse curses. When a tramcar was attacked, its windows smashed and its passengers terrorised, the police, who had been observing the scene from a distance and waiting for something to break, moved in and cleared the street.

By then the air was pregnant with menace. There was an almost palpable aura of impending violence, a feeling that had swept through the surrounding streets, climbed the stairs of the tenements and taken root in every flat the Gallowgate.

All through the night groups of men and women ran through the streets, screaming and swearing, smashing shop windows and harassing what policemen they could find. One officer was attacked as he went to help a woman who had been hit by a car. As he bent down over the injured woman he was attacked by a group of rioters who kicked him on the head and body. Dragging himself to his feet he ran down the street, the gang on his heels, and leaped on to a passing tram.

Senior officers feared an attack on the Central Police Office, where the suspects were being held. As a precaution, a detachment of soldiers was placed on duty at the station.

In the days that followed the initial attack and the riots of Wednesday night, the police picked up thirty-four people in connection with the murder and rescue bid, plus another twelve for rioting.

During the various searches of flats in the area, police also found a variety of guns, ammunition and explosives, including a haul in a cellar at 74 Abercrombie Street which was at the time the largest quantity ever found in Glasgow. It included thirty-five revolvers, six hand grenades, gelignite, detonators, revolver and rifle ammunition and a bayonet.

Following the arrest of Father McCrery, the then Chief Constable J. V. Stevenston received a number of threatening letters, purporting to be from IRA sympathisers. They claimed that an officer involved in the Father's arrest, a Constable Martin Loudon, was guilty of sacrilege, that he had entered the chapel 'in possession of a firearm to arrest a Catholic priest'. The letters went on to say that Constable Loudon was a marked man and that he would not escape the consequences of his 'rash action'.

However, the Chief Constable claimed that the constable had not been involved in the arrests in any way and that Father McCrery had actually been taken into custody in his own rooms. At no time did an armed police officer enter the chapel.

Ultimately, only thirteen people appeared in Edinburgh's High Court charged with attempting to rescue Carty, alias Somers, and discharging firearms, killing Inspector Johnston and wounding Detective Sergeant Stirton. They were also charged with conspiracy. Each of them pleaded 'Not Guilty'.

Although Detective Sergeant Stirton positively identified nine of the accused, counsel for the defence managed to provide an alibi for each of the thirteen. Police methods of identification were also brought into question with claims that crown witnesses were allowed to see the accused while they were in custody prior to an identification parade.

On 19 August 1921, all thirteen accused walked free from the courts. Six had been found Not Guilty and the other seven had received Not Proven verdicts.

Carty himself had been smuggled out of the city soon after the rescue bid. He was taken to Dublin on the Saturday after the attack, guarded by armed members of the Royal Irish Constabulary.

Inspector Johnston's body was transported from Glasgow to Castle Douglas, the dead man's home town, where he was buried.

Large crowds turned out at both ends of the journey to watch the hearse move slowly past, while Stipendiary Neilson paid tribute to the fallen officer, saying: 'He was of the most blameless character, a man of fine disposition, a quiet, intelligent, energetic and most capable officer.'

He left a wife and two children.

The police had failed to prove their case against the suspects. Perhaps the person who had actually fired the gun which killed Inspector Johnston had escaped police attention entirely. Perhaps he – or she – had fled back to Ireland immediately.

The case remains officially unsolved.

Chapter Four

THE HARD MEN

One of Glasgow's most enduring myths – if one of the least endearing – is that of the hard man. To generations of movie-mad Glaswegians, steeped in the lore of the Hollywood West, he was a man who lived by the 'Code of the Gunfighter'. Tough and prone to swift and terrible violence, the hard man also possessed a nobility that could only be found in the city's darker and meaner streets.

To listen to the stories, he was a one-man 'Magnificent Seven', who would answer the call of a friend in trouble without thinking, wading into a fray without fear of physical danger. He would be called upon by neighbours to settle a dispute with a grasping landlord, or to dissaude a wayward son from a destructive path. He would fight, it is said, out of a sense of honour, for the sheer hell of it or, Glasgow being Glasgow, over religious differences. He was a streetfighter who kow-towed to no man and who never hurt anyone undeservedly.

This is an appealing portrait and it is tempting to accept its heavy romanticism as the truth. Sadly, it is a far from accurate picture. Certainly, there were men who worked hard five or six days a week and who lived only to get 'tanked up' (roaring drunk) in the pub or shebeen (illegal drinking houses) on Friday and Saturday night. These men may also have found themselves involved, either through accident, design or just sheer ill-nature, in a brutal bout of bareknuckled fighting before making their way through the dark and gloomy streets to their tenement homes. But, for every one of them, there were ten lesser men who disdained the 'square go' – a no-holds-barred, knock-down, drag-out fight without the use of weapons – in favour of a short, sharp affair in which a knife, razor, bayonet, broken bottle or similar edged implement was brought into use.

These men – not so much hard men as 'chib' men or razor kings – were often graduates of the notorious razor gangs from the twenties and thirties. They lived on the edge of crime, acting as strong-arms in robberies or as enforcers for the money lenders who fixed themselves like leeches on the so-called slum communities – and who still operate to this day in the city's housing estates.

Some of them operated crude extortion schemes, working in concert with fellow ex-gang members to squeeze money out of local shopkeepers. These were the bullies and the braggarts; many were alcoholics who, when they had no innocent victims to pick on, would practise their 'art' on their wives, girlfriends or their children.

Patrick Carraher was the first of such men to receive national notoriety. He was an alcoholic who suffered from a psychopathic personality which manifested itself in a persecution complex and what one psychiatrist, described as 'a gross lack of moral and social responsibility'. However, unlike others of his kind, Carraher never at any time aligned himself with any gangs. As a child he was a loner and he remained that way throughout his adult life.

Eventually, this slight, sinister man would be dubbed 'The Fiend of the Gorbals', even though the murder for which he was finally hanged was committed in Townhead, on the other side of the river from that notorious slum district.

Carraher was born to decent, hard-working parents in the Gorbals on 19 October 1906. Four years later, his mother died and his father remarried. From the start, Carraher and his stepmother did not get along. He was a surly and moody child and no amount of beatings from his father would change his temperament. If anything, they made him worse until by the age of fourteen he took to staying away from home for long periods, being seduced by the twilight world of the area – a world where swift violence was commonplace and crime was the norm. He realised that easy money could be had by someone who was good with his fists and willing to use them and when he was seventeen years of age he was sent to prison for fourteen days on an assault and theft charge.

Three weeks after his release he was back in court again, this time for simple theft. From then on he was seldom out of prison on various charges of theft and assault. In fact, from his seventeenth year until his fortieth, when he was executed in Barlinnie Prison, Carraher received prison sentences amounting to fourteen years plus another three-year stint in Borstal – a total of seventeen years in penal institutions, leaving him only six as a free man. But during those six he battered, slashed and hacked an untold number of people and killed at least two.

In prison, he refined his violent skills until he had developed a considerable reputation in the underworld as a knife-man. He used a blade – any blade – often and he used it well, drawing it speedily from a place of concealment and lunging swiftly at his target.

As he grew older, he began to drink to excess, the alcohol making his already nasty temperament even more vicious. He would pick fights with anyone, sometimes to prove his growing reputation as a hard man, sometimes merely because it was expected of him. Carraher had no real friends, although on a number of occasions he would 'mix it' for the sake of others. Ultimately, it would be this hunger for a fight, coming to the aid of a partner-in-crime during a street brawl, that would lead him to the gallows – the man he was helping inevitably scampering away from the trouble like a frightened rabbit.

Before that fateful night in 1945, though, Carraher would murder another man and receive a three-year prison term, the charges being reduced to culpable homicide due to lack of evidence.

On 13 August 1938 a drunken Carraher, by then a notorious figure in the Gorbals, was staggering through the streets. He had been drinking heavily all day and suddenly felt the need for some female companionship: in particular, Katie Morgan, with whom he had enjoyed a brief affair which had only recently ended. He met eighteen-year-old Margaret McNicol and drunkenly asked her to take a message to his one-time girlfriend. The girl, knowing that Katie Morgan had no particular desire to see or speak to Carraher ever again, refused and ran to the waiting arms of her boyfriend, James Durie, a nineteen-year-old window cleaner, who was then walking down the street.

Carraher was none too pleased at having his instructions ignored by a slip of a lassie and followed the couple, grabbing the girl's arm. Durie, already in possession of the other arm, held on and there followed a fierce tug-of-war between the two men with the hapless young girl in the middle. Eventually, Margaret managed to break free and ran a short distance down the street, leaving her boyfriend to face Carraher. And his knife. Carraher's first impulse was always to draw his blade and he saw no reason to resist that impulse on this occasion. The young man ran off, leaving the notorious knife-man swaying and cursing alone in the street.

However, that was not to be the end of the affair. Honour was a powerful force in the Gorbals at that time and the Durie family had lost a considerable amount of face when young James had fled from the knife-wielding Carraher without even striking a blow. Discretion may have been the better part of valour, but the Durie family had no desire to see any of their members branded a coward by the likes of Carraher.

So, accompanied by his older brother, John (twenty-four), his brother-in-law Charles Morgan (sixteen) and a family friend, Peter Howard (twenty-three), James Durie searched the streets for Carraher, determined to challenge him to a 'square-go' to be carefully supervised by his companions. They eventually found Carraher not far from Gorbals Cross in Ballater Street, where James issued his challenge. Carraher declined the invitation, stating that he was in no condition to fight, which was probably true. However, this did not prevent him from hurling a few choice epithets at the Durie clan.

Matters might have ended there, if twenty-three-year-old soldier James Sydney Shaw had not happened upon the scene. He, too, was somewhat the worse for drink, having returned home on leave and was out enjoying himself on the town. He asked if this was a private argument or could anyone join in. Perhaps he was trying to cool what was turning into a heated situation, or perhaps he was another would-be hard man looking for a scrap. Whatever his reasons, he found himself bearing the brunt of Carraher's foul-mouthed tirade and did not ease the tension by accusing the drunken knife-man of 'speaking like an Englishman'. It was an unfortunate choice of insult as no Scotsman wishes to be associated with his neighbours south of the border.

A police officer walking his beat tried to break the argument up, telling the participants to 'take a walk'. The Durie clan began to move away, realising that their honour would not be salvaged this night, while Carraher and Shaw both continued to aim insults at each other.

Then, as one of the Durie boys would later tell the court: 'Suddenly, I heard a scuffle. When I turned round, Carraher had disappeared and Shaw was holding his neck.'

Blood was spurting from the wound in the soldier's neck as he staggered to the corner of Thistle and Ballater Streets where he collapsed. Only Peter Howard remained to try and help the injured man as he dragged himself to his feet and ran towards Gorbals Cross, leaving pools of blood on the pavement as he moved. Police would later disguise these with sand.

He lost a great deal of blood in his 150-yard journey from the scene of the slashing to where he finally slumped unconscious in front of a cinema beyond the railway bridge that carried trains to St Enoch's Station. Here a policeman rushed to his side, trying to staunch the flow while he waited for an ambulance to arrive.

Shaw was rushed to the city's Royal Infirmary at the top of the High Street but he died soon after being admitted. Carraher, meanwhile, had slipped into the night and Peter Howard was arrested for Shaw's murder. He had been seen in the area of the slaying, after all, and he did have blood on his clothes.

News of the killing spread through the Gorbals like wildfire. Carraher heard that Howard had been arrested and nobly declared that he would hand himself in to the police. The girl he was with asked him why he had stabbed Shaw and Carraher said the soldier had been 'very cheeky'.

'But I'll not let Peter Howard swing for it,' he continued. 'I'll give myself up.' Then off he went, almost cheerfully, apparently to hand himself in at the police station and confess to the murder.

In the end he could not bring himself to do the decent thing. What he did do was throw the knife into the dark and muddy waters of the River Clyde, where it probably still rests to this day.

Later, the police came for him, by then satisfied that Howard had not delivered the fatal knife blow. The street telegraph had been buzzing with Carraher's involvement in the fatal scuffle and he was found sitting by the fire in a flat in Florence Street by Detective Sergeant John Johnstone.

Carraher looked at the detective through his cold, heavily lidded eyes and said: 'Is he dead right enough? Well, I was expecting you. I'll give you the full strength of it.'

However, at his trial, a case was made in Carraher's favour. There was no doubt that he had actually struck the killing blow, but the fact that no one actually witnessed the slashing worked against the Crown.

The question of how drunk Carraher was at the time was also raised. According to the courts, intoxication could be taken into view when considering if an act was committed with 'full malicious intent' or with 'culpable recklessness in a minor degree'.

The jury took two hours to find Carraher guilty of Culpable Homicide. He had avoided the gallows but would not avoid a prison sentence. The judge, Lord Pitman, sternly pointed out that 'drink is no excuse whatever for assault resulting in death' and promptly sentenced him to three years in Barlinnie.

While he languished in prison, the world outside was changing. In September 1939, Britain declared war on Nazi Germany and most able-bodied men either volunteered for duty or were conscripted. When the United States entered the war in 1941, Glasgow became the magnet for their armed forces, many of whom were based within easy reach of the city. Soldiers, sailors and airmen seeking the high life before being posted to one of the various theatres of war were not disappointed with what they found in the city.

Glasgow became the entertainment centre of the west of Scotland. Dance halls, public houses, cinemas and night clubs enjoyed a boom period – as did what was left of the Glasgow underworld. For with a war comes what the eastern Europeans call 'the invisible hand' – the black market.

In a country reeling under strict rationing, the black marketeers could lay their hands on just about everything from petrol to nylons, while there was also a nice turnover on illegal alcohol and prostitutes. The black-outs also acted as a useful cover for these illegal enterprises while a much reduced police force also proved a boon.

It was into this heady atmosphere of profiteering that Carraher emerged from Barlinnie, immediately realising that a man could thrive in this new Glasgow – as long as he was not too choosy as to how he made his money.

Many of his old acquaintances were already abroad, fighting the Germans or the Japanese. Many of these hard men were proving themselves to be more than able soldiers, although taking none too easily to the regimented life. Some would return from the war totally sickened by their experiences, their desire to fight satiated by the blood and horrors of warfare.

Carraher himself was declared unfit for service, thanks to a weak chest and a stomach complaint. He decided to move closer to the city centre and based himself in Townhead, the oldest section of Glasgow. Here, amid the winding streets and dark lanes that cut through the crowded tenements, the denizens of the twilight world could exist and operate happily and relatively free from the prying eyes of the police and authorities.

But the violent streak that ran deeply through Carraher's character was always determined to rise to the surface and it was not long before he was once again involved in 'rammies' (fierce street fights).

By this time, he had found the love of his life, one Sarah Bonnar, with whom he shared a flat. He also forged a bond with her brother, Daniel, and together the two rampaged through the area, fighting, stealing and terrorising.

In February 1943 the two embarked on what one contemporary chronicler described as 'an orgy of violence', culminating in Carraher threatening three women with a razor and then attacking another man in George Street, punching him, kicking him and finally slashing him. This man was lucky, however: Carraher's aim was off and he managed only to slice through the lapels of the man's jacket, drawing just a little blood. For this, Carraher was given another three years in jail.

Carraher's days were numbered – and it would be his friend Bonnar who would cause his downfall.

On Friday, 23 November, the three Gordon brothers left their home at about 4.30 p.m. intent on enjoying an evening's drinking. The family was known to the police although they were by no means criminals. Like many men in the Townhead and Gorbals area they enjoyed a good fight. In this regard their paths had crossed before with those of Carraher and Bonnar. Later that night their paths would cross again – and John Gordon would die, blood spurting from a four-inch wound in his neck.

The forty-year-old regular soldier had served for twenty years with the Seaforth Highlanders and was at the time on demob leave. He had been captured by the Germans at Dunkirk and had spent the remainder of the war in a POW camp. His brother Joseph was a gunner on leave from Gibraltar.

The brothers first went to a flat at 139 McAslin Street, Townhead, where their sister lived with her husband, Duncan Revie, an army deserter on the run from the authorities. Like many another deserter, he went into hiding in the warren-like streets of Townhead, confident that he would never be found.

At 5 p.m. the four men walked into the Coronation Bar in McAslin Street and drank steadily there until 7 p.m. when they moved on to Cameron's Public House in Rottenrow. There they stayed until closing time at 9.30 p.m., by which time Joseph and Edward Gordon had drunk themselves senseless, slumping unconscious over a table littered with empty beer and whisky glasses.

At some time during the drinking session, John Keatings joined the company. He was another deserter, this time from the navy, and like John Gordon and Duncan Revie proved to have a strong head for drink. The three men weaved their way out of the bar, drunk as lords and itching for trouble.

They would find it.

Three-quarters of an hour earlier, Carraher and Bonnar had left another pub in Rottenrow, Thomson's Public House, also somewhat the worse for drink. They had spent most of the afternoon and all evening drinking and had joined up with Thomas Connolly Watt, known in Townhead as 'Wee Watt'. Making their way back to Bonnar's flat in Rottenrow, they met some women and decided to have a party. At some point, Bonnar decided to go out and buy some more drink and find some other revellers.

What he found was the Gordon clan. He bumped into the drunken crew outside Cameron's and the old grudge was revived. It was Keatings who first stirred up the trouble, announcing that he was willing to take on all comers, particularly Bonnar about whom he made some disparaging remarks.

Bonnar, his honour insulted, took off his jacket, laid it on the pavement in front of him and displayed his willingness for a 'square go'. However, when both Keatings and Revie lunged at him, he took to his heels down the street, leaving his jacket lying on the road. Keatings and Revie ran after him, catching up with him. A few blows were struck but Bonnar managed to get away without any serious damage.

Once Bonnar was out of sight, Keatings decided that he was in no condition for any further activity and bade his farewells to Revie and Gordon. He disappeared into the darkness of the November night, unaware that he had set in motion a chain of events that would end in murder.

Meanwhile, Bonnar had run to his sister's flat in College Street. There he armed himself with an axe and, donning a woman's costume jacket to keep out the winter chill, rushed back to the street to find the Gordon clan again. He was armed now and felt confident that he could take on all three. If they wanted to mix it, he was just the fellow to satisfy them.

His undignified flight down the street after the first skirmish had been witnessed by a woman cleaning her windows. Recognising Bonnar, she felt it her neighbourly duty to tell his sister Sarah, who in turn told Carraher, still enjoying the party in the Rottenrow flat.

Wordlessly, Carraher donned his jacket and made for the door, accompanied by Wee Watt. On their way down the tenement stairs, Carraher showed Wee Watt a wood carver's chisel in his pocket, running his thumb along the sharp blade, saying ominously: 'This is the very tool for them.'

In the street they met the strangely dressed Bonnar who told them what had happened. Together, they set out to find the Gordons and exact just revenge for Bonnar's humiliation. They came upon Gordon and Revie at the intersection of McAslin and Taylor Streets. Revie immediately went for Bonnar who, after another brief scuffle, decided to take flight again, closely followed by his opponent. That left Carraher and John Gordon.

Witnesses later said that they heard men shouting and came upon the pair grappling at the ill-lit corner. They said they saw one man

– Carraher – 'punching' the other – Gordon. He fell to the ground, blood streaming through his fingers from a deep wound in his neck. Carraher meanwhile had slipped like a shadow into the darkness, leaving another victim lying in a pool of blood on the city streets. A passer-by tried to help the wounded man while another attempted to hail a taxi to take him to hospital. Meanwhile, the drunken Revie appeared back on the scene having lost Bonnar in the twisting streets and alleyways. For some reason, probably making sense to his alcohol-fogged brain, he decided to take his brother-in-law home and, pulling him to his feet, proceeded to carry him up to the second-floor flat at McAslin Street.

However, by this time a taxi had been hailed and two witnesses managed to wrestle the injured man from Revie's drunken clutches, then took him to the Royal Infirmary. But it was too late. Gordon died just a few seconds after a harassed doctor had conducted an initial examination.

Word of the murder circulated swiftly around the area, eventually reaching the ears of Bonnar and Carraher, by then back in the Rottenrow flat. The news was brought to them by a taxi driver and a friend, a complete stranger to Carraher.

When he heard the news, the killer took the stranger into another room and gave him the chisel, instructing him to dispose of it. The man knew of Carraher's reputation and, no doubt in fear of this cold-eyed killer, did as he was told, breaking the wooden tool in two and dropping the halves down separate drains in the High Street.

The fracas had been witnessed by a number of people and it did not take police long to identify the various parties involved. In the early hours of the following morning, John Johnstone – the very same officer who arrested him on the previous murder charge and who was now a detective inspector – arrested Carraher as he lay in bed with his common-law wife, Sarah Bonnar.

It was all over for the man the press called 'The Fiend of the Gorbals'. Bonnar turned King's Evidence, determined not to be dragged down with Carraher over what he saw as only a street fight. Wee Watt told the court about Carraher's remarks on the stair well. Witnesses identified him as the man who had fatally 'punched' Gordon during the fight.

Defence counsel tried desperately to plead diminished responsibility on behalf of their client, who sat through the three-day trial showing no emotion at all. However, two distinguished psychiatrists both testified that although Carraher displayed psychopathic tendencies, he could distinguish between right and wrong and was fit to plead.

Dr Angus McNiven, physician superintendent at Glasgow's Royal Mental Hospital in Gartnavel said that Carraher had described the events of that night in a 'jaunty' manner 'as if he were just describing a frolic'. He said that the accused's attitude was 'very abnormal' and that he had a gross lack of moral sense and social responsibility.

Professor William Blyth of the Anderson College of Medicine agreed with his colleague, saying that Carraher displayed a psychopathic personality and had a persecution complex. He pointed out that Carraher was in the habit of checking cupboards and suddenly opening doors, convinced that people were hiding behind them, waiting to jump on him.

The jury remained unimpressed by descriptions of Carraher's mental state and took only twenty minutes to find him guilty. The judge, Lord Russell, sentenced him to be 'hanged by the neck upon a gibbet until you be dead and your body thereafter to be buried within the walls of the said prison and order your whole moveable goods and gear to be escheat and inbrought to His Majesty's use; which is pronounced for Doom'.

At 8 a.m. on 6 April 1946, after losing an appeal and having a petition for reprieve dismissed, Patrick Carraher was hung in Barlinnie Prison.

As the notice of execution was pinned to the door, only one person showed any emotion. Sarah Bonnar read the typewritten notice with tear-filled eyes, then turned and slowly walked away from the prison gates.

Carraher was only the second man to be executed in Glasgow in eighteen years. The first had been John Lyon, hung by Albert Pierrepoint in Barlinnie in February 1946 for the murder of John Thomas Brady during a gang fight in October 1945. The last execution prior to that was in Duke Street Prison on 3 August 1928, when George Reynolds, a vagrant, was hung for the murder of a fireman.

Between 1928 and 1946, the newspapers were filled with much controversy over the introduction of mixed juries. It was felt that women were too delicate to find men guilty of murder and so consign them to death by hanging. However, the guilty verdicts on Lyon and Carraher showed that the fairer sex did indeed have the stomach for executions.

Had Capital Punishment not been abolished in 1965 (at that time only a temporary measure: it was not made permanent until 1969) another Gorbals hoodlum would almost certainly have faced the gallows.

Jimmy Boyle broke Patrick Carraher's record of being the only man to face murder charges twice in Glasgow's High Court. This baby-faced hard man was three times brought before judges on homicide charges. On each occasion, there were accusations of witness intimidation; threats were made and gelignite bombs were thrown. However, on the first two charges at least, these suspicions could not be proved – and neither could the murder charge. Boyle was subsequently lionised by his peers as 'The Man They Could Not Hang'.

But, on the third, Boyle was found guilty and sentenced to life in prison – and, for the first time, the claims that witnesses had been 'got at' were proven in a court of law, with Boyle's lawyer eventually receiving an eight-year sentence.

Boyle's early life is one of the utmost barbarity, filled with gang fights, stabbings, slashings and beatings. In 264 blood-spattered pages of his autobiography *A Sense of Freedom*, Boyle often quite graphically describes not only some of his own quite vicious acts but also the brutality he experienced at the hands of the notorious prison 'batter squads' – groups of prison officers whose delight it was to beat up troublesome convicts.

He also maintains his innocence of the murder charge for which he was finally jailed, suggesting that he was framed by the police who were determined to have him off the streets. The evidence against him, though, appeared to be unimpeachable.

He speaks warmly of his childhood in the Gorbals, talking frankly about the attractions a life of crime held for an impressionable youngster, desperate for the adulation of his peers and the recognition of his heroes – in Boyle's case the local hard men, thugs and crooks.

Jimmy Boyle was born in May of 1944 into a family already well acquainted with violent crime. His father, Tommy, was a notorious figure in the Gorbals of the thirties and fourties, thanks to his membership of the Bee Hive Gang, a street gang which not only indulged in battles with rival gangs but also organised itself into a criminal fraternity, committing robberies and blowing safes.

After the Bee Hive Gang disbanded at the end of World War II, Tommy Boyle and his friends continued in their criminal ways. He died when young Jimmy was five, leaving his wife Bessie to bring up the four children. Gradually, the young Boyle was drawn into the twilight world of the Gorbals underworld. His heroes were the streetfighters who congregated in the many pubs in the area and he and his young friends did everything they could to be noticed by these men.

Eventually, they began to steal, small amounts of money at first, then graduating to the 'big time': breaking into shops and selling the stolen goods to households in the area. This was common practice in those days and even those many families who were honest – but painfully poor – were involved in what amounted to mass reset.

During this period Boyle revelled in the admiration of his schoolmates, an admiration that grew after his first arrest at the tender age of thirteen for breaking into chewing-gum machines.

After spending four hellish nights in Larchgrove Remand Home, a young offenders institution in the East End, a much chastened Jimmy Boyle appeared in the Central Police Court and received two years' probation. During the hearing he promised to be a good boy and to stay out of trouble. At the time, he said, he meant it: his experiences in Larchgrove had been terrifying and he had no desire to return there.

This resolve did not last though and he was soon back to his old thieving ways until he was arrested again, this time for breaking into a hut which usually housed show pigeons. On this occasion the hut was empty but Boyle and his accomplices were caught in the act by police. Back he went to Larchgrove, for two weeks, once again promising to go straight on his release.

However, by this time he had formed his own street gang, which he called 'The Skull', and was throwing himself wholeheartedly into a series of gang fights and struggles over territory. He discovered his own propensity for violence during a so-called 'dummy fight' with an older gang leader.

Boyle and his cronies had been recruited by a gang of older boys to help them in a fight with rivals. However, when the proposed battle did not take place, the leader invited Boyle to take part in a 'dummy fight' with him. Boyle agreed and proceeded to beat his opponent senseless using a set of knuckledusters with which he had been supplied. Boyle enjoyed the increased adulation he received, both from his friends and the girls who hung around the gangs.

A further spell in Larchgrove failed to quell his increasingly rebellious spirit. If anything, it only served to strengthen it when he found that his reputation for being a crime 'king pin' had spread to the young inmates. Even on the inside he was treated to hero-worship.

The first time he used a blade on another human being was during a fight with a rival gang from Castlemilk, a housing estate to the south of the city. Boyle was attacked by a rival gang member wielding a hammer and he retaliated with a butcher's knife, slashing the youth viciously on the face. Once again, this act served only to strengthen his burgeoning reputation.

Eventually, 'The Skull' transformed itself into the 'Wild Young Cumbie' – and Boyle found himself in an approved school for three years for stealing a cash box from the annual Christmas carnival in the Kelvin Hall. Just as he had been leaving the building he was spotted by detectives who knew him. They stopped him for routine questioning and found the stolen cash box.

Boyle said in his book that his time spent in the St John Approved School provided him with criminal connections that he used when embarking on an adult life of crime. Among the inmates was Larry Winters, a Glasgow youngster who would share many of Boyle's experiences in Peterhead and Inverness prisons before taking his own life in the experimental Barlinnie Special Unit while he and Boyle were 'guinea-pig' prisoners.

During a leave of absence from the school, Boyle ran away. He made his way for the first time to London – a trip he would often make when life grew too hot in Glasgow. Eventually he was picked up by London Police for trying to steal a transistor radio from a shop. He served the remainder of his sentence in St John's and returned to London on his release, becoming involved in the drug scene – mixing with some highly dubious characters and – of course, stealing.

Once back in Glasgow, Boyle lost no time at all in landing himself in trouble and ended up in Borstal on a shop-breaking charge. He made more criminal contacts here and learned new tricks, tricks which he would put to use once free.

On the streets, violence once again flared, with Boyle and his friends in the centre of it. A feud with another gang led to a particularly bloody confrontation in Crown Street, a battle in which a number of innocent people were injured.

Battles such as this were becoming increasingly more common in the Glasgow of the sixties with the resurgence of the gangs in the city's outlying housing estates like Castlemilk and Easterhouse. Harold MacMillan may have told the nation that they had 'never had it so good', but this was not enough for dissolute youths in Glasgow who, whether they were spurred on by religious differences, tribal loyalties, alcohol or just a need for violent action, would face each other on city streets.

Such conflicts were not the invention of the sixties' street gangs, nor were they new in the days of the razor gangs in the twenties and thirties. In fact, Glasgow had a tradition of gang clashes going back to the late 1830s.

Boyle and others were arrested for their part in the Crown Street incident and, while on bail in January 1963, Boyle was badly beaten up by members of the rival gang.

Realising that life was proving too hot for him in his home town, Boyle made a return trip to London, setting up a money-lending racket, but soon found himself in Wormwood Scrubs for assaulting a police officer. When it was learned that he had jumped bail in Glasgow, he was taken back to face trial and was jailed for two years.

This time he was not sent to a remand home or an approved school. Boyle was eighteen now and had hit the big time. He was to serve his two years in Barlinnie Prison.

His term in prison affected him deeply, although he presented a 'hard' face to both prison officers and fellow convicts. He did not enjoy being penned up in a small room for hours on end, but at that time did not consider giving up his violent, criminal activities. He would do his time, keep up his hard man façade, but that did not mean he would enjoy it.

Ultimately though, he could not keep out of trouble even when inside. Boyle's life is characterised by a defiance of authority, whether it be teachers, police or prison officers and it was while doing his first stint in the Bar-L, as the prison is affectionately known, that he struck his first 'screw' and ended up in solitary confinement. It was also the first time he was severely beaten by a batter squad.

On his release, Boyle moved his criminal activities from his old Gorbals stomping ground to Govan, where he became involved with the tallymen (money-lenders) and the shebeen owners.

Money-lending had always been prevalent in the poorer Glasgow areas. The tallyman would lend cash, with no questions asked, to anyone who wanted it. No collateral was needed: as the saying goes, the borrower's body was his collateral.

The money was borrowed at usurious rates, at least twenty-five per cent. For instance, if someone borrowed ten pounds, they would be charged £2.50 interest. If at the end of the loan period – generally a week – they could not repay, a further 25 per cent was added on. After seven days the debt would then be almost £16. And for each additional week, another twenty-five per cent would be added. Some people only managed to pay off the interest, leaving the original debt still outstanding.

Consistent failure to maintain payments could result in the borrower being visited by the tallyman's heavies, who would issue a reminder – perhaps in the form of physical damage. Stories of their brutality are rife in Glasgow: one rumour even contended that heavies once crucified a man to the wooden floor of his home; another that they smashed their way into a house by hacking at the front door with an axe.

Boyle paints a very rosy picture of the practice in his book, claiming that if anyone could not pay all they had to do was explain their difficulties to the money-lender and new arrangements would be made. Very seldom, he said, was a borrower beaten up, violence being reserved only for those 'toe-rags' who borrowed money with no intention of ever paying it back. Reports of beatings and terrorising were inventions of the police and the press, he claimed.

But stories of beatings persisted although police could never make a charge stick. Witnesses were then – and are still – loath to testify against the tallymen – also known under the American nickname 'loan sharks' – who still operate widely throughout the country.

However, Boyle would soon be accused of something a great deal more serious than money-lending. In December 1964, while Boyle lay in bed with his girlfriend, police burst into his flat and arrested him for murder.

A man called Lynch had been stabbed and robbed while a second man had been slashed – and Boyle's name was in the frame. Boyle denied the charge, claiming an alibi: he had been in the Wheatsheaf pub in the Gorbals with two girls all night.

He contended that he had become involved in an argument with a man outside the pub, falling into a muddy puddle in the process. He said the entire incident had been witnessed by the girls. He also said that he had asked two youngsters to get him a taxi to go home. And, finally, he denied even knowing Lynch.

In the end, the police could not corroborate the charges and Boyle walked away from the High Court a free man. However, he was soon on the run again, following a fight in a pub with two men. Armed with a broken bottle, Boyle defended himself with his now customary zeal, using the jagged edge to gouge out one man's eye and to seriously injure the other on the hand.

It was while he was in hiding from the police for this incident that he found himself implicated for a second time in murder. While at a party in Renfield Street, in the city centre, he and his friends became involved in a fight – a common enough occurrence at these parties. During the battle, eighteen-year-old Henry Savage was stabbed with a broken bottle. His brother Charles was also slashed. Eventually, detectives caught up with Boyle and his friend, Willie Smith. Co-accused Tony Smith and Willie Bennett were still at large. (They had actually gone into hiding in New York but were later arrested.)

Boyle, who denied any involvement in the murder, was also charged with the earlier assault on the two men who had challenged him in the pub. However, police once again had difficulty in tracing witnesses and, while Boyle awaited trial for the assault, he was told by the procurator-fiscal that the murder charge would be held in abeyance. So, while the procurator-fiscal continued to gather evidence on the murder charge, Boyle was sentenced to two years for the assault and found himself back in Barlinnie.

In October 1965, the four murder suspects appeared in the High Court, amid speculation of witness 'nobbling'. One witness even had her house blown up with gelignite by overzealous friends of the four men.

Prosecution witnesses also mysteriously disappeared prior to the trial and Boyle's lawyer made a formal complaint to the court about his inability to interview them. Obviously, the authorities had moved them to a place of safety, to prevent any coercion attempts.

But the prosecution case against Boyle and his cronies was not strong enough and eventually the murder charge was reduced to one of jostling and pushing; sentences of three months were handed out. In addition, Willie Smith was later cleared on a second murder charge – two brothers had attacked him in a Govan street, slitting his throat. Despite his injury, Smith had managed to get the knife away from one of them and struck out, killing the man.

Once again, Boyle had walked away from a murder charge. His reputation in the underworld was blossoming. He was now a force to be reckoned with, as it was generally accepted – on both sides of the law – that he and his friends were expert 'fixers'. Boyle, however, consistently proclaims his innocence on all charges.

The authorities transferred him from Barlinnie to Peterhead, reputed to be the toughest prison in Scotland. Here he once again fell foul of the batter squads, managing to win himself only a brief respite from their attentions by stripping naked and smearing his body with his own filth. His attackers could not gain a sufficient hold on him and, in any case, were hesitant to even approach him lest they become contaminated. Eventually they overcame their distaste and, donning overalls and gloves, managed to move in again.

Finally he was thrown into solitary confinement, a situation that would become more and more common during Boyle's prison life.

In January 1967 Boyle was released and immediately returned to his work with the tallymen and running his own shebeen. His gang also developed strong links with the Kray twins in London, who made regular recruiting drives in Glasgow.

In general there was a certain amount of antipathy between Glasgow heavies and London crooks. The former thought the latter was soft, while the Englishmen felt their Scots counterparts were lacking in sophistication. However, Boyle is on record as saying he thought highly of the twins and it was to them that he turned when he found himself once again on the run, fleeing from another murder charge.

It was on the night of 4 July 1967 that Boyle and his partner William Wilson turned up at the door of one, Babs Rooney, a small-time crook and pimp who owed Boyle's people money. Rooney lived with his twenty-one-year-old girlfriend Sadie Cairney and her four-year-old child in Cornwall Street, Kinning Park, on the city's south side and had for some time been teaming up with Willie Bennett, an old cohort of Boyle's. Bennett, however, had since fallen out of favour after what Boyle described as a 'series of dirty tricks'. These tricks included borrowing money and not paying it back.

A light drizzle was falling as Boyle and Wilson called at Rooney's flat; they had already been involved in a fight that night. On their way to Kinning Park they had called in at Wilson's Crown Street flat to collect a jacket. In the dark close mouth, they had bumped into two strangers.

Words were exchanged and the argument degenerated into a fight, with Boyle eventually drawing a knife from his boot and not only cutting one of his opponents, Charles Rae, but also fifteen-year-old Edward McGill who had been taking a short-cut through the close.

The boy would later testify against Boyle in court – a brave thing to do considering that the gang's intimidation machine swung once again into full gear with a gelignite bomb being thrown through the window of his home.

He said that he and his brother chanced upon the four men fighting in the back court when Boyle came up to him, told him that he should not have been there and promptly stabbed him in the stomach and on the arm.

So, blood having already been drawn that night, Boyle and Wilson carried on to Kinning Park. The stage was now set for murder. According to Boyle – who of course denied all charges – they were admitted into the flat by Sadie Cairney. Rooney was in bed, but got up to greet them. He was bare-chested and the meeting was cordial at first.

However, drink was consumed and soon Boyle and Rooney fell into an argument during which Boyle once again drew his knife and carved a deep furrow on Rooney's chest. He spent some time outside the flat assuring Sadie that Babs was not seriously hurt and warning her not to say anything about the blooding.

Wilson, meanwhile, was still in the kitchen with Rooney. Boyle waited for his friend to come down but when he did not reappear, he assumed that Wilson had left through a back door.

Boyle claims that the first he knew about Rooney's death was when two friends came to his home the following morning, telling him that Wilson had been arrested. He knew that it was only a matter of time before he would be implicated – in the end, his fingerprints were found on a beer can – so he decided to run off to London, where he was welcomed by the brothers Kray.

However, Glasgow police traced him and he was arrested while drinking with three Glasgow heavies in an East End pub. A large furniture van pulled up outside and armed police burst out. At the same time, other bar 'customers' leaped to their feet, waving revolvers – they were undercover officers who had been tailing Boyle and his henchmen.

Boyle was transported back to Glasgow where preparations were being made for his third – and final – appearance in Glasgow's High Court on a murder charge. This time, the police were determined not to let the man they saw as the most evil man in Glasgow slip through their fingers.

Boyle's mysterious friends were equally determined to prevent him from being convicted. Once again, witnesses were terrorised. Threats were made. Bombs were thrown. Witnesses had to be rehoused at secret addresses for their own protection while Sadie Cairney had to be hidden outside Glasgow to prevent gang members from getting to her. Soon after the murder she had fled to Manchester, claiming that she had been told that a 'team' (gang) in Glasgow was looking for her.

However, in court she told a different story, completely exonerating Boyle. She admitted that she had let Boyle and Wilson into the flat but that five minutes after they arrived there was another knock at the door and she opened it to two strange men in light raincoats, asking for her boyfriend. Rooney went to the door to talk to them and a few minutes later she heard raised voices. She went back out into the hallway in time to hear one of the men say to Rooney: 'You're going to get it and Bennett is next.'

Then, one of the men's arms darted out and down in a vicious

slashing movement. Rooney staggered back and, with blood streaming down his face and over his body, pleaded with the men to take
Sadie away 'because I love her too much. Don't let anything happen
to her.' It was these men, she contended, who had killed Rooney and
not Boyle and Wilson.

After she had given her evidence, Sadie Cairney was interviewed
again by police officers. Her story was at odds with what she had
told them earlier and they believed that she had somehow been
intimidated. The accused, however, claimed that any intimidation
had been carried out by the authorities.

When the court sat again, prosecution counsel asked for permission to put her back on the stand but was refused. The jury did not
believe her story. They took only forty-five minutes to unanimously
find Boyle guilty of murdering 'Babs' Rooney, a man who owed the
tallymen only £7. Wilson was found not guilty of murder but was
given twenty-one months for assault and for stealing £7 and a lighter
from Rooney's house.

In his summing up, Lord Cameron said that the case had been
heard against a 'sinister background of terror and intimidation'. He
further went on to describe Boyle as a 'dangerous man'.

Jimmy 'Baby Face' Boyle was sentenced to life for the slaying,
the judge recommending that he serve no less than fifteen years.
He was only twenty-four years of age.

The trial had struck a public nerve. Concern was mounting
over the increasing violence in the city. Violent crime was seen
as a major problem in 1967 – in the first ten months of that
year there were no fewer than twenty-one murders in Glasgow.
With Boyle out of the way, the authorities felt they had made a
breakthrough in their fight against the scourge. They did not know
that he would continue his one-man war against society behind
prison walls.

In prison, Boyle raged and fumed against the authorities. He
punched the governor of Barlinnie Prison, breaking his cheekbone.
He received beatings. He was unco-operative, feeling he had nothing
to lose.

Finally, he was taken to Inverness's Porterfield Prison, which was
ostensibly for local offenders but did have a punishment block for
troublesome inmates. Here he was able to renew his acquaintance
with old friends from the Gorbals but soon found himself in solitary
for smashing up the governor's office.

He purposely fouled his cell, urinating and defecating where he
felt like it, to make it more unpleasant for the prison officers to
come in and collect his dirty meal plates. He kept one small space

clear of contamination though, to enable him to run on the spot, to keep himself fit and to generate some heat.

Once back in the segregation block he contemplated suicide. He lay in his cell at night, holding a razor blade against his wrists. But he did not draw his own blood the way he had drawn the blood of so many others. In the end, he decided to keep rebelling, to become even more unco-operative – even more violent.

He was transferred to Peterhead and was no sooner through the gates of the Aberdeen prison than he was in solitary again following an attack on a prison officer. This incident could have turned into a full-scale riot, with other prisoners grabbing officers' batons. However, in the end good sense prevailed and Boyle was led quietly to the solitary cell. That night, he said, he received yet another beating.

And so his prison career continued. A seemingly never-ending stream of fights and beatings, of barbarity and inhumanity on both sides. How much of it is true can only be guessed at: naturally, the official versions of the various incidents differ greatly from Boyle's.

It was only a matter of time before Boyle's rebellious nature and the prison authorities' hatred of their violent charge would explode in a welter of blood and brutality. That explosion occurred on a December day back in the winter wonderland of Inverness.

By 1972 the authorities had devised a new way to deal with prisoners like Boyle. Six cells in Porterfield Prison were converted into cages. Food was pushed to the raging prisoner under the bars of the cage, rather like animals in a zoo. However, according to the prisoners, the beatings continued and it was one such beating which led some of them to make what they claimed was a 'peaceful' protest. The prison officers in turn claimed that it was an escape attempt.

Whatever the truth, three prison officers were seriously injured – one was stabbed fifteen times, another lost an eye – while the four prisoners each received further beatings, Boyle's quite severe. In court later, a doctor who had examined him said that he hadn't expected Boyle to last the night.

Altogether four inmates were involved in the 'riot' – Boyle, Larry Winters, William McPherson, serving twenty-five years for bank robbery, and Howard Wilson, a one-time Glasgow police officer who turned cop-killer (see Chapter Nine) and who, ironically, once 'staked out' Boyle's flat while he was on the run from the law.

They were in the recreation room when the trouble erupted. The prisoners alleged that they were conducting a peaceful protest and were forced to protect themselves when the prison officers just launched themselves at them, beating them with batons. The prisoners maintained that they were merely protecting themselves. The officers for their part held that the four men went for them with knives and other weapons, trying to kill them. Whatever happened, the room was wrecked during the ensuing battle, blood smearing the walls and the floor.

At the subsequent trial, the four prisoners were found Not Guilty of attempted murder but were each sentenced to an additional six years on assault charges. Meanwhile, twelve prison officers resigned from the service.

Boyle felt that he and his friends had won some sort of victory, a feeling reinforced when he was found Not Proven of stabbing Willie 'The Thug' Bennett while in Peterhead Prison in February 1973 – the same Bennett who had once been a friend but who fell out of favour when he teamed up with the late Babs Rooney.

In court, Bennett stated that he had been high on drugs at the time of the prison stabbing and did not remember the incident. Bennett himself died in July 1991, aged fifty, after being stabbed during a brawl outside a pub in Craigton, Glasgow.

The authorities finally decided to take a new direction in dealing with congenitally violent prisoners like Boyle and set up the experimental Special Unit in Barlinnie Prison. Here, prisoners would no longer be treated like animals but as responsible human beings. They would be trusted and even make their own rules. The unit would be more or less run by the prisoners, under close supervision by trusted prison officers.

Boyle and his fellow inmates, including Larry Winters, treated the new régime with some suspicion. They could not at first take to being treated as equals by the hand-picked officers. They found being trusted difficult to understand, let alone relate to. (The prisoners discuss their conditions and the running of the unit at weekly meetings with prison officers. If any prisoner breaks the rules or becomes unco-operative then he is forced to sit through a sometimes gruelling interrogation by his peers.)

Eventually, the inmates were even allowed to prepare their own food – unheard of in prisons as this meant entrusting them with sharp implements. (Books and newspapers are freely available and visiting periods are far more flexible than in the mainstream prison. Inmates are also allowed to have their own television sets and hi-fi equipment.)

It was in this atmosphere that Boyle discovered latent artistic talent, not only writing his own memoirs, *A Sense of Freedom* and *The Pain of Confinement*, but also collaborating on a successful play with Tom McGrath entitled *The Hard Man*, dealing with his experiences in prison. His books, although highly subjective, are engrossing portraits of one man's life of crime. In addition, he took to sculpture and is now a highly regarded artist.

In Boyle's case, the Special Unit proved a tremendous success. For his old friend Larry Winters it proved less than satisfactory. Winters had received a life sentence for shooting a barman and had served thirteen years before he was found dead in his cell. He had taken an overdose of tranquillisers.

From the beginning, Winters had failed to integrate properly. His depressions deepened as did his dependence on the officially prescribed tranquillisers. He did, however, begin to show promise as a poet – some of his poems were published after his death under the title, *The Silent Scream*.

His life story was later filmed, with Scots actor Ian Glen playing Winters. Coincidentally, the film was directed by David Hayman, the respected actor and artistic director of the 7:84 Theatre Company who played Boyle in the television version of *A Sense of Freedom*.

Winters' death in September 1977 placed the future of the unit at risk. Security was tightened amid rumours that drugs, alcohol and even women were freely available to the prisoners. The unit had never been popular among the 'hang 'em, birch 'em' sections of society who believed that life inside was too soft and who demanded its closure. However, the Special Unit managed to weather the storm and is still in operation.

Boyle has served the fifteen-year sentence laid down by the courts. He is now free and has put his former life behind him. He is married – to Dr Sarah Trevelyan, a psychiatrist who visited him in prison and daughter of the former British Film Censor, Lord Trevelyan – and has a family of his own.

But, wherever he goes, Boyle will not be able to shake off his past completely. Many police officers and even tabloid journalists are waiting for him to slip back into his old ways, convinced that a leopard cannot change his spots.

Boyle has disappointed them – but the tension must be there. He is, after all, Jimmy Boyle, once Scotland's most violent man. He must be walking a very fine line, unable perhaps to return to certain parts of Glasgow where the cult of the hard man still exists.

What would happen, for instance, if he walked into a pub and was challenged by a young pretender, desperate to forge himself a reputation? Boyle cannot lose his temper the way that ordinary citizens can. He cannot lash out when threatened.

In a way, he is still in prison.

Chapter Five

THE SCIENCE OF DETECTION

Just after 5 p.m. on Friday, 26 September 1947, twenty-two-year-old Archibald McIntyre made his way up to his family's cottage, perched high on a hill above the River Tay in Perthshire. Across the valley the trees were still green: it would be a few weeks before they would slowly turn golden brown under the autumn sun, erupting in the riot of colour that makes that season the most beautiful of the Highland year. But on that day in 1947 the serenity and casual beauty of the area was to be marred by bloody murder.

Tower Cottage, the home of Archie and his parents Peter and Catherine McIntyre, was part of the Tombuie Estate between Aberfeldy and Kenmore. When Archie reached the cottage at the top of the steep track about a mile from the main road he found all the doors were locked. The young man was not surprised. He knew that his father, a shepherd, was in Perth at the sheep sales, while his mother had been due to go to the big house to prepare the rooms for the return of the young Laird, Mr J. D. Hutchison.

Archie quietened the family dog, a cairn terrier, which was barking furiously at the door and settled himself down on the doorstep to read the newspapers that had been delivered earlier by the postman.

Meanwhile, estate gamekeeper Duncan McKerracher had called at Tombuie House to ensure that everything was ready for the owner's return that weekend. To his surprise he found the fires unlit and the rooms unaired. The man frowned: it wasn't like Mrs McIntyre to ignore her duties. Something must be wrong at Tower Cottage and he had to find out what it was.

The gamekeeper found Archie sitting outside the cottage, still reading the newspaper in the fading September sun. He told him that his mother had not shown up at the big house that day.

Now the young man began to grow concerned. He found a ladder and forced his way into the house through the kitchen window. The kitchen was a mess. The breakfast dishes were still lying unwashed in the sink and there was an unfinished letter to his sister Annie in Arran lying on the table.

Quickly, while Duncan McKerracher waited outside, Archie ran through the house. Every room was in disarray. Drawers had been pulled out, furniture turned over, papers strewn across the floor. It was as if someone had been searching for something.

But there was no sign of Mrs McIntyre. Archie ran upstairs, looking in every room, calling out her name, his movements growing more and more frenzied. Finally he came back down and tried the door of his own bedroom.

It was locked. This was puzzling. He never locked his bedroom door, and there was no reason for any other member of the family to do so. Picking up an axe he started to hack at the wood, finally breaking in.

His mother was lying on the bed. A mattress had been dragged from another bed and thrown on top of her, her mouth gagged with a scarf, her hands and feet tied so tightly together with black bootlaces that the ligatures bit deeply into her flesh. And there was blood. A lot of blood.

She had been battered to death.

Local police alerted County Headquarters in Perth and Chief Constable A. J. Sim, a Detective Inspector, and fingerprint men sped to the lonely farmhouse while all roads from Kenmore were patrolled for fifteen miles in every direction. Officers were also sent out on foot to interview farm and estate workers who may have had reason to be in the vicinity of Tower Cottage that day and who may have seen something suspicious.

But they were too late – the murderer was already miles away.

Meanwhile, Mrs McIntyre's husband was making his way from Perth unaware of the bloody events in his home. He climbed down off the bus at the end of the road leading to the cottage at about 7 p.m. that night, to be met by a pale-faced Duncan McKerracher. The gamekeeper broke the tragic news to the shepherd and took him back to his own house for the night.

The murder also attracted the attention of the press, who were told by Chief Constable Sim: 'She had been brutally murdered, probably in the course of the forenoon. Theft appears to have been the motive and £80, mostly in £5 notes, is missing.'

The money was mostly wages, for some of the estate workers, in Mr McIntyre's keeping. Also missing was a forty-year-old silver watch, some ration books, a man's new blue suit and the dead woman's wedding ring.

A rough time of death could be established by the unfinished letter on the kitchen table. Had Mrs McIntyre been killed in the afternoon she would have completed the letter and handed it to postman Jim Seaton when he made his regular call between 11 a.m. and 12 noon.

However, a post-mortem was still necessary and pathologist Professor John Glaister was recalled from his holiday in Loch Lomond to carry it out. His evidence would be crucial in bringing the killer to justice.

Professor Glaister's autopsy report stated that death resulted from 'fractures of the base of the skull, with subdural haemorrhage, the result of very considerable violence, together with superimposed respiratory embarrassment'.

There were four deep wounds on the head. Whoever had hit the poor woman had done so with tremendous force, using a very substantial weapon indeed. At the time, police believed a golf club found in the cottage to be the murder weapon. Professor Glaister found nothing to contradict them.

They were wrong all the same. The true murder weapon was found two days later during a painstaking search of the high bracken around the cottage. About 400 yards away police found a spot where the vegetation had been broken and flattened, as if it had been used as a hiding place.

Archie, meanwhile, had recalled seeing a movement in the bushes that morning as he left for work. However, he had assumed it was a deer.

No deer had hidden in the four-foot-high bracken that morning. Police found a set of overalls, a sawn-off shotgun, a bloodstained handkerchief and a used safety-razor. Each of these items would prove damning for the culprit, while the razor in particular would be essential in the prosecution case.

The overalls were old and worn and had bloodstains on them. The shotgun was broken into two pieces and blood smeared all over the butt. Professor Glaister immediately told police that it was more likely to be the murder weapon – the wounds on Mrs McIntyre's head matched the stock of the shotgun more closely than that of the golf club.

But, perhaps more importantly, the blade of the razor still had traces of a man's hair clinging to it, as if he had given himself a dry shave before the murder, then thrown the razor aside.

The hairs were carefully scraped off and retained for study by Professor Glaister and his forensic team. The razor itself was then sent for fingerprint examination. There were no fingerprints but the hairs would prove vital in placing the murderer at the scene of his crime.

A further search of the man-made clearing uncovered a return railway ticket, dated Thursday, 25 September – the day before the murder. Railway officials told police that it was the type of ticket issued to soldiers in uniform.

More information flooded in. Witnesses told police of a Pole with a bad cough and dirty shoes who leaped into a taxi in Aberfeldy on the morning of the murder.

Chief Constable Sim told the press: 'It is desired to interview a Pole who travelled on Friday September 26 by taxi from Aberfeldy to Perth, where he probably joined the 1.40 p.m. train which runs to Stirling, Larbert and Edinburgh.

His description is: about thirty-five years of age, five foot, six inches in height, slim build, thin face, pointed chin, clean-shaven, dressed in a light coloured raincoat, soft felt hat, probably dark grey.'

Mr Sim continued: 'His shoes were so dirty that it could not be said whether they were black or brown.' The suspect also wore brown kid gloves, carried a brown leather despatch case and suffered from a spasmodic cough which was at times quite severe.

The hunt for this coughing killer spread throughout the country. Border police joined the search when a man answering the description was spotted on the Glasgow to Carlisle road two miles north of Lockerbie trying to thumb a lift north. But this man was never found.

Meanwhile, Detective Superintendent Ewing and Superintendent McIlwraith of Glasgow police joined the search. Murder is uncommon in the rural areas of Scotland and perhaps the local police felt a bit out of their depth. In the cities – Glasgow in particular – violent death is commonplace and it was no doubt felt that their expertise would be invaluable.

Although the search for the suspect had spread to other parts of Scotland, inquiries continued locally: investigating officers could still not rule out the possibility of local knowledge, someone who perhaps knew that there was a larger than usual sum of money in the cottage.

Nearby Taymouth Castle, once the home of the Duke of Breadalbane, was being used at the time as a resettlement centre for over 800 Polish soldiers who had decided to stay on in Britain rather than return to their communist-controlled country. Men would come and go from the castle regularly and, with the help of interpreters, police interviewed all the Poles they could locate who had been in the area at the time of the murder.

But the one man they really wanted to talk to – the mysterious coughing Pole with the dirty shoes – eluded them.

However, a break in the case was not far off.

Appeals were made to trace the origin of the twelve-bore shotgun found in the bracken. It was an old weapon, only recently sawn off. A description was issued to the newspapers and then broadcast on BBC radio.

A gardener in Oldmeldrum in Aberdeenshire heard the broadcast and recognised the shotgun as one which he had loaned to a local farm labourer. Further investigations showed that the shotgun had been stolen around the same time as Polish labourer Stanislaw Myszka had left the farm to seek further work in the south. The man had left in the week that Mrs McIntyre was murdered. The bloodstained handkerchief was also identified as one that had been given to Myszka by the labourer's wife.

Aberdeenshire police were alerted to Myszka's return to the area by another Polish exile, Mr Wladystow Szwec, who had settled in the area with his wife, Agnes, a local girl.

Myszka had arrived at the door of Mr Szwec's farm cottage at Upper Kinknockie Farm, Ardallie in Buchan, north of Aberdeen, on the Saturday following the murder. He had not found work in the south but he did have money.

During his stay, Agnes Szwec read reports of the murder to Myszka. 'His face reddened up like a fire when he heard the details,' she said at his trial. 'He could not sit still after it.'

However, by the time her husband realised that Myszka fitted the description of the man the police were looking for, their short-term lodger had moved on again, ostensibly to look for work in Peterhead, ten miles away.

Police set up roadblocks, cordoning off Peterhead. However, Myszka had not gone as far as the east coast fishing port. He had actually hidden in a former RAF station near Longside in Aberdeenshire – and it was here that two police officers making a routine search of the disused huts found him on Thursday, 2 October.

Constables Duncan and McLaren surprised the man and he immediately took to his heels, running like a scared rabbit through the deserted air base and into the nearby fields, the two police officers in hot pursuit. They finally caught up with him in a small field. Once captured, Myszka put up no further resistance and was led away to Peterhead.

In the huts, police found some of the items of clothing he had stolen from Tower Cottage and, when searched in Peterhead police station, Mrs McIntyre's gold wedding ring was discovered concealed in his shoe.

Word of Myszka's capture quickly spread and when he appeared at Perth Sheriff Court a crowd of several hundred people had gathered on the steps. Women and children had already verbally abused him as he was taken from Peterhead police station to a police car. The authorities suspected that feeling would be even stronger in Perth, so Myszka was manacled to a plain clothes police officer and for his own protection hidden away among four other prisoners as he was led into the court.

Once he was inside, the crowd quickly scrambled for places in the public gallery. Once again though, the authorities outsmarted them: Myszka was bundled upstairs and appeared in private before the Sheriff. The hearing lasted only a few minutes. The charges were read out to the accused man and interpreted for him. He made no declaration and was remanded for trial.

While Myszka awaited trial, Professor Glaister asked the authorities for samples of his beard to compare with the hairs found on the razor outside Tower Cottage. The samples matched.

Myszka's trial for murder took place in Perth High Court in January 1948. He had originally pleaded insanity, saying that he was worried to distraction by the fate of his children whom he had heard were to be moved from France back to Poland. He had not been responsible for his actions.

However, after three psychiatrists – one a Pole – judged him to be sane, his plea was amended to Not Guilty. He admitted the theft but not the murder and his lawyer said he was still not capable of instructing his defence counsel.

Ultimately, the defence's hopes rested on demolishing the evidence of Professor Glaister.

As a Polish army officer sat in the dock with Myszka, translating all the questions and answers, Professor Glaister was grilled over his findings and opinions. It was, the scientist later wrote, a 'picture of the extent to which the forensic scientist can commit himself on the subject'.

The Professor testified that the two samples of beard – from the razor and from Myszka – were 'so similar as to be consistent with a common source'.

Defence counsel leaped on this, wondering if the samples were 'not too similar to exclude the possibility of it being someone else's hair altogether'.

'We can never say that hair comes from the individual unless it is taken from that individual,' said the expert witness. 'As far as we can go is that the characters are so common as to be consistent with a common source.'

The study of the characteristics of hair was not as exact as that of fingerprints, he explained. It involves a more prolonged study and more protracted study of hair of all types, beginning by taking the cellular characters of each, the general and detailed structure, the pigment distribution, the general range of colouration and by comparing one sample with the other, a match can be found. But no forensic scientist could say for certain that two samples came from the same person, only that certain characteristics were so similar as to suggest a common source.

Professor Glaister's testimony, along with the discovery of the shotgun and handkerchief, placed Myszka at the cottage on the morning of the murder. The evidence was strong enough for the jury of eleven men and one woman to return a verdict of guilty after retiring for only twenty minutes.

And on the morning of 6 February 1948, twenty-three-year-old Stanislaw Myszka, a deserter from the Polish Army in Exile, was hung in Perth Prison.

The conviction of Stanislaw Myszka is just one example of the use of forensic science in detecting murder. Forensic evidence is now of vital importance in the investigation of any crime, from the study of bloodstains to complex genetic fingerprinting.

Known at one time as 'Medical Jurisprudence', forensic medicine has been in use in some form or another for centuries, although it was not taught in universities until the seventeenth century.

The first British chair in the field was established by George III at Edinburgh University in 1807 and, ever since, professors in Edinburgh and Glasgow have been at the top of the profession. Text-books on the subject would come from graduates of those cities' universities – Sir Sydney Smith, Professor Harvey Littlejohn and Professor John Glaister.

The field was described by Professor Alfred Swaine Taylor, whose *Principles and Practice of Medical Jurisprudence* was for years the Bible of the profession, as 'the application of every branch of medical knowledge to the purposes of the law'.

Without the expertise and evidence of these expert witnesses, many a murderer may never have been caught, let alone tried and sentenced. On the other hand, poorly researched forensic evidence has not only led to the acquittal of some guilty men and women, but also the imprisonment of the innocent, as in the case of the Birmingham Six.

Apart from the information that can be obtained from the victim's body during the post-mortem, the most important clues that the forensic expert can provide for investigating detectives stem from what they call 'contact traces'.

It was French criminologist Edmond Locard who first said that every contact leaves a trace, words echoed by Professor Glaister, one of the legends of Scottish expert witnesses, when he said that it was all but impossible for someone to enter or leave the scene of a crime without either leaving some trace of his presence, or taking some trace of the location away with him.

These contact traces can point scientists and detectives in the direction of a killer. Fingerprints, footprints, tyre tracks, blood, fibres, semen, oil, dust and, as we have already seen, hairs can place a suspect at the scene of the crime, if not actually implicate him.

One of the earliest recorded applications of simple techniques in Scotland dates from 1786 when a Dumfriesshire crofter and his wife found their young daughter murdered. The authorities' suspicions fell on a local man called Richardson, but he was able to claim what seemed like a cast-iron alibi.

However, eventually, plaster casts were made of some boot prints outside the cottage and it was found that the pattern of nails on the sole matched a pair of Richardson's boots. They also found bloodstains on the man's stockings while mud and sand on his boots and clothes could be traced to that found around the cottage. Finally, Richardson was arrested and hanged in Dumfries in 1787.

The victim can leave marks on the killer. Blood and fragments of flesh can be wedged under fingernails, fibres and dust can be transferred from one to the other, hair can be torn out during a struggle and found clutched in the dead person's hand.

Occasionally, the killer can leave a mark on his victim which will prove to be so unique that he will lead detectives and the expert witness straight to him almost as easily as if he had left his name and address.

Such was the case of the so-called 'Beast of Biggar', in which a bite mark would not only prove crucial to the identification of the killer but also make Scottish legal history.

Pretty Linda Peacock was an ordinary fifteen-year-old girl. She was bright, lively and had an interest in records and horses. When she grew up she wanted to be a vet. She also had the average fifteen-year-old girl's interest in boys. Like all popular, good-looking teenage girls she could flirt unconsciously. But she was not promiscuous, and it was her unwillingness to submit to an older boy's sexual advances that would lead to her violent death in a dark, deserted graveyard in a small Lanarkshire town.

Her body was discovered under a leafy bush in Biggar's St Mary's churchyard by a police officer at about 6.45 a.m. on Monday, 7 August 1967. The officer was part of a massive search party made up of police and locals which had been hunting for the young girl since 1.30 a.m.

Linda had been beaten viciously across the head and strangled. She had not been raped, although her anorak, blouse and bra had been pulled up to expose her breasts. And it was on the right breast that the killer had left his mark, a clearly defined bite.

The customary photographs were taken of the body as it was found, including no less than fifteen of the bite mark, deemed even at that early stage in the hunt to be important.

She had been strangled from behind: the marks of the cord used to throttle the life out of her were deeper at the front of the neck than at the back. Her left wrist also showed marks of a ligature which had been burned off, leaving scorch marks on the flesh. From the look of the ground beneath the body the girl had put up a struggle. However, her killer had proved too strong for her, beating her with some sort of weapon, then strangling her.

Led by Detective Chief Superintendent William Muncie, head of Lanarkshire CID, the murder squad set out to fill in the poor girl's final few hours. She had spent the afternoon at a friend's farm, they learned, tending to some ponies. Then, after having dinner with her own family at Swaire Cottage on the outskirts of the town, she accepted a lift from a family friend into the town centre, where she was to meet some school friends.

By 9 p.m. she was heading home, stopping for almost half an hour to chat to twelve-year-old Sylvia Cleplock. Linda left the girl at 9.30 p.m., saying she was going to walk home. She was last seen alive by someone other than her killer at 9.45 p.m., when she exchanged a few words with two elderly townfolk.

When last seen by the couple, Linda was walking very slowly along the quiet road leading to her home, a mile away. It was as if she was waiting for someone. But who? Nine hours later, her battered and strangled body was found in the graveyard, only yards from the grave of her grandmother.

The murder squad was made up of members from both Lanarkshire Crime Squad and the Regional Crime Squad in Glasgow. Officers were called in from all over Central Scotland to help with the wearying legwork that forms the centre of any murder hunt. Within one week, over 3500 people had been interviewed in connection with the case.

Biggar was, and is, a small county town with a population at that time of only 2000 people. News of the murder stunned the community. A weekly dance in the town hall was cancelled because the local group, The Counts, felt it would be inappropriate to carry on as if nothing had happened.

Meanwhile, a Mrs Mae Armstrong from Gartcosh, whose mother had been murdered in 1965, began to raise a petition calling for the return of capital punishment, then under 'temporary' abolition.

Every person over fourteen in the town and surrounding area was interviewed, while appeals went out to others to come forward with any information.

A woman who lived near the graveyard said she heard a scream at about 10.20 p.m. Other witnesses recalled seeing a man and a girl in conversation near the gates of the churchyard at about 10.15 p.m.

'We would like this couple to come forward,' said D.C.S. Muncie, 'so that we will know whether or not it was Linda.'

As they would subsequently discover, it was indeed Linda – and she had met her killer before.

Men and youths drifted in and out of the picture as the inquiry progressed. Hundreds of people phoned the murder incident room in Biggar town hall with information and offers of help. Detectives travelled to Dunbar to talk to three girls on holiday in the east coast town believed to have had the address of a man who could perhaps assist them with their enquiries.

A man was taken from his home in Galashiels to Biggar for questioning. He was later allowed home.

A mysterious Irish hitchhiker with scratches on his face turned up at a nearby farm, looking for a drink of water. The farmer was suspicious, mindful of the announcement that Linda Peacock had fought with her attacker, and phoned the police. The man was traced and he too was cleared.

A *Daily Record* photographer hired a plane and flew over the area, taking photographs for his newspaper. The police borrowed these pictures to help them plan their extensive search of the fields and farms that cluster around Biggar.

Bank manager Thomas Aitken remembered seeing the couple at the gates of the cemetery, although he was not sure of the exact time. However, he did know that when he finally got home he switched on his TV just in time to hear comedian Dickie Henderson introducing Frank Sinatra Jnr on *The Blackpool Show*.

The witness was taken to STV studios in Glasgow, where a tape of the programme was screened. Mr Aitken pinpointed the exact time he switched on his TV – exactly twenty minutes and ten seconds into the show.

Then, again using a stopwatch, Mr Aitken retraced his route on the night of the murder and found that it took him twenty minutes to get home from the cemetery gates. That meant he had seen the couple at 10 p.m.

The routine that is part of any murder hunt went on and on . . . a mini-skirted policewoman recreated Linda's last walk one week after the murder in the hope that it would stimulate the memories of witnesses; . . . household and industrial vacuum cleaners were used to carefully examine the murder scene. Special power cables were run from a house over 100 yards from the graveyard to allow police to suck up dirt, grass, leaves, gravel and litter from a thirty-square-yard area. The items were then taken in large bags to the murder headquarters where other officers patiently sifted through them in the hope that they would glean any clue that could point them to the killer; . . . detectives combed the area carefully on their hands and knees, using pens, pencils and even nail scissors to help them retrieve and pick up anything that might help; . . . a special device called 'The Retriever', a form of geiger counter, was pressed into use. 'By tuning it in, we can eliminate other things that we are not interested in,' said a detective.

And, all the while, Linda's killer remained at large. But not for long. By Monday, 14 August, D.C.S. Muncie was telling the press: 'We need one more vital part of information to clinch our inquiry.' The veteran police officer then hinted that they had something that belonged to the killer, but he refused to say what. That mysterious 'something' was the bite mark.

While the legwork was continuing in and around the town, forensic experts had been making an intense study of the teeth marks in the photographs taken by the police photographer. Dr Warren

Harvey, an expert in forensic odontology and lecturer and consultant at the Glasgow Dental Hospital, had been called in to lend his considerable expertise to the case.

By this time, investigations were centred on the Loaningdale Approved School, and in particular on a short list of twenty-nine boys and staff. The bite marks were deemed to be so unique it was felt that the corresponding set of teeth would be as distinctive as a fingerprint. Dental impressions were taken from all twenty-nine suspects, models were made from the casts and these compared with the transparencies of the wound.

The particular peculiarities they were looking for included two canines with holes, or pits, in the cutting edges and a broken upper left central tooth. Another tooth also had a hole.

The examinations by Dr Harvey and Inspector Osborne Butler of the Police Identification Department resulted in five of the twenty-nine suspects being recalled for further dental impressions. Only one person was called for a third – Gordon Hay, a seventeen-year-old Aberdeen youth who had been convicted in 1966 of breaking into a factory. He had arrived at the school in January 1967 but during his few months there had proved to be something of a troublemaker and had been transferred to a tighter security unit at Montrose shortly after the murder.

During his interviews with the police, Hay was truculent and aggressive. At his trial, he would be described as 'cold and cunning'. D.C.S. Muncie was convinced that they had their man. He and his expert witnesses were about to make Scottish legal history.

Hay's trial began in Edinburgh's High Court on Monday, 26 February 1968. He was charged with striking Linda Peacock with an instrument, biting her, tying a ligature round her wrist, another round her neck and strangling her.

The youth pled Not Guilty, submitting a special defence of alibi. Quite simply, he claimed to have been in the school dormitory at the time. He also alleged that he had been beaten up by the police.

Revelations of friendships between local girls and the boys of the approved school were to shock the adult population of Biggar. Witnesses told of a special owl hoot signal that certain girls of the town used to call their boyfriends from the school at night for dates in the fields. Linda Peacock had also been known to date boys from the school.

Hay was not one of these regular boyfriends, but an inmate told the court of Hay's first meeting with Linda, only the day before she died.

He had been with Hay, another pupil and a member of staff in Biggar on Saturday, 5 August, when Linda came up to speak to them. The conversation had only lasted a few minutes but when she walked away Hay said to the witness: 'I wouldn't mind a night with her.'

The next night he would meet Linda, take her into the graveyard and, when she refused to have sex with him, he hit her with a boat hook stolen from another boy, sank his teeth into her breast – making her scream in doing so – and then strangled her.

Then he ran back into the school, where he later threw the remains of the cord he had used to choke the girl into the incinerator. What was left of the cord, similar to the type used on a dressing-gown, was found by police. They would also find bloodstains on Hay's clothing.

Another witness from the school told the court that at 10.15 p.m. on the night of the murder he went to the dormitory he shared with Hay and two other boys. Hay was not there – although he claimed that he was. The witness then stated that when he woke up later that night, Hay had returned.

And even more damaging to Hay's alibi was the testimony of another boy who said that he was awakened that night by the slamming of the dorm door and he clearly saw Hay come in, his hair windswept, his face dirty and the knees of his jeans covered in mud.

But it was the dental testimony that was to prove most damning of all – and Hay's defence counsel tried his best to prevent it from being heard.

On the third day of the trial, the trial judge, Lord Grant, cleared the court while opposing lawyers argued over the admissibility of the expert evidence. Counsel for the defence contended that the warrant used to obtain impressions of Hay's teeth was illegal and any evidence gleaned through it was therefore tainted – what the Americans call 'fruit of the poisoned tree'.

After a three-and-a-half-hour debate, Lord Grant and his two colleagues on the bench decided that the evidence could be heard. The medical evidence was lengthy. Of just over 1000 pages of foolscap pages of evidence, almost 400 were medical and dental.

Professor Keith Simpson, the Home Office pathologist who had been asked to help by D.I. Butler and Dr Harvey, testified that he had studied all twenty-nine of the impressions from the staff and boys of the school.

'I have looked at this with the greatest of care,' he said. 'There are

78

a number of points of comparison, two of which in my experience are remarkable and unique.'

In more than thirty years of practice, he said, he had not seen a bite mark with better defined details.

Dr Warren Harvey had also examined the teeth of 342 teenage soldiers in a bid to trace the killer. He said that he spent almost four hours examining the boys, seeing between eighty and 100 an hour.

'As an army exercise it was splendid,' he noted. 'They came in one door and out the other.'

But out of those 342 he found only two with one hole in a canine tooth – and none had two.

One of the marks in the bite was quite unlike anything he had ever seen before.

He said later: 'This boy's teeth were absolutely unique. There were pits on the two opposite eye teeth – but these were not hollows which would normally be made by grinding.

'The boy could not grind these teeth against one another in his mouth and they were natural pits which might have stemmed from a childhood illness.'

Hay's counsel was still determined to undermine the expert testimony and produced dentists of his own to testify that although the marks could have been caused by the accused, it was far from beyond a reasonable doubt.

Among them was Professor George Beagrie, professor of restorative dentistry at Edinburgh University, who believed that photographs of the bite were not sufficiently well defined to make an accurate comparison. Neither did he accept that the pits in the canine teeth were rare.

The jury were not convinced by the doubts the defence had tried to cast and after withdrawing for two and a half hours, they found Hay guilty. It was the first occasion in Britain in which forensic dentistry, then a relatively new science, was used to help identify a murderer from only three characteristic bite marks on the body. Hay was also the first person in Scotland to be convicted on the strength of his teeth marks.

It was rare for police to find identifiable bite marks on a corpse, the marks usually being found in some soft food near the scene of the crime: for example, a piece of cheese or an apple.

It was the latter which, in 1976, tripped up a Southport arsonist when he took a bite out of a piece of the fruit and then left it behind at the scene of one of his fires. When he was arrested, forensic odontologists found a total of forty-six corresponding points between the marks on the apple and a cast of his teeth.

At the time of the murder, Hay was only seventeen and so was sentenced to be detained during Her Majesty's Pleasure. A subsequent appeal was refused by a panel of five judges.

Throughout his trial, his mother sat just behind him. When his sentence was announced, she burst into tears and had to be led from the court by a policewoman. Later, she was allowed to speak to her son for a few minutes before he was driven away in a police van. She told newspaper reporters that she would stand by her son. Naturally, the dead girl's mother was not so forgiving.

'For as long as I live,' she said, 'I can never forgive that boy.'

Meanwhile, the provost of Biggar called for the closure of Loaningdale Approved School or at least the complete replacement of the staff. Prior to the murder there had never been any trouble between locals and inmates. The authorities had no reason to expect trouble from Hay, they said, who had no prior history of violence. However, to prevent any further nocturnal expeditions by inmates, they did install an alarm system.

But the security precautions were too late to help Linda Peacock.

At the height of the search for her killer, the teenage victim was buried in the same graveyard in which she had been murdered. A huge crowd of over 600 people gathered for her funeral, lining the streets as the coffin was taken from the local parish church to the graveyard. Shops and offices closed for an hour as a mark of respect.

The coffin was carried by four of Linda's brothers and among the mourners were three high-ranking police officers, including D.C.S. Muncie.

As the service ended, Linda's seventy-year-old father, George, stooped and laid a wreath of white chrysanthemums on the grave. The wreath was in the shape of a pony.

Chapter Six

A MAN CALLED PETER

The hangman entered the condemned cell at precisely 8 a.m. on Friday, 11 July 1958. He paused briefly in the doorway of the small room, surveying the men already there – three prison guards, a priest chanting softly from his Bible and the condemned man himself, short but powerfully built, his thick black, glossy hair combed tightly back from his face, the widow's peak jutting sharply on to his forehead like a knifeblade.

The executioner, Harry B. Allen, nodded once and the short, dark-headed man was taken from the cell into an adjoining room where the gallows were waiting. His arms were tied behind his back and he was led on to the scaffold. A white hood was pulled over his head, the noose looped around his neck. And then the trap was sprung.

It was all over in less than a minute. Sixty seconds to bring to an end the life of a man who had terrorised Lanarkshire for two years. A man who had been found guilty of seven murders, but who almost certainly committed another five. A man who showed no sign of remorse over his crimes or any sign of pity or compassion for his victims or their grieving relatives.

A man called Peter Manuel.

Peter Thomas Anthony Manuel was the man who talked too much. He was a boastful, arrogant and psychopathic petty criminal with aspirations. He wanted to prove to the world that he was smarter than anyone else, that he could outwit the authorities, that he could pull off the ultimate crime – mass murder – and get away with it.

He was a cruel, remorseless killer who enjoyed terrorising women, experiencing a sexual thrill when he did so. He needed to feel powerful. He needed to impress his peers.

He did possess an extraordinary animal cunning. He was intelligent, capable of defending himself in court on both a rape charge

– winning a Not Proven verdict – and later, unsuccessfully, when being tried for his life.

Ultimately, though, all his sly skills foundered on his own inability to keep himself out of the spotlight. It was his deep-felt need to be centre stage, to be a somebody, that proved his undoing.

He was a curiously contradictory man. He was capable of cold-blooded murder and brutal acts of violence, yet he was devoted to his family. He could not form any lasting attachments with people outside his family circle – at one point he was engaged to be married but the relationship was broken off. He deeply loved his pet alsatian, Rusty. When the animal was killed in a road accident, Manuel was desolate.

Later, amid the carnage of the Smart household after he had murdered the entire family, he would take time to feed the family cat, returning to the house over the following six days to fill its bowl. Yet he callously killed a cow in a field by shooting it up one nostril.

Peter Manuel was born on 15 March 1927 in a hospital on the island of Manhattan, New York. His father, Samuel Manuel, and mother Bridget had emigrated from Lanarkshire to the USA where, they had heard, the poor and huddled masses of Europe could find happiness and make their fortune. They soon discovered that life there was no easier than in Scotland. In many ways, it was even harder.

At first, the couple and their eldest son, James, lived in Detroit but eventually moved to New York in search of work. Soon after little Peter's birth, the family returned to Detroit where Samuel found work in a car plant.

Six years later, Samuel fell ill and could not work. The family decided to return to Scotland, eventually moving again to Coventry where, in 1937, Bridget gave birth to a baby daughter, Teresa.

Peter Manuel proved to be a troublesome individual from an early age. He sported a strong American accent, which he later lost but could adopt at will, but failed to impress the tough Coventry children and found himself living outside the accepted circles. Thus cut off, he began to play truant from school.

By the age of eleven he was on probation for breaking into a shop. From then until he was eighteen, he spent the majority of his time in remand homes, approved schools and borstals. He developed a knack for escaping from these institutions, partly as a means to draw attention to himself and also to prove that he was smarter than the authorities.

As he grew older he became increasingly more violent. At fifteen he broke into a girl's room, woke her up and then proceeded to beat her on the head with a hammer. He then stole the contents of her purse. There was no reason for the brutal attack – he woke her up specifically to go for her with the hammer. It was these sinister urges that would later lead him to mass murder.

Charges of violent and sexual assault would appear all too regularly on his record. While on the run from an English remand home he attacked, indecently assaulted and robbed a woman, fleeing to Glasgow before being recaptured.

In Lanarkshire in 1945 he attacked a pregnant woman, dragging her over a fence to a railway embankment and indecently assaulting her. Twelve years later he would murder a girl on the same footpath.

At the time of the attack on the pregnant woman, Manuel was on bail for fifteen housebreaking charges. The rape charge was added and he received a total of nine years in Aberdeen's Peterhead Prison.

Once inside, he began to develop the boastful personality and attention-grabbing activities that would eventually lead him to the gallows. He tried to impress his fellow inmates with skills he did not possess, claiming to be an expert safecracker or a champion boxer.

When his cellmates remained spectacularly unimpressed, Manuel tried another tack, desperate to show them that he was a force to be reckoned with, that he was, indeed, one of them. He became a troublesome prisoner. He refused to obey orders. He attacked prison officers. In years to come and for different reasons, another Glasgow crook, Jimmy Boyle, would adopt the same attitude to much greater effect.

For his pains, Manuel was treated to considerable stretches of time in solitary confinement. But still he failed to convince the hardened criminals that he was anything more than a petty crook with a penchant for sex offences.

Once free, Manuel tried the same technique to ingratiate himself with Glasgow's underworld. They were also unconvinced by this fanciful little show-off. Much later, they would band together to help bring him down, putting an end to his reign of terror.

To please his parents, on whom he doted, Manuel tried to go straight. He attempted to develop his artistic talents, showing some promise with a few short stories and some sketches.

However, in July 1955 his inner urges proved too much for him and he once again attacked a woman as she walked home alone. She claimed that he dragged her into a field and, holding a knife to her throat, threatened to cut off her head. He did not rape her. It would later be proved that Manuel was incapable of sexual gratification, achieving orgasm only through instilling terror.

At the subsequent trial in Airdrie Sheriff Court, Manuel defended himself – a dress rehearsal for the big show three years later in Glasgow's High Court. On this occasion, though, he was successful and the jury brought in a Not Proven verdict.

Manuel was free to commit murder. The catalogue of horrors began in East Kilbride on Monday, 2 January 1956.

Now a sprawling modern town ever encroaching on the green fields which separate it from Glasgow and Hamilton, East Kilbride was at that time little more than a village, although a number of new estates were growing out of the farmland. It was mid-winter and the nights were dark and freezingly cold.

On that night, pretty, fair-haired Anne Kneilands, a seventeen-year-old machinist with a Glasgow knitwear factory, had been due to meet a boy she had met the previous Friday night at a dance. However, her new boyfriend had failed to show up.

So she was making her lonely way home to the Calderwood Estate, past the golf course that was slowly being churned up to make way for new roads and houses.

She never made it home. Anne met someone else that night. A man grabbed her and dragged her screaming over a fence and into the long grass beside the fifth tee. And there he beat her viciously over the head with an iron bar, caving in her skull, and interfered with her clothing, pulling off her underwear. The girl, though, was not sexually molested.

At about 3 p.m. on Wednesday, 4 January, forty-year-old labourer George Gribbon was taking his regular walk across the golf course with his dog. He veered off the fairway and into the long grass, intending to search the line of trees nearby for lost golf balls. Instead, he found Anne's body lying in a small hollow on the ground.

The horrified labourer dashed out of the golf course to some workmen who were building a new road. Gasping for breath, he told them about the body in the woods, but they did not believe him. He ran on to find a phone and alert the police.

Sergeant William Woods of Lanarkshire constabulary was first on the scene, soon to be followed by detectives and forensic scientists. The area was cordoned off and a search was conducted for clues. Darkness was falling steadily and the hunt had to be continued under the harsh glare of land-rover headlights. Pressmen huddled together in a far corner, waiting for news.

There was little the police could tell them. A girl was dead. There were signs of a struggle in the loose earth. Her clothing had been disarranged. Her killer may have blood on his clothes.

Investigations spread out from the scene of the crime to the township. The boy who had arranged to meet Anne on that fateful night was traced. He had gone to a party with some friends and had decided not to show up for the rendezvous. A bus conductress told of a conversation with the dead girl. Anne had been laughing and joking, she said, particularly about the dark stretch of road she had to walk along to get home.

Detectives made a midnight appeal to dancers in the Blantyre Co-operative Hall the following Friday. Anne had attended a dance there the previous week and detectives wanted to know who she had danced with or talked to. Perhaps she had met her killer there. Only two men volunteered information.

Police traced a Mr Hugh Marshall, who had been walking his dog between 8.30 p.m. and 9.00 p.m. on the night of the murder, and who had heard a girl scream from the direction of the golf course. The road was a popular 'winching' spot for youngsters and a young girl crying out might not have been an uncommon occurrence, even on a dark and cold January night. Mr Marshall did not investigate and there were no more screams.

Manuel's name cropped up early in the investigation, when he was one of a group of gas board workers interviewed by a police constable checking on George Gribbon's story. The young police-man noticed that Manuel had fresh scratches on his face. Those same scratches were also noted by another officer, investigating a series of thefts from the work site.

Manuel's violent reputation and history of sex offences coupled with those scratches were more than enough to pique the curiosity of the murder squad detectives. Manuel was visited at his parents' home in Birkenshaws, near Uddingston, by Superintendent James Hendry of Lanarkshire CID. He and Manuel were old adversaries and he knew Manuel to be a boastful and fanciful man – as well as a dangerous one.

Manuel claimed that he had received the scratches in a fight in Glasgow on Hogmanay. This was not altogether improbable: Manuel saw himself as something of a hard man and if he was indeed out carousing on arguably the most drunken night of the city's year he was likely to talk himself into some sort of trouble and so receive a summary kicking.

However, Superintendent Hendry was not convinced and a warrant was obtained to search the house. Items of Manuel's clothing were taken away for forensic examination. No evidence was found and Manuel was freed.

The trail ran cold and the murder of Anne Kneilands remained unsolved. The story slid off the front pages of the newspapers. Anne's parents grieved, slowly trying to bring their life back to normal.

Manuel smiled contentedly.

Tragic and senseless though the murder was, it was merely to be the opening scene of an increasingly grisly tale. The real horror was yet to come.

In September 1956 Mr and Mrs Henry Platt and their sixteen-year-old son, Geoffrey, returned to their Bothwell home from holiday to find that they had been visited by a burglar. The thief had ransacked the house, opening tins of soup and pouring them all over the kitchen floor. A tin of pears had also been opened, the juice drunk and the fruit scattered over the house. There was dirt on the bed – obviously someone had lain there with his shoes on – and mysterious holes had been made in the quilt and mattress. The carpet bore the marks of cigarette burns.

Among the items taken were a stopwatch, an ordinary watch and a unique electric shaver – an experimental type produced by Phillips in their Hamilton factory and not on sale to the public. Both the shaver and the holes in the mattress were to become significant almost eighteen months later.

When she arrived for work at 5 Fennsbank Avenue, High Burnside, shortly before 9 a.m. on Monday, 17 September, home help Mrs Helen Collison was puzzled to find the back door still locked. The door was normally left open for her by the daughter of the house, seventeen-year-old Vivienne Watt when she left for classes at Skerry's College, Glasgow.

Mrs Collison looked through Vivienne's bedroom window. The curtains were drawn but hung slightly loose and she could just make out the young girl's figure under the bedclothes. Assuming she had overslept, the domestic help rapped loudly on the glass. The girl did not move.

The woman walked round to the front of the bungalow, where she noticed that a pane of glass had been smashed beside the door. As she stood there, postman Peter Collier walked cheerily up the path. Concerned, she asked him to help her open the door. The postman put his hand through the broken pane and turned the Yale lock on the door.

Mrs Collison called out but there was no reply. She moved to the bedroom of Mrs Marion Watt, Vivienne's forty-year-old invalid mother. She knocked on the door and called the woman's name softly. Then she turned the door handle and walked into the room.

Mrs Watt and her sister, Mrs Margaret Brown, lay in bed, the bedclothes pulled up neatly under their chins. At first glance they looked as if they were fast asleep, but they were both dead, shot through the head at point-blank range. The only tell-tale sign was a thin trickle of blood from their noses.

Stunned, Peter Collier ran for the phone to call the police. Mrs Collison stumbled out of the room and into Vivienne's room. The girl's pillow was saturated with blood. She, too, had been shot in the head. But she was, miraculously, still alive. As the cleaning woman bent over her body, the young girl groaned once. The woman screamed to the postman in the hall to ask for an ambulance, too. It was, however, too late. The young girl died with a slight moan long before the police or an ambulance arrived. There was nothing anyone present could have done for her.

News of the charnel-house horror swept up the quiet residential street. Police and forensics teams descended on the bungalow like locusts, grimly searching the house for clues.

They were told that Mr William Watt, the father, was on a fishing trip at Lochgilphead. A Glasgow baker and one-time policeman, Mr Watt had recently recovered from a slight illness and had gone off to the country for a breather, taking the family dog, a black labrador named Queenie, with him. He had been expecting his wife and daughter to join him at the weekend.

Word was sent to his hotel of the tragedy, but the husband had left early that morning to go fishing. The owner knew where he was and rushed out to tell him of the murders.

The women had been murdered at some time early that morning. Detectives swiftly established that Vivienne and her friend Deanne Valente, who lived next door, had been listening to Radio Luxembourg's *Top Twenty* programme the night before. The show started at 11 p.m. and ended after midnight.

Deanne had gone home at about 11.50 p.m. and could hear from her own bedroom the sound of Vivienne's radio, playing the current number one record – Doris Day singing *Whatever Will Be, Will Be*. Reporters pounced on this snippet of information, almost gleefully dubbing the triple murderer 'The Top Twenty Killer.'

Deanne did not hear the shots later that night. Neither did a night-watchman at a building site only yards from the murder house.

Before she went to bed, Vivienne apparently ordered a wake-up telephone call for 7 a.m. the following morning. The operator's records showed that the call was made, but no one answered. By that time, of course, all three women were dead or dying.

Another break-in was discovered at Number 18 Fennsbank Avenue, a few houses down. This was owned by the Misses Martin, two sisters who had luckily been on holiday. As at the Watt house, access had been gained by breaking a small pane of glass on the door, slipping in a hand and turning the Yale lock. Once inside, the thief helped himself to some items of jewellery – but not before he had also helped himself to a tin of soup and a tin of spaghetti. As he ate the food, the intruder rested on a settee stubbing his cigarettes out on the carpet beside him.

Then the newspapers were told that Vivienne had been 'criminally assaulted'. Her pyjama trousers had been pulled off, her top ripped open and her bra wrenched from her body. She had not been sexually molested.

The *Evening Times* of Thursday, 20 September, was the first newspaper to raise the possibility of a link between the Watt murders and that of Anne Kneilands earlier that year. There were similarities in the way both girls' clothing was disarranged, they noted, quoting a police source.

There was also speculation that the killer may have been a nervous gunman who had walked into Mr Watt's bakery in London Road, in the city's east end, scaring a shop assistant half to death before running away.

On Sunday, 9 September, the man entered the shop at 800 London Road, a hat pulled low over the his eyes and his coat collar turned up to conceal his face. Stopping at the counter, he pointed a revolver at assistant Margaret Lambie, aged thirty-eight, who screamed in terror. The gunman, startled by the scream, ran out of the shop. He was never identified.

Could it have been Manuel? Or was it just a coincidence that a nervous armed raider tried to rob the bakery of a man whose family would be senselessly slain seven days later? We will probably never know.

The image of an unknown killer calmly walking into a suburban residence in the dead of night and slaughtering the sleeping occupants terrified the public. As the investigation progressed, worried Glaswegians began to sense that the police were baffled. One man from the west end of the city decided to offer detectives some advice on how they could clear up the mystery swiftly.

He sent a letter to Glasgow's Lord Provost suggesting that police call on the services of Dutch clairvoyant Peter Hurkos. Hurkos had been astounding Europe with his psychometric skills, the ability to sense events and identify people simply by handling objects or shaking hands.

The Lord Provost passed the letter on to Lanarkshire Chief Constable Thomas Renfrew who declined to take up the suggestion. The idea of using occult means to help solve a murder was perhaps too outlandish a notion to a hard-headed Scottish policeman.

(Fourteen years later, psychic Gerard Croiset would assist police in their investigations into both the disappearance of Annan teenager Pat McAdam and the Bible John murders in Glasgow. Despite impressive displays of his uncanny sixth sense, Croiset failed to produce any tangible leads and both cases remain officially unsolved (see Chapters Seven and Ten).)

Again, Manuel's name cropped up early in the investigation. An informant told a Lanarkshire detective that he had seen him in a pub before the triple slaying, boasting that he was going to rob a wealthy house and that if anyone caught him at it, he had 'the right thing' for them. With a knowing wink, he tapped something bulky in his jacket pocket. The informant suspected it was a gun.

Manuel later claimed to drinking cronies that he had tested the gun by shooting a cow up the nostril. A vet confirmed that a cow had, indeed, died mysteriously and he could find no cause. He had noticed slight bleeding around the nose but the thought of the cow dying from a gunshot had not occurred to him. Unfortunately, the carcass had already been disposed of.

Manuel was at the time out on bail on a charge of breaking and entering a canteen at Hamilton Colliery. A warrant was obtained to search his home. The search proved fruitless and, once again, this cold killer had to be set free.

Suspicion began to fall on Mr Watt. Although countless people testified to his being devoted to his invalid wife, police discovered that the Glasgow businessman had been unfaithful on more than one occasion.

He had claimed that on the night of the murder he had been asleep in his hotel room, intending to get up at 5.30 the following morning to go fishing. He had even borrowed an alarm clock to make sure he woke up. However, he said he slept through the alarm and did not wake up until 7.30 a.m., when he went out to find a good spot for his fishing before returning to the hotel at 8.30 a.m. for breakfast.

Another hotel guest confirmed that he had heard the alarm going off at 5.30 a.m. and ringing for some considerable time before shutting itself off. However, the police were of the opinion that it should have aroused the sleeping Mr Watt.

Meanwhile, the suspected man's claim that the drive from the hotel to his home in Glasgow took him two and a half hours was disproved by a police driver who made the trip in just over two hours. The theory was that Mr Watt slipped out of the hotel in the middle of the night, drove to his home in High Burnside, murdered his wife, daughter and sister-in-law and then returned to Lochgilphead after the alarm had gone off.

The theory was backed by the evidence of a ferryman on the Renfrew ferry who positively identified Mr Watt as the man who had driven onto his boat on the north side of the river at 3 a.m. on that fateful morning. The man had a big black dog in his car.

On Thursday, 27 September, William Watt was charged with the three murders. He would spend sixty-seven tense days in Barlinnie Prison. While, in another wing, the real killer was serving eighteen months for the colliery break-in.

In prison, Manuel kept himself up to date with the developments in the Watt case by avidly reading the newspapers and picking up bits of news from inmates. He knew that William Watt was being kept in the untried prisoners wing of Barlinnie. He even showed signs of sympathy with the man's plight.

Slowly though, it began to dawn on Manuel's warped mind that Mr Watt was receiving all the attention. Manuel knew that the police had the wrong man and he did not like that man receiving 'credit' he did not deserve.

Manuel began to talk, at first to other inmates. He whispered that he knew something about the killings. He suggested that he knew who the real killer was. He boasted that he knew details about the house's interior that would back up his story. He hinted that he would be willing to talk.

His story fell mainly on deaf ears. Manuel was well known as a spinner of tales, a weaver of fantasies in which he cast himself as an important central character. He exaggerated his American birth, often sporting what was by then a fake accent. He also liked to claim that he was once the henchman of Chicago mobster Al Capone – despite the fact that he had never been near the Windy City and that Manuel had only been three years of age when Capone was at the height of his career.

He was known for writing tip-off letters to the police, claiming knowledge of crimes that he plainly did not have. He told fellow inmates that he had been the mastermind behind two daring raids –

one a £40,000 bullion raid in London in September 1954, the other a £50,000 bank raid in Glasgow in 1955.

One of his fantasies did bring the desired result. During his sojourn in Peterhead, serving eight years on the rape charge, he claimed to have become friendly with an unnamed man who had intimate knowledge of the escape route used by Burgess and Maclean, the Soviet spies.

Unlike his other tales, this was given some credence by the authorities. The US Government, seriously concerned over the state of British security following the spy revelations, sent two FBI agents from Washington to interview Manuel, who was flown to London for the occasion. It did not take the agents long to realise that this small Scot was fantasising.

But Manuel had what he wanted all along – attention. He was centre stage and all eyes were on him, if only for a comparatively brief moment. And now he saw William Watt receiving the attention that he, Peter Manuel, rightly deserved.

Manuel eventually wrote to lawyer Lawrence Dowdall, who was representing Watt, repeating his claims of insider knowledge of the murders. He backed up his claims with detailed descriptions of the interior of the Watt house – and the information that one of the women had been shot twice in the head.

Mr Dowdall checked this latter piece of information with the police, who confirmed that one of the victims had, indeed, received two bullet wounds, information that had not been made public.

Manuel also stated that during an earlier housebreaking, his nameless informant had fired his gun, a .38 Webley, into a mattress. Apparently he had been arguing with his female accomplice and the gun had gone off.

The lawyer visited Manuel in prison, going over the man's story in painstaking detail, not believing for a minute that a third party had told Manuel what happened on that dark and bloody night in such minute detail. The prisoner insisted that it was true.

At the same time, police received information from another confidential source that Manuel had bought a Webley revolver the week before the Watt murders.

Once again, police officers searched Manuel's home, this time even going over the small garden with mine detectors in case he had buried the weapon. But they came up empty handed. What they did not know was that the gun was already lying at the bottom of the River Clyde.

Lawrence Dowdall, a legend among Glasgow criminal lawyers, managed to demolish the flimsy evidence against his client. The crucial ferryman's identification was called into question when the lawyer pointed out that it was a very dark night and that Mr Watt's photograph and that of his dog had been all over the newspapers for some days.

On 3 December 1956 William Watt was released from Barlinnie, the charges against him dropped. However, the dark stain of suspicion was never fully washed away and even today there are a few people who remember the case who whisper of hired killers and murder plots which went wrong. But there is no evidence, no proof.

Publicly, the police now theorised that the murders had been committed by a burglar who had panicked and shot the three women. Secretly, a growing number of detectives suspected that Manuel was the real killer. Newspaper editors were also convinced of his guilt and reporters were sent out to gather background copy on Manuel, ready for publication on his eventual conviction.

William Watt, his prison ordeal behind him, now set out to conduct his own enquiries. The police had already arrested the wrong man once; they could do so again. He visited certain bars in the city known to be the haunts of Glasgow's underworld. The word was spread and certain forces within the city's twilight people were only too willing to furnish him with details about Manuel's stories.

Manuel himself was released from prison in November 1957, still insisting on his version of events. Eight days after receiving his liberty, he made a trip to Newcastle in search of a job. He did not find employment, but he did commit murder.

Taxi driver Sydney Dunn could not believe his luck when he picked up the man outside Newcastle railway station and was told to take him to Edinburgh. But as he neared the village of Edmunbyers in County Durham, his luck ran out. Manuel drew a gun and shot him in the back of the head and then cut his throat.

Exactly why he killed the taxi driver was never discovered, although there was a theory that the man had somehow made a wrong turning, sending the deranged Manuel off into a frenzy. Certainly the cab was badly smashed up when it was discovered on a lonely stretch of moorland. Mr Dunn's body lay a few yards away.

In Glasgow, Manuel suggested that he and Watt meet in the Whitehall Restaurant in Glasgow. At that meeting, and in subsequent conversations in a bar in Crown Street, Manuel sketched his story, implicating a petty thief and his girlfriend in the murders. They had broken into the Watt house by mistake, he claimed, expecting to find a safe filled with money.

By this time, Mr Watt was convinced of this man's guilt. It must have taken a great deal of self-control to keep his anger and hatred from spilling over. He knew, perhaps on Lawrence Dowdall's advice, that the only way they were going to get this man was to let him talk. Perhaps his own words would hang him.

However, at one point, Watt did crack and he told Manuel that if he thought he had had anything to do with the murders he would 'not only lay hands on him, he would tear him into little pieces'.

Manuel looked at the grieving husband and father coolly, sat up straight and said: 'People don't do that to Peter Manuel.'

He then took out a photograph of a girl and ripped it up into little pieces, dropping them into an ashtray. With horror, Mr Watt recognised the picture of Anne Kneilands.

Meanwhile, Mr and Mrs Platt had moved house and just before Christmas of 1957 had noticed lumps in their mattress – lumps that had not been there before. It was as if something had been dislodged during the flitting. Ripping open the holes that had been made by the burglar the year before they found one of their missing watches.

Probing further into the mattress they made a more sinister discovery – a spent bullet from a .38 revolver.

They passed it on to the police and a ballistics expert confirmed that the bullet came from the same gun used in the Watt murders.

Whoever had killed those three people had also broken into the Platt house in September. As with the Martin sisters in High Burnside, it was only by sheer good fortune that they had been on holiday.

The Reverend Alexander Houston and his wife also narrowly escaped death. Luckily, they had been visiting friends when a thief forced his way into their home at 66 Wester Road, Mount Vernon, on Christmas Day, 1957. The burglar made off with a camera, a new pair of men's gloves and £2 from a missionary collection box. At the time, no one saw anything more evil in the crime than a petty theft. However, had the Reverend Houston and his wife been at home, they might have become the next victims.

The gloves and the camera would later prove to be Manuel's undoing.

On 28 December a young man stood at the bus stop in Uddingston, waiting for his girlfriend to arrive. He waited for some time but the girl never appeared.

The girl, Isabelle Cooke, had left her home at 5 Carrick Drive,

Mount Vernon – only a short distance from Reverend Houston's Wester Road home – earlier that evening. She had made her way along a quiet, deserted footpath that ran across the Shettleston to Bothwell railway line. She had been heading for London Road, where she would have caught a bus to Uddingston.

At about 7.30 p.m., a woman who lived near the footpath heard a girl's voice, crying out in fear. There were no other sounds and the woman lost interest.

Isabelle Cooke had become Manuel's next victim.

The following day, the girl's father reported her disappearance to the police, who immediately started a search. There was no sign of Isabelle, although they did find her cosmetic bag under a railway bridge in Mount Vernon Avenue.

The hunt continued but proved fruitless. The river was dragged. North Calder Water was dammed by the fire brigade and the water pumped out. The countryside was combed. Reports were received from all over the country that she had been seen alive and well. Each report was carefully checked and proved either a mistake or a hoax.

Police formed a theory that her body might have been thrown off a bridge on to an open wagon of a passing goods train. Railway goods vans were searched in sidings all over Scotland.

Reverend Houston appealed from his pulpit for volunteers to help the police conduct their search. But they did not find Isabelle's body.

Soon, Uddingston would be rocked by another terrifying tragedy.

On 2 January a car owned by Peter James Smart of 38 Sheepburn Road, Uddingston, was found abandoned in Florence Street, Gorbals. Police officers tried to contact both Mr Smart and his employers, a civil engineering company in London Road, but the office was closed for the New Year and there was no answer from Mr Smart's home.

Mr Smart left work for the holidays on 31 December. Before he went home to Uddingston, he had drawn £35 in new notes from the Commercial Bank at Parkhead Cross. He and his family had intended to visit his parents in Jedburgh over the New Year period. On Hogmanay, a neighbour said she saw the lights of the house on, while next morning the garage doors were open and the car was gone. On 2 January the neighbour shut the doors, noticing that the bedroom and dining-room curtains were drawn. Other neighbours also noticed this, while a family friend passing by said the lounge curtains were drawn but the windows

St Mary's Roman Catholic Church in Abercrombie Street, Glasgow – the focus of a riot following the ambush of a police van carrying an IRA officer in 1921

Tower Cottage, high on a hill overlooking Loch Tay, where Stanislaw Myszka brutally murdered shepherd's wife Catherine McIntyre in 1947

Quiet Fennsbank Avenue, High Burnside, where Peter Manuel murdered Marion Watt, her daughter Vivienne and her sister Margaret Brown in 1956

Peter Manuel, perhaps Scotland's most notorious murderer
(Courtesy of the Sunday Mail and Daily Record)

Attractive Sheila Garvie and her husband Maxwell in happier times
(Courtesy of the *Sunday Mail* and *Daily Record*)

St Mary's Kirk, Biggar, where pretty Linda Peacock met her death

Glasgow's Barrowland Ballroom, the haunt of the shadowy Bible John in 1969/70

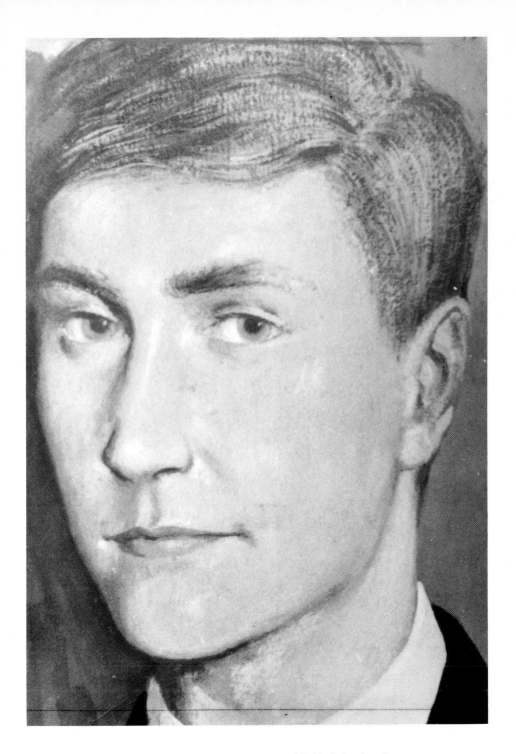

The face of a killer? An artist's impression of Bible John, based on witness descriptions. His true identity remains a mystery to this day
(Courtesy of the *Sunday Mail* and *Daily Record*)

Detectives on the Edinburgh rail line where the first piece of the Torso Murder puzzle was found. To their right can be seen the woman's leg, wrapped in a blanket, which sparked off the massive murder hunt in 1969
(Courtesy of the *Sunday Mail* and *Daily Record*)

The tenement at 51 Allison Street, Glasgow, where Howard Wilson gunned down three policemen in 1969, killing two of them

Howard Wilson being led from Glasgow's High Court
(Courtesy of the *Sunday Mail* and *Daily Record*)

The multi-storey car park in Waterloo Street, Glasgow, where Thomas Young allegedly took prostitutes

The face of Archibald Hall, The Demon Butler
(Courtesy of the *Sunday Mail* and *Daily Record*)

were open – a curious thing for a family to do in the middle of winter.

At about 7.30 p.m. on Friday, 3 January 1958, a light was seen in the dining-room of the Smart home. The witness assumed that the family had returned home. The following day, the lounge curtains were open again and the windows closed. Someone had obviously been in the house during the night.

On Monday, 6 January, Mr Smart failed to turn up for work. His employers sent a foreman out to look for him. The man found milk and newspapers piled up on the doorstep but there was no sign of life in the house.

The foreman alerted the police who forced open the back door. In the hallway letters, newspapers and magazines dating from 31 December were found lying on the carpet.

In the master bedroom, Mr Smart and his wife were lying in bed, shot trough the head at point-blank range. Mrs Smart's nightdress had been ripped open. In the smaller bedroom, eleven-year-old Michael Smart had also been shot.

The family had been dead for some days. The house had been ransacked and it was obvious the killer had spent some time there. He had made himself some food in the kitchen and had fed the family cat with a tin of salmon. Police suspected that he had returned to the house on a number of occasions between New Year's morning, when he had killed the family, and the following weekend. Perhaps he had come back to feed the cat, they thought.

Manuel's callous audacity knew no bounds. He had been able to return many times to the house and relax and eat while the dead bodies of his victims lay nearby. On 2 January he had even coolly given a lift to Constable Robert Smith in the car stolen from the Smart's garage. Constable Smith had been on his way to join in the search for Isabelle Cooke and Manuel had chatted to him during the journey in a friendly manner about the girl's disappearance.

And as the policeman climbed out of the stolen car, Manuel smiled, nodded towards the gathering search party, and said: 'They're searching in the wrong place.'

Then he drove off, leaving a perplexed and slightly chilled young police constable standing on the pavement.

In the days that followed the discovery of the murdered Smart family, terror held sway over the streets. As in Burnside just after the Watt murders, local people became increasingly security conscious. One ironmonger told reporters that in the seven days after the discovery of the bodies he had sold six dozen door chains and was sold out of door bolts. Normally, he said, there was very little demand for these items.

This new atrocity horrified even the most hardened criminals. It was common knowledge in the underworld that Peter Manuel was the culprit and by this time they were heartily sick of his boastful ways. They preferred to keep their activities shadowy and silent; Manuel was a publicity seeker, a man who wanted to impress others with his deeds.

Certain information was steered towards police investigating the case, including the fact that Manuel had been seen spending money freely after 1 January – money which he had not had on 31 December. Police were told that they were new notes and were also informed in which pubs Manuel had been seen.

The information was checked and some of the notes recovered. The serial numbers tallied with those of the notes given to Mr Smart by the Parkhead bank.

Once again, police swooped on the Manuel home. This time, they found what was left of the money, the unique razor from the Platt break-in and the camera and gloves taken from the home of the Reverend Houston. Samuel Manuel, Peter's father, was arrested for the break-in and Manuel himself was taken for questioning.

Even now, he tried to lie his way out of the situation. At police headquarters in Hamilton, Manuel blamed Samuel 'Dandy' McKay, a well-known Glasgow criminal, for the Smart murders. He claimed that McKay had given him the banknotes.

McKay was a thief and a hard man but was not one to kill a family in cold blood and the police knew this. However, they pulled the man in and made Manuel repeat his allegations to his face. McKay's expression darkened when he heard the accusation. He then told Manuel that he had made the biggest mistake of his life, and one that he would swing for.

Angrily, McKay told the police everything he knew about Manuel – and he knew a great deal. He knew about the guns. He knew about Manuel's boasting. He could give times and dates.

Eventually, Manuel himself cracked. Detectives had gathered a vast array of evidence linking him with the Smart murders. Manuel's cool reserve crumbled. His arrogance washed away on a sea of self-pity, Manuel spilled all in a meeting with his parents and Detective Inspector Robert McNeill of Lanarkshire police. Also present were Detective Superintendent Alexander Brown and Detective Inspector Thomas Goodall of Glasgow police – the latter the nemesis of many a Glasgow criminal, including Jimmy Boyle.

His mother started it off. She sat at a table with her son

and said quietly: 'Tell us everything, Peter. Tell the truth about everything.'

Just as quietly, Manuel said: 'I have been fighting this for years. There is no future for me. I have done some terrible things.'

And out it all came – how he killed Anne Kneilands on that dark winter's night two years before, the slaying of the Watt and Smart families, the murder of Isabelle Cooke. It was a chilling montage of murder unique in the annals of Scottish crime.

Manuel made two written statements, and led the police to the newly ploughed field on Burntbroom Farm near Uddingston where he had buried Isabelle Cooke's body. At first he could not find the exact spot but then he stopped, pointed at the ground beneath his feet and quite calmly said: 'I think she is in there.' He glanced around him again, then continued: 'I think I am standing on her.'

Grimly, police began to dig, unearthing Isabelle's half-naked, strangled body, her bra still tied tightly round her neck.

Manuel also told them that he had dropped both guns in the Clyde, ironically near the High Court where he would soon stand trial.

This posed a problem to police: How could they search the bottom of the murky river? First, they used a large electromagnet, but succeeded in attracting only a variety of knives and pieces of scrap metal.

Then, for the first time in Scotland, a civilian diver was recruited. He searched the river bed for only twenty minutes before bursting to the surface with a Webley revolver in his hand. Tests would later prove that it was the weapon used in the Watt horror. A further two fruitless days followed, before the diver appeared triumphantly on the surface again, this time with a Beretta automatic – the gun used in the Smart killings.

The horror was over, but the drama would continue.

The trial of Peter Manuel began on Monday, 12 May 1958. For weeks it had been the main talking point of Glasgow. The name Peter Manuel was on everybody's lips. He was, at the time, the greatest mass murderer Scotland had ever seen. To countless children he was the personification of the bogeyman; a threat issued by parents for poor behaviour – 'If you don't get to your bed, Peter Manuel will come and get you.'

Hundreds of citizens wanted to be in the court to see the monster on trial for his life. However, there was room only for sixty persons in the public gallery. At 8.20 p.m. on Sunday, 11 May – the day before the trial began – a queue began to form outside the North Court. People brought flasks, food and sleeping-bags, prepared to camp out in the street.

At 10 a.m. the following morning, the first sixty people were allowed in. They expected grisly tales of foul murder and high drama. They were not disappointed.

There were surprises right from the opening moments of the trial. Manuel sat in the dock, neatly dressed in a blazer and slate grey trousers specially bought for the trial. He was flanked by two policemen, wooden batons held loosely in their white-gloved hands.

The jury was made up of nine men and six women. Manuel's lawyers had tried to talk him into pushing for an all-male jury, fearing that details of his crimes would alienate the female members, but he refused, claiming self-confidently: 'I have a way with women.'

He pleaded 'Not Guilty' to the eight charges of capital murder, three charges of theft by housebreaking and one of simple theft. If he was found guilty of any one of the murder charges, he would hang.

Manuel's lawyers invoked special defences on the murder charges. He claimed alibi on the Kneilands, Cooke and Smart murders. For the Burnside murders, he shocked the court by accusing William Watt.

Press, public and the jury were stunned. The following day the newspapers were filled with the accusations. Once again, Manuel enjoyed the full glare of publicity.

For the first three days of the trial he seemed to satisfy himself with that, sitting impassively as he listened to the case against him. There was no sign of emotion as William Watt gave evidence from a bed wheeled into the court – a few days before he had been injured in a car accident.

For three days Manuel sat there, without saying a word. Then he sprang his next surprise.

On the fourth day, just as Detective Inspector Thomas Goodall was about to give evidence, Manuel asked for permission to speak to the court. He stood up and said to the judge, Lord Cameron: 'My Lord, before the examination of this witness begins, I would like an opportunity to confer with my counsel.'

Permission was given and just under an hour later, Manuel's QC, Mr Harold Leslie, told the court: 'I have to inform your Lordship that I am now no longer in a position with my colleagues to continue with the case, Manuel being desirous of conducting the remainder of the trial. Unless I can be of any further service, I and my colleagues will accordingly withdraw.'

Now Manuel really was where he had always wanted to be – in the spotlight. The eyes of not only Glasgow but the rest of Britain were upon him, for the trial was being covered by newspapermen from all over the country. It was as if he was reliving one of the great triumphs of his life, when he successfully defended himself on a rape charge in 1955.

Over the next twelve days he displayed a flair for cross-examination and some considerable courtroom skill. But his position was indefensible – and it was not helped by his constant accusations that the police had conspired to frame him. Neither did his constantly changing stories go unnoticed by the jury.

He put William Watt back on the stand and openly accused him of murdering his wife, daughter and sister-in-law. Mr Watt coldly called him a liar. He put his own parents on the stand in a vain attempt to uphold his various alibis. He questioned a stream of petty criminals. And then he went on the stand himself. He denied his guilt, even claiming that he had supplied Mr Smart with the gun which was used in the Uddingston murders. He said that just after New Year he visited the Smart home, found the bodies and took the gun from the dead hand of Peter Smart, who, he claimed, had killed his wife, son and then himself. Manuel said he threw the gun away to protect himself.

He repeated his accusation against Mr Watt, using the already discredited testimony of the ferryman as the basis of his evidence. As for his written confessions, Manuel claimed that he had made them to protect his family, who were under threat from the police. The confessions were all part of an elaborate conspiracy to frame him. He further claimed that he did not lead detectives to the site of Isabelle Cooke's makeshift grave: they in fact took him.

In his summing up, Lord Cameron warned the jury not to allow their judgment to be 'clouded by any feeling of revulsion at the nature of the crimes'.

He added: 'Innocent blood has been shed and young lives have been cut short in conditions of tragedy and horror, but neither you nor I are here as avengers of blood. You and I are here as Ministers and servants of the law and, I hope, justice.'

He also said that Manuel had conducted his own defence 'with a skill that is quite remarkable'.

It was not skilful enough. After a sixteen-day trial, the jury took only two and a half hours to reach their verdict. As they filed back into the courtroom, a slight sheen of sweat broke out on Manuel's face. It was his only outward sign of nervousness.

The jury found him guilty of seven murders. He was found 'Not Guilty' of the Anne Kneilands killing due to lack of corroborative evidence pointing to his guilt – his signed confession was not enough under Scots law. As for the murder of the Newcastle taxi driver, Sydney Dunn, the court had no jurisdiction over a killing committed on English soil and so that case would remain untried. Justice would be served though, a Newcastle detective had been waiting in court to take Manuel into custody should he be freed by any strange quirk of fate.

A grim-faced Lord Cameron stared fixedly at Manuel as he intoned the fateful words of the death sentence.

'Peter Thomas Anthony Manuel, in respect of the verdict of guilty of capital murder and of murder done on different occasions, the sentence of the court is that you will be taken from this place to the prison of Barlinnie at Glasgow to be detained until the nineteenth day of June and on that day within the said prison at Glasgow and between the hours of eight and ten to suffer death by hanging.'

Then the judge placed the ominous black cap on his head and added: 'This pronounced for doom.'

Manuel's subsequent appeal was turned down, the court of Criminal Appeal in Edinburgh ruling that his confession was made when he was 'fully and rationally aware of what he was doing and deliberately made up his own mind to unburden his soul of the dark deeds which he narrated with such convincing detail'.

When he heard that his appeal had been refused, Manuel tried to cheat the hangman by stealing some disinfectant from a guard cleaning his cell and swallowed it. His suicide attempt failed, and from then until the day of the execution he was guarded constantly by three prison officers.

During his time in prison, waiting for the end, Manuel confessed to three other murders: that of Helen 'Red Helen' Carlin, a prostitute found strangled in Pimlico, London in September, 1954; Anne Steele, a fifty-five-year-old woman battered to death in Glasgow in June, 1956; and Ellen 'English Nellie' Petrie, stabbed in June 1956 in Glasgow. Police believe that other unsolved killings were also the work of this lone madman but will never know for certain.

At 8 a.m. on Friday, 11 July 1958, Manuel's older brother James knelt in a Motherwell chapel, praying to God for the soul of his brother.

In Barlinnie Prison on the other side of Glasgow, Manuel was taken from his cell into the room next door. The apparatus had been tested by hangman Harry Allen the night before, rubber silencers fitted to the trapdoor so as not to disturb the condemned man. The executioner had also observed Manuel through a spyhole before completing his fatal calculations.

Manuel had been silent for three weeks, refusing to speak to anyone except his parents or his brother. He did not break that silence on the scaffold on that grey, rain-swept July morning.

At 8.01 a.m. it was all over.

He would be the last man to be hanged in Glasgow. Hangman Harry Allen would execute Peter Anthony Allen (no relation) in Liverpool on 13 August 1964. The man had been found guilty of murdering van-driver John West during a robbery attempt. His accomplice Gwynne Owen Evans was hung on the same day in Manchester. They were the last people to be executed in Britain. The last Scottish execution was in 1963 when Henry John Burnett was hanged in Aberdeen.

At the time of Manuel's death, his home in Birkenshaws lay empty. His parents had left town before the end of the trial. The street, a cul-de-sac, was empty. A prayer light which had been burning in the window from the first night of his arrest was finally extinguished.

A few miles away, what was once the home of the Smart family in Uddingston was deserted, the windows boarded. Locals claimed it was haunted. No one would move in. Some time later it would be bought by a family unafraid of gossip. By a chilling coincidence, their name would be Watt.

Later on the day of the hanging James Manuel would travel by bus to Barlinnie Prison, where his brother was to be buried in a grave marked only by his initials, and as a slight rain fell from a slate grey sky, would deliver a simple wreath to the gates.

The card would read: 'To my brother Peter from James.'

It would be the only sign of mourning for the monster known as Manuel.

Chapter Seven

TRAVELLING MAN

When the lorry stopped it must have seemed like a miracle. The two girls had been standing in the cold of a Glasgow February morning trying to thumb a lift home to Dumfriesshire – not an easy task on a drizzly Sunday.

Seventeen-year-old Pat McAdam and her nineteen-year-old friend Hazel Campbell had travelled north to Glasgow the day before, spending the day shopping and then going out dancing at night.

The girls had then gone on to an all-night party in the East End and were now hitch-hiking their way back home, standing in the city's London Road, desperately trying to flag down one of the few vehicles heading south at that time of the morning.

The heavy lorry pulled into the side of the road ahead of them, its brakes screeching in the damp morning air. The driver seemed to be a friendly sort, smiling as he leaned out of the cab to ask the girls where they were going. Hazel was going to her home in Annan, Pat to Dumfries. The girls were in luck – the driver was heading for Hull. He could take them all the way.

The truck steamed down the road, stopping at the Star service-station at Lesmahagow where the man very kindly bought the girls something to eat. He was full of patter, this driver. Charming even. So charming that he managed to lure young Pat, a pretty brunette, into the back of the lorry where they kissed and cuddled while Hazel slept in the cabin.

Finally, Hazel was dropped off in Annan at about 2 p.m. She closed the large door behind her, waving to her friend Pat, shouting to her that she would see her later. And then the driver heaved his vehicle into gear and drove off in the direction of Dumfries. But Hazel would never see Pat again. No one would – except perhaps her killer.

It was Sunday, 19 February 1967, and Pat McAdam was about to become one of the country's most celebrated mysteries.

The girl's worried parents contacted the police when Pat did not come home. Detectives spoke to Hazel and through her description traced the haulage firm which owned the lorry – and the driver who had picked the girls up.

But the driver insisted that he had dropped the girl off just outside Dumfries – although he admitted that he had made love to her in a lay-by just outside Annan first. However, Hazel had said that Pat had rebuffed a young man at the party by telling him it was her time of the month. Why then would she give in to a stranger in the cab of a lorry?

Police were suspicious. A lorry like the one driven by the man had been seen speeding through the maze of narrow roads between Annan and Lockerbie – and the driver had not turned up at his digs in Hull that evening as planned.

There was, however, no firm evidence to link the man with the girl's disappearance and the police were eventually forced to let him go.

The search for the missing girl continued. Police would use every means at their disposal in a search that would continue for months, including tracker dogs, frogmen, helicopters and uniformed officers conducting door-to-door enquiries in the rural area around Dumfries and Annan.

They would even use the mysterious skills of a Dutch clairvoyant to try and trace her body – and hopefully lead them to her murderer. Gerard Croiset had often been called upon by the authorities in Holland to help in murder cases and had achieved some fame through his involvement in a case of kidnapping and child murder in New York. His countryman, Peter Hurkos, had also been involved in the search for the Boston Strangler, with disappointing results.

However, British police are a hard-headed bunch who would rather deal in hard facts than airy-fairy notions of the divination of clues through the supernatural.

It was the *Daily Record* which first contacted Gerard Croiset and asked him to use his psychometric skills to help them in the search – and of course sell a few more newspapers. One of their reporters flew to Utrecht with Pat McAdam's bible. The psychic held the book and announced that the girl was dead, that she had been killed near a bridge and her body thrown into a river. This was interesting: the lorry had been seen parked near a bridge over the River Annan which flows out into the Solway Firth. Croiset then went on to describe a house nearby with an advertisement sign on the side. In the garden, he said, there was a wheelbarrow and a car with no wheels. Once again, this fitted the facts: there was such a house near the bridge – complete with wheelbarrow and old car.

The psychic then stated that the body was caught in tree roots and the girl's clothing could be found along the riverbank.

A search was made . . . and women's clothes were found at the side of the river. However, they were not Pat McAdam's – and her body was never found.

Croiset visited the area to see if he could pick up any other vibrations and said he felt water every time he thought about the missing girl. Perhaps her body had been washed out into the Solway Firth, where strong currents could have carried it out to sea or forced it into any of the stretches of quicksand for which the area is notorious. During his visit to Scotland, Croiset would be called on to help Glasgow police in their search for Bible John (see Chapter Ten).

The search gradually wound down and the Pat McAdam case faded from the public consciousness. But ten years after the girl disappeared, that same public would be reminded of the unfortunate teenager when a Glasgow man was arrested for multiple rape and murder.

That man was Thomas Ross Young. And he was the lorry driver who picked up the girls in London Road on that cold February morning.

Thomas Ross Young was described as a 'text book rapist'. He had no respect for women, even loathed them.

After his trial for murder in 1977, Young's ex-wife, Alice (not her real name), said of him: 'They were just there to be used and abused by him. He always felt he had been rejected by a woman – his mother – when he was young.'

Young was an illegitimate child born in Kirkintilloch in 1934. From the start, his mother wanted nothing whatsoever to do with him and left it to her parents to bring the boy up. In 1946 they adopted him officially. But by then the damage had been done.

He found himself in trouble with the law at nine years of age when he was admonished in Kirkintilloch Burgh Police Court on a charge of theft. A few months later, in November 1943, he was given a year's probation on three charges of housebreaking.

More telling was his conviction at thirteen years of age for indecent assault and theft. For this he received his first taste of institutional life, being sent to Oakbank Approved School. Five years later, while in the army, he received ninety-one days detention by a military court in Catterick for going AWOL.

In 1955 he met the woman he would marry while working in an iron foundry in Kirkintilloch. Her parents did not approve of their daughter's choice of a husband and the couple ran away to Chesterfield where they were married in March, 1956.

At first the newly-weds were very happy. They lived in England for a time before they moved back to Kirkintilloch and finally to a flat – a single end – in Glasgow.

And then Young began to change from a loving, even considerate, husband to a violent monster. His temper would flare up suddenly and he would lash out at his wife. He also took to staying out all night.

Alice later said that she believed he was jealous of their son. She felt that she had not paid enough attention to her husband. And when his violent, highly sexed nature led him to rape and murder, she would even blame herself, feeling that perhaps her lack of sexual drive forced him to seek satisfaction elsewhere.

She was, of course, wrong: Young's sex drive was tremendously high but also abnormal, according to one psychiatrist's report at the time of his trial. When the need for sex came over him he felt he must have it – at any cost.

Another report suggested that Young may also have been sexually inadequate, becoming frenzied when he could not find satisfaction. He would then turn to deviant acts, becoming violent when his partners refused to give in.

His aggression often found expression at home. He continued to beat his wife – once kicking her around the house before throwing her into a cupboard which he then sealed with six inch nails. He left her in there for over an hour before he let her out.

The woman spent six weeks in hospital after that incident. She had been beaten so badly that doctors thought she would lose her sight.

His womanising continued unchecked. At one point, one of his girlfriends came to their flat looking for him. When she discovered that he was married she terminated the relationship immediately.

Young seldom told his fancy women that he was married. He spun them tales, sometimes lying about his name and his address. He told others that he had been married but that his wife had died.

One Christmas he brought home a sweater with a card saying – 'With Love from Margaret'. His wife promptly threw it on the fire – and received another beating for her trouble.

But his wife stuck with him, despite an abortive attempt at

divorce in 1963. She stayed with him for one simple reason – fear. She was frightened of what would happen if she tried to end the marriage or get some sort of help.

She even stuck with him through his trial at Shropshire Assizes in 1967 when he was accused of raping a nineteen-year-old girl. He told her that the girl had been a prostitute and had demanded more money than he cared to give.

Mrs Young believed him, putting his dalliance with a prostitute down to her own lack of interest in sex. But he still received eighteen months in prison.

His violence was not solely aimed at his wife. He once viciously slashed one of their three sons across the throat with his lorry-driver's clipboard. He also assaulted his two daughters-in-law.

But for his only daughter he had nothing but love. Penny (not her real name) was the apple of his eye and he often gave her presents. It was one of these presents that would help convict him of murder.

Finally, in 1970, Mrs Young began divorce proceedings. By this time her husband had once again been arrested for rape; on this occasion the victim was a fifteen-year-old girl in the cab of his lorry at Abington in Lanarkshire. When he heard what his wife was doing, Young threatened to kill her.

But this time the woman was determined to see things through and in 1973 the decree was made final. She hoped she had seen the last of the man she once called husband. But in 1975, Young was released from jail having completed two-thirds of his eight-year sentence.

He went to live in a flat in Ashley Street, near St George's Cross in Glasgow's north side. He would continue to call in at his former wife's flat in Crow Road, Glasgow, ostensibly to see the children.

He still spent some of his spare time at home, reading war comics as well as such dangerous literature as *The Dandy* and *The Beano*. He also loved the cinema, although by that time his favourite star, Doris Day, had retired from the screen.

And at the same time, he had embarked on a two-year orgy of rape and violence that would end in murder.

Young claimed that he had had sex with over 200 girls in the cab of his lorry over the years.

'Picking up girls is easy,' he once smilingly told detectives. And if the girls proved unwilling to give in to his demands he simply attacked them and raped them.

He was not a big man – only five foot, eight inches tall – but he was powerfully built, using chest expanders and karate training to keep himself fit. He could easily have overpowered the girls and women he picked up in his lorry, and later, when he prowled the night-enshrouded streets of the city.

He liked to keep himself neat and tidy, spending an hour in the bathroom every morning grooming himself. He liked to be clean-cut and neatly dressed. It was a compulsion that he carried with him to work. His employer said that he was the best driver he had ever had. He was always on time and kept his lorry spotlessly clean, but seldom mixed socially with his fellow workers, keeping himself to himself. Naturally, this employer knew nothing of Young's criminal record for theft and rape.

It is impossible to say exactly how many assaults he was responsible for as so many rapes go unreported. It is also impossible to say how many willing sexual partners he picked up on his innumerable long-distance trips to the south of England.

He also took to cruising the streets of Glasgow at night, sometimes with a taxi sign on top of his hired car to attract 'fares'. Occasionally he would pick up a prostitute, take her to a multi-storey car park in Waterloo Street – in the heart of Glasgow's red light area – and beat her up if she refused to indulge in bouts of sadistic sex. One of these working girls even claimed that he had stubbed a lighted cigarette out in her face, although this was found Not Proven in court.

It was only a matter of time before he turned to murder.

On Monday, 27 June 1977, farmer's son Henry Morgan was helping his father on South Medrox Farm, Glenboig. He was driving his tractor on a small road leading to Inchneuk Farm when he caught sight of something lying half concealed beneath leaves and bushes.

He climbed out of his cab and went to investigate. The smell was overpowering as he pushed the leaves back to reveal the half-naked, almost mummified, body of a woman, lying face down with her hands tied behind her back and her pants thrust into her mouth.

The body was later identified as thirty-seven-year-old bakery worker Frances Barker, who had been missing since 10 June. Police believed that she had accepted a lift from her killer in the streets of Maryhill in Glasgow.

The damp conditions of the lane meant that the corpse was badly decomposed by the time pathologists were able to make their examination. Establishing the cause of death was difficult, but they were in no doubt that it was murder.

Doctors found a small bone in her throat had been broken and showed traces of blood. They were of the opinion that there was no question of the injury occurring after death. They decided that auburn-haired Frances Barker had died from strangulation or suffocation – or a combination of both.

The road in which her body was found was a well-known lovers' lane where, two months before the discovery of the corpse, a prostitute had been attacked by a lorry driver. The man had refused to pay her, raped her and then hit her on the mouth with an iron bar. Badly beaten, she had managed to stop a car driving by and so escape the same fate that befell Frances Barker.

The prostitute's evidence led detectives to a string of rapes and brutal assaults, including that of a sixteen-year-old girl. All the facts drew the investigating officers inexorably to Young, but when they called at his Ashley Street flat their bird had flown.

When he heard that the net was tightening on him, Young had fled to Alice's flat. He hit her as soon as he walked in, then grabbed her by the throat and said: 'I'm going to do you in. It won't make much difference. I'm going away for a long time anyway.'

The terrified woman agreed to hide the man she had once loved, lying to the police when they finally arrived. But the police sensed her nervousness and decided to keep a close watch on the Crow Road flat. They waited outside, watching the close entrance and the windows for any sign of their quarry. Their hunch paid off. Eventually, Young was spotted at the kitchen window and subsequently arrested.

During a search of the flat a detective found his feet sinking into the floor of the bedroom. Jerking back the carpet he found a hole leading to specially constructed shelter where Young had hidden earlier.

They also found some vital pieces of evidence – a number of articles which could be traced to the dead woman, including a powder compact, a make-up bag and a lipstick.

Young had also given his beloved daughter a bracelet which had belonged to Miss Barker. He later claimed that he had bought it for £8 from a pawnbroker.

His Scania Super Eighty lowloader lorry was placed under scrutiny. Forensic scientists vacuumed the interior of the cab, finding a hawthorn leaf which could have come from the murder lane and a sample of hair. The blood type on the roots matched that of Frances Barker. Scratches on the roof could also have been made by the low-lying branches hanging over the lane.

Detectives spent days in a similar vehicle, timing the route that Young had claimed to have travelled. They even drove up and down the scene of the crime to check that the branches did, indeed, touch the top of the cabin.

Meanwhile, his makeshift hiding place in his ex-wife's flat was also examined carefully, mud being scraped from the floorboards to see if it matched the mud where the body was found.

They also found four small buttons, three white and one blue, which could not be traced to any of Young's known victims forcing detectives to suspect that there may have been other women who had fallen victim to the man over the years. Forces throughout Britain were contacted and officers investigating various unsolved murders were alerted. Files on missing women were reopened, samples of Young's blood were sent out. In addition, Young's possible involvement in the unsolved Bible John murders in Glasgow in 1968–69 (see Chapter Ten) and the strange disappearance of Mrs Renee MacRae and her three-year-old son in 1976 were also investigated. But Young was ruled out in every instance. And once again the case of Pat McAdam resurfaced. But Young would not say anything more, and senior officers from Dumfries visiting him in his Glasgow cell would leave disappointed.

Although Young denied it in court, detectives claimed that the man broke down and wept soon after he was arrested. Admitting the various offences, he said that he often suffered blackouts.

According to the police, Young told them: 'Youse bastards don't believe me anyway that I need help. Nobody believes me. It's going to be the same as last time. I am going to come out when I've done my time and be a maniac again if I don't get treatment.'

According to police, when Young completed his statement he seemed to slip into a trance, staring straight ahead, his arms folded.

It was a pose that would become all too familiar at his trial in Glasgow's High Court in October 1977. He would sit in the dock, his deathly white face set and emotionless, his arms folded, his cold, hazel eyes staring straight ahead. Even as his ex-wife and his daughter gave evidence against him, he did not move, never once looking in their direction.

Penny could not bring herself to look at her father. She wanted nothing more to do with him. He had sent her passes to visit him in prison, but she had refused to go.

'He's brought nothing but heartbreak to me and the family,' she said.

The jury of eight women and seven men took only fifty-seven minutes to return their verdict. They found Young:

*GUILTY of murdering Frances Barker;

*GUILTY of raping and attempting to murder the prostitute in the Glenboig lovers' lane;

*GUILTY of raping a prostitute at knifepoint in the Waterloo Street multi-storey car park;

*GUILTY of raping a sixteen-year-old girl in his home after he had struck her with an iron bar. During a struggle he bit her through the nose and then put her through a ten-hour sex ordeal, taking Polaroid pictures of her continually;

*GUILTY of attacking and robbing a sixty-five-year-old pensioner, but NOT GUILTY of raping her. She had thought Young's car was a taxi and once inside he had hit her with a screwdriver and robbed her;

*GUILTY of brutally attacking a twenty-year-old woman at a bus stop in Edinburgh Road, Carntyne, and attempting to murder her. He had offered her a lift and when she refused he came out of the car, his face white, his hands clutching and opening as they reached out for her. He lunged at the screaming girl, holding a knife to her throat and then began to bang her head against the side of the shelter. Once he had knocked the girl senseless, he picked her up and tried to bundle her into his car, but was seen by a passing eighteen-year-old youth who shouted out. Young dropped the girl, leaped into his car and drove off, leaving his would-be victim bruised and battered on the ground. Had he been successful in his kidnap attempt, that young woman could well have been his next rape and murder victim;

*GUILTY of attacking his ex-wife, punching her on the head and body and threatening further violence;

*NOT GUILTY of assaulting a forty-six-year-old prostitute near Charing Cross and the rape of a Paisley woman in 1977;

*NOT PROVEN of the assault of the prostitute who claimed he burned her with a lighted cigarette.

In sentencing him to two terms of life imprisonment, the judge, Lord MacDonald, recommended that Young not be released for at least thirty years – the longest sentence ever imposed in Scotland – saying: 'It is clear from the verdict of the jury that you are a dangerous man and the public should be protected from you.'

Young, wearing a brown safari suit, sat in the dock as he had done throughout the eight-day trial, unmoved, his eyes fixed on some point directly in front of him. Then he was taken away to begin his sentence. He left the court quietly, much to the relief of detectives who had watched him grow increasingly more aggressive in the cells: on the second day of the trial he even fought with two of his guards as they were taking him to the court. But once in the court he sat silently in the dock. Cold. Emotionless. Heartless.

As a Category 'A' high-risk prisoner, he would be kept for a lengthy period in solitary confinement in Aberdeen's Peterhead Prison. He would eat and sleep in a cell in which a light would burn constantly to allow prison officers to observe him.

By the time Young is released from prison he will be seventy-three years old. It is even possible that he will die in prison, a thought which prompted the then secretary of the Scottish Prison Officers Association to tell the press: 'A man like this faces a slow, lingering death rather than a quick one. He is the perfect example of a murderer who should be hanged.'

If he is ever released it is to be hoped that those urges which forced him to commit his unspeakable acts have dimmed; urges which are summed up by two tattoos on his arms. Both are of naked women, one with a snake curling round her body, the other lying on a champagne glass with some musical notes dancing alongside.

'That's me,' he used to boast, 'wine, women and song . . .'.

Chapter Eight

CRIME OF PASSION

The sixties were in full swing when the Garvie murder trial spread itself across front pages up and down the country. Gone were the stern moral strictures of Madeleine Smith's day. Sex was no longer something to be ashamed of. It was now something to be enjoyed, discussed and even explored. The new morality was epitomised by the Garvie affair, an eternal triangle tale with extra angles.

Max Garvie wanted to carve his own particular niche in the new permissive society. His search for gratification saw him experimenting with drugs and perversion and pushing his wife headlong into an affair with a younger man. But that search came to a brutal end when the flood of passion he had unleashed in others engulfed him.

When he married Sheila Watson in 1955, they seemed like the perfect couple. He was handsome, charming and wealthy. She was attractive, bubbly and loved him deeply. Over the following nine years the Garvies would have three children, two girls and a boy. It was a match made in heaven. It would end in hell.

On 15 May 1968 Max Garvie vanished from his luxury farm home in Fordoun, Kincardineshire. His wife said that she had woken up that morning to find the bed beside her empty. She had no idea where he had gone. Suggestions were made that he had run away with another woman, that he had flown with her to Hamburg or Ireland. His car, a blue Cortina, was parked on the runway of Fordoun Flying Club, which he had helped to form. Police conducted a massive search but there was no sign of the missing man.

Three months later, on 17 August, his putrefied body was found in an underground culvert leading from Laurieston Castle, near the east coast town of St Cyrus. He had been bludgeoned and shot once through the head.

Sheila Garvie was arrested for her husband's murder. Also

charged were her lover, Brian Tevendale, and twenty-year-old
Anthony Paul (not his real name). Their trial in Aberdeen High
Court in November 1968 was dubbed the trial of the century. Not
since the dramatic revelations of Madeleine Smith and Edward
Pritchard in Glasgow one hundred years before had a murder case
so fired the public imagination.

The judge called it 'a long, tiring and, in some ways, sordid case'.
Sheila Garvie's solicitor, Lawrence Dowdall, made it clear from the
beginning that their defence would involve 'attacking the character
of the deceased in respect of his unnatural and perverted sexual
practices'.

It was a tale of high passion and sexual deviance among the rich
and glamorous. It was a tale of lust and murder that could have been
torn out of the pages of a Harold Robbins novel. Reporters thought
they had died and gone to heaven: they poured into Aberdeen from
all over the country and abroad. The events of the courtroom were
faithfully and sensationally reported to an eager public, thirsting
for every sordid detail.

There was drama in and out of the courtroom – Mrs Garvie's
mother collapsed on the stand during her testimony; the judge had
to call a recess to allow the accused woman to recover from the
sight of her murdered husband's skull, produced in evidence; and
a female juror took ill and had to be excused duty, leaving the jury
one person short for the remainder of the trial. And outside the
court building, angry crowds attacked and jeered at the woman
who admitted to being the dead man's mistress and a willing
participant in curious sex weekends with Mrs Garvie and Brian
Tevendale.

It was, indeed, the trial of the century.

Sheila Watson was no stranger to wealth – although her family had
never had much cash of their own. For three years, until she was
fifteen years of age, she had lived on the royal estate at Balmoral
where her father was a stonemason. When she was thirteen, the
young girl had even performed before members of the royal family,
playing Queen Victoria in a pageant.

She would often see Princess Margaret walking around the
estate with King's Equerry, Peter Townsend – a liaison which
would eventually cause controversy. At the time, young Sheila
could not have known that she would create something of a stir
herself.

Leaving school at fifteen, she worked first on the local telephone
exchange before returning to Balmoral as a maid. One day, she

was among a dozen women to have tea with the queen, to thank them for the gift of an embroidered tablecloth.

When her parents moved to a cottage in Stonehaven, she took a job as a clerkess with an Aberdeen bus company. In 1954 she met Maxwell Garvie at a summer dance in Stonehaven Town Hall. He was twenty-one, she was eighteen. They were married within a year, on 11 June 1955.

Now Mrs Garvie, Sheila took readily to life in her husband's luxurious farmhouse at West Cairnbeg, Fordoun. She was married to a good-looking, successful and extremely wealthy young farmer. Everything in her garden was particularly rosy.

But in 1962, her charming, handsome husband began to change in a way that only his wife would notice. It had begun with an interest in nudism. He forced his young, attractive wife to go with him to nudist camps in Britain and abroad. He also wanted his daughters to take part and even bought land near Alford in Aberdeenshire, planted 1000 trees and set up his own private nudist club.

He developed a taste for pornography, forcing Sheila to pose for nude photographs which he showed to his friends: at one point a complete stranger told her: 'I've seen more of you than you think.' And he indulged in deviant sexual practices, forcing his wife to gratify his peculiar lusts.

At her trial, Sheila Garvie said that her husband became 'obsessed with sex'.

'He seemed to get sex all out of proportion,' she said. 'He sent to London for literature and books and pornographic pictures. He just seemed to change.'

As time went on, his behaviour began to depress her and make her increasingly morose. She sought medical and psychiatric treatment and at one point was taking tranquillisers fourteen times a day.

Finally, he pushed her into a sexual liaison with a young friend, whom he once said he loved more than his wife. That friend was Brian Tevendale and he was an unwitting participant in Garvie's sex games. At least at first.

Twenty-three-year-old Tevendale was born in St Cyrus, halfway between Dundee and Aberdeen. His father was a war hero and ex-policeman who owned the town's Bush Hotel but who had died when the boy was fifteen.

Tevendale was working as a barman when he first met Max Garvie. They were both members of the Scottish National Party – Garvie was an ex-office-bearer – and both took part in a trip to the site of the Battle of Bannockburn. Garvie took a shine to this young man, but at the time Tevendale did not realise exactly how much of a shine.

The wealthy farmer invited the young man to stay overnight at the farm on a number of occasions, always making sure that Tevendale and his wife were left alone together for extended periods of time. Later, he would ask his wife what had happened between them.

'They were absolutely revolting questions,' she would say in court. 'I can't describe them.'

What Garvie wanted to know was whether she and Tevendale were having sex – and if so, he wanted details.

Although Sheila and Brian Tevendale were attracted to each other, nothing had happened between them – until September 1967 when Garvie grabbed his wife, who had had quite a bit to drink, and thrust her bodily into Tevendale's bedroom. She stayed all night.

'In the morning I went through to my own bedroom and Max demanded I have sex with him,' she said. 'It appeared it excited him that I had been with Brian. He got a kick out of it.'

But it seemed that forcing his wife into the arms and the bed of another man was not enough for Max Garvie. According to Tevendale, he even had designs on the other man himself.

Garvie made his first pass at the younger man while driving in his car. Tevendale made it clear he was not interested. But later that night, Garvie came into Tevendale's bedroom in West Cairnbeg, wearing a red nightgown, which was open down the front. He was naked underneath and he sat on the edge of the bed until Tevendale told him to leave.

And, again according to Tevendale, Garvie made a dangerous drunken boast to him during a flight in which they were 'shooting up' motorists on the road below. This was a game Garvie devised, a variation on 'Chicken', in which he flew his plane as low as he could towards an approaching car until the driver skidded to a halt or swerved off the road.

It was during one such expedition that Garvie confided to Tevendale that he was going to go home and try out a new type of homo-sex on his wife – and if she objected he would break her neck.

Meanwhile, Tevendale had introduced Garvie to his sister, Mrs Trudi Birse, who was married to an Aberdeen policeman. She was attracted to him immediately and soon they were also sexually involved.

115

At one point, Sheila Garvie overheard her husband making a date with Trudi. She pleaded with him not to go, but he just smiled and reminded her it was 1968 and 'people did this sort of thing'. Later he would tell her that he got more pleasure out of Trudi in a fortnight than he did in an entire marriage with Sheila.

Soon, the two couples were travelling all over the country, staying in hotels – Tevendale sleeping with Sheila Garvie, Trudi Birse with Max Garvie.

And when he had had his fill of Trudi, he would send her to fetch his wife and would make love to her. Mrs Birse was also to ask Sheila and Brian about their sex life and then pass it on to him.

On one occasion he threw a small party in his home – and lined up a girl for Trudi's husband, Fred. The girl was to keep the policeman happy while he took Trudi to bed.

There were times, though, when Trudi was not available for the sex parties and cosy weekends for four – and on those occasions Garvie decided that he and Tevendale would toss a coin to see who slept with Sheila. The agreement was best out of three, but when he lost twice in a row he decided that the three of them would all go to bed together.

Garvie said he liked to see Brian with Sheila, and he liked to see her happy. But his pleasure palled when he realised that the couple had actually fallen for each other. This was not part of his plan – sex for kicks was fine, love was out of the question.

He cut short his own sexual relationship with Trudi and demanded that Sheila do the same with Brian Tevendale. Sheila refused. Once, in anger, he grabbed his wife, twisted her arm up her back and forced her to her knees. Then, as he held a broken glass to her face, he insisted that she say 'Tevendale's a bastard'. When she would not do so, he threw her across the room with all his strength, sending her crashing into the wall. He later told her mother that he had done this under the influence of drugs and drink.

Matters deteriorated from there. Tevendale was beaten up twice, once by a man who attacked him in Stonehaven, slashing him slightly on the face while saying that it was a 'present from the Skipper'.

Tevendale called Garvie 'Skipper' when he was flying and when he next saw Max the older man said 'You won't get the chance to run next time.'

Sheila left Garvie twice, but returned on both occasions because, according to Tevendale, he threatened to shoot the lover and the children if she didn't.

The situation was desperate. And desperate situations call for desperate remedies.

It was Max Garvie's sister, Mrs Hilda Kerr, who reported her brother's disappearance. When questioned, his wife insisted that he would return in time for an important meeting of the flying club. When he missed that, she agreed that something was amiss.

His car was found on the runway. Tevendale hinted that 'Maxie' had run off with another woman.

The *Scottish Police Gazette* published a notice of his disappearance, using information gathered from the missing man's wife and sister. It stated that Maxwell Garvie was a free spender, a heavy spirit drinker and was fond of female company but had strong homosexual tendencies: he was often seen in the company of young men. He took 'Pro-plus' pep pills and tranquillisers, the report claimed, often in conjunction with drink.

The *Police Gazette* continued: 'Of late he has been very impulsive, probably brought about by his addiction to drink. Has threatened suicide on at least one occasion. Deals in pornographic material and is an active member of nudist camps and an enthusiastic flyer. May have gone abroad.'

Then, on 16 August, three months after Garvie's supposed disappearance, Mrs Edith Watson, Sheila Garvie's mother, told the police that her son-in-law was in fact dead.

She had come to stay at West Cairnbeg to help Sheila look after the children. Her daughter was splitting her time between the farm and Trudi Birse's home in Aberdeen, where Tevendale was staying. Soon after Mrs Watson had arrived, Sheila told her that Max was dead.

Mrs Watson said in court that the word murder was never used and she never asked if Max's death was accidental or planned. However, Sheila did talk about 'a strong man at her back' and wondered about tidal forces: clearly, she thought the body had been buried at sea.

Finally, on 14 August, she told her mother that she was taking the children and going to start a new life with Brian Tevendale. It was this announcement that forced Mrs Watson to break her silence and tell the police the grim secret she had kept for three months.

She did it because Max Garvie had once asked her to look after the children if anything ever happened to him – and above all to keep them away from Tevendale. He knew that Mrs Watson had never liked Tevendale.

Police promptly arrested Sheila Garvie, Brian Tevendale and

twenty-year-old Anthony Paul. When charged, they would be the first people to appear for murder in Stonehaven Sheriff Court for seventy years.

Tevendale told detectives that he had received a phone call in the middle of the night on 14 May from Sheila Garvie. He said that she was hysterical, that there had been a fight with Max over sex and when she had refused to give in to his demands he had threatened her with a rifle.

'He said that if she didn't let him put it up her arse, he'd shoot her,' he told police.

Sheila had struggled with her husband and the rifle had gone off, killing him instantly.

Tevendale agreed to hide the body, taking it to the tunnel running from Laurieston Castle in which he had played as a child.

It was this story that Tevendale allegedly tried to get Sheila to agree to tell soon after their arrest. Police had allowed them to talk for a few minutes in the police station. Sheila refused.

After his brief meeting with Sheila in the police station, Tevendale agreed to lead detectives right to the body. Afterwards, he believed that he would only be called as a witness.

However, on the day after the murder he had given his sister another version of that night's events. Mrs Birse testified that she had found Brian sitting alone in the kitchen, looking worried and pale. She had asked him what was wrong and he eventually told her that he and Anthony, whom he had met while employed in an Aberdeen garage, had gone to West Cairnbeg, where Anthony had hit Max over the head with an iron bar.

Believing the man to be already dead, Brian had shot him in the head. He and the young mechanic then dumped the body in the culvert. Paul, on the other hand, gave another version of the events of that dark and violent night. He said that he had agreed to go with Tevendale to see Max Garvie, that they had been met by Mrs Garvie who greeted them warmly and gave them drinks before leading them upstairs to an empty room.

Tevendale, Paul claimed, had lifted a rifle from the wall as he entered the house and had loaded it with shells taken from his own pocket. They waited for forty-five minutes in the room until Mrs Garvie returned and said: 'He's asleep now.'

She took them into her bedroom where Paul saw a man lying face down on the bed. Without any warning, Tevendale beat the man over the head with the butt of the rifle, then threw a pillow over his head and fired through it.

Paul said that Mrs Garvie was not in the room at the time of the murder. The two men then dragged the body out of the house and threw it into the boot of Paul's old Ford Zephyr car. Tevendale told the young man to follow him as he drove Garvie's blue Cortina to the flying club runway where he abandoned it.

Then he guided Paul to the culvert where they dumped the body. When they returned to their car they found it had become stuck in a rut and they had to arouse a farmer who lived nearby and ask him to use his tractor to drag the vehicle free. The farmer, Mr Kenneth Thompson, recognised Tevendale but did not let on.

He would be able to identify Tevendale in court.

Sheila Garvie gave yet another version of events. She admitted that she and Garvie had argued – over sex as usual – but that they had then made love and both went to sleep. She was awakened by someone pulling at her arm. At first she thought it was one of the children but then she recognised Tevendale's voice. He urged her to get out of bed and took her to the bathroom, telling her to wait inside. As she moved across the room she saw there was another man with him.

She had taken sleeping pills and was still in a drugged state. She did as she was told and once she had locked herself into the bathroom she heard a series of terrible thumping sounds from the bedroom.

Then there was silence – until Tevendale came to get her again, telling her to go and hold the door to the children's bedroom closed. As she did so, she heard Tevendale and the other man dragging something heavy out of the room. She glanced around and saw them manhandling a large heavy object wrapped in a white sheet down the stairs.

It would be up to the court to decide which version of the events was the true one.

The trial began on Tuesday, 19 November 1968. Criminologists believed it would be a classic of its kind and this only served to pique the public's curiosity further. People who at one time claimed to be friends of the Garvies found themselves pursued by pressmen waving chequebooks, intent on purchasing any photographs of the couple. These so-called friends promptly sold the snaps and they duly appeared in newspapers.

Queues began to form early in the morning for the limited number of spaces in the small courtroom. The crowds grew so large that police had to erect crash barriers in a bid to control them. In the end only 100 people were allowed in. Another 200 had to be turned away disappointed.

Each of the three accused had their own counsel. Lionel Daiches, QC, represented Sheila Garvie, Kenneth Cameron, Advocate – the son of Lord Cameron – appeared for Tevendale, Dr R. Taylor, QC, for Paul.

All three pleaded Not Guilty to the charges, with Garvie and Paul each lodging a special plea of impeachment – Garvie that the murder was committed by Tevendale or Paul or both; Paul that the culprits were Garvie or Tevendale, or both. Prosecuting were Solicitor-General Mr Ewan Stewart, QC, assisted by Mr H. Morton, advocate depute and Mr John Wheatley, advocate and son of Lord Wheatley. The trial was sensational from day one.

On the first day, Mr Daiches probed witnesses about the activities in 'Kinky Cottage', the name given by locals to Max Garvie's Aberdeen cottage which formed the headquarters of his nudist camp.

And soon after taking the oath, Mrs Watson, Sheila's mother, collapsed on the witness stand. She had to be helped away, shouting hysterically, while her daughter sat in the dock, weeping silently.

The fifty-nine-year-old woman was recalled the following day. Sipping occasionally from a glass of water, her hand shaking, she told everything she knew about her daughter's stormy relationship with Max Garvie, of the violence, of the man's unnatural sex demands, of his drug taking. She talked about Max's machinations regarding Tevendale and Sheila; of the three-in-a-bed episodes; of why she finally went to the police.

Trudi Birse also gave evidence, talking frankly of her relationship with Garvie, the sex foursomes and the story her brother had told her after the murder. She also admitted helping Sheila Garvie after the murder, washing Tevendale's bloodstained clothes and, with her husband, burning sheets from the bed. Later, Fred Birse admitted to telling Sheila how to wipe fingerprints from a rifle using an oily rag and burning the blood-soaked mattress.

Max Garvie's skull was produced twice as evidence. The first time it was shown to a police officer in a cardboard box, although two of the female jurors and Mrs Garvie still looked away when it was produced.

However, the second time it was taken out of the box by forensic scientist Dr Douglas McBain from Aberdeen University. The sight of the grisly exhibit proved too much for Sheila Garvie, who took ill. The judge, Lord Thomson, called a five-minute recess to allow the accused woman to recover. One of the other female jurors had taken ill earlier and was excused duty. The judge ruled that the trial could continue with only fourteen jurors.

The court heard from the Garvies' cleaner, who testified that the day after Garvie's disappearance the furniture of the bedroom was rearranged and she was told not to clean it. Later examinations of the room turned up traces of blood – and showed that the mattress on the bed was too narrow. The real mattress had been burned by Fred Birse in a rubbish dump.

The local minister was called. He said that local gossip held that Garvie had invited a friend to seduce his wife. The minister had also been active in talking Sheila Garvie into returning to her husband on one occasion. He said that she had told him that her husband had subjected her to 'perverted intercourse' and that he had homosexual tendencies.

'I found this difficult to attribute to the man I knew,' he said.

A book belonging to the victim was produced, entitled *Sexual Techniques of the Human Female*. The court heard that a section dealing with husbands encouraging wives to have affairs was turned down – and a paragraph circled in pencil.

Paul insisted that he had no idea that murder was to be committed when he went to the farmhouse. He said that he had remained silent after the murder because he was frightened of Tevendale and that, if he talked, he would go the same way as Garvie. He even had Tevendale as the best man at his wedding on 26 July, two months after the slaying. Sheila Garvie was a maid of honour.

A police sergeant testified that in his opinion Paul was a young man who could be easily led. He also said that he had known Tevendale before his arrest and that he was a 'very dominating character'.

Eventually, Sheila Garvie spent a total of nine hours in the witness box. The ex-Sunday School teacher talked about how happy the marriage had been until 1962, when Max developed a taste for unnatural sex. She also said that she had never been unfaithful prior to his engineering of the Tevendale affair.

Although she denied having anything to do with the murder, she had decided to protect the man she loved – Tevendale.

'What Brian did, he did to protect me,' she said. 'I thought that I could not betray him.'

She blamed herself for the events on the night of 14 May.

'I felt morally responsible for what happened that night,' she said. 'I had got Brian involved so deeply that I felt I had unconsciously provoked him into an emotional state and he had acted upon it.'

She had told her mother that Max would not be coming home because she wanted her to think she was involved in his death.

121

She knew of her mother's dislike for Tevendale and felt the woman would have gone to the police otherwise.

In the three months between the murder and her arrest, she had often thought of suicide, she claimed.

'It was terribly difficult,' she said. 'I did not know how long I could live with the secret.'

Naturally, in his summing up, the prosecution counsel tried to blacken her character. The Solicitor-General, Mr Ewan Stewart, QC, suggested that Sheila was in fact the real brains behind the plot, while Paul's defence counsel claimed that there was little doubt that she 'played the part of Lady Macbeth'.

Tevendale's story of the accidental shooting was dismissed by Mr Stewart, who said that had such a call been made in the middle of the night from a frantic Mrs Garvie there would have been a record of it at the telephone exchange. In addition, if the rifle had gone off at close range there would be powder or burn marks around the bullet hole. There were none.

Mr Lionel Daiches, QC, described the case as being like a 'Lady Chatterley with a tragic ending' saying the murder was 'cowardly'.

'. . . a sleeping man lying in bed and his body put down a shaft into a culvert to rot under stones,' he said.

As for the dead man, he had created 'not only a permissive society in his own home, not only a foursome group which he thought was in the best tradition of a modern enlightened society, but was creating a Frankenstein's monster which eventually rose up and slew him.'

Lord Thomson took over an hour in his directions to the jury, reminding the nine men and five women: 'This is a court of law and not a court of morality. You must try and exclude from your deliberations all considerations based on sympathy or emotion.'

He said that the jury had heard a great deal of evidence regarding sexual behaviour and perversion.

'It has been said that Maxwell Garvie was a sexual pervert and one who tried to force his perversions on his wife,' said Lord Thomson. 'It is just as much murder in our law to kill such a man as it is to kill a man who is sexually normal and whose morals are beyond reproach.'

He said that the jury may decide to accept what Mrs Garvie said, that she had gone to bed after taking tablets and knew nothing of what was happening.

'But if you accept (Paul's) version of the events that night, that Tevendale was shown into the house by Mrs Garvie, taken upstairs to the bedroom and told by her that her husband was asleep, there can be no doubt in law that Sheila Garvie is guilty of murder . . .'.

He added that there was no doubt that Tevendale had pulled the trigger and that there was an abundance of evidence from which an inference could be drawn in corroboration of his guilt. The only question for the jury to consider was not whether the persons involved were moral, immoral or amoral but whether each of the accused was guilty of murder.

Just under an hour after they filed out to debate the case, the jury came back into the court. A breathless silence hung over the room as their verdict was announced. Sheila Garvie clung tightly to the rail as they heard that the case against Anthony Paul was found Not Proven, but that she and Brian Tevendale had been found Guilty and were to be sentenced to life imprisonment.

According to newspapers, Sheila Garvie had, as she left the courtroom, whispered to her lover's mother 'I want to marry Brian.'

In the cells beneath the court, again according to the press, she and Tevendale were allowed a few moments together. In their final few tearful seconds together they kissed and embraced. Then they were parted.

Sheila Garvie has denied this, although she did admit that Tevendale wrote to her in prison to tell her that he had asked the Secretary of State for Scotland for permission to marry her. He wanted her to do the same, but she decided against it, she said.

The court case was over, but the drama would continue.

As they left the High Court after the sentence, Trudi Birse and her husband were mobbed by a bitter and angry crowd. Over 2000 people pressed around them, spitting and hissing and shouting out 'Hang them . . . lynch them . . .'.

The couple were pushed and jostled by the furious mob and had to hide in the nearby offices of the *Daily Record* until police could clear a way to allow them to escape in a taxi.

Meanwhile, at least one person was not satisfied with reading about the case: he or she wanted a memento. Someone broke into the cottage on Max Garvie's nudist camp in Alford, forcing open the door and ripping several pages from the visitor's book.

Six months after the trial, Sheila Garvie's mother died and was buried in Stonehaven. Her daughter was refused permission to attend the funeral.

In September 1978 Sheila Garvie was freed. She had served her sentence, first in Gartside Prison in Greenock and was then transferred in 1975 to the new Corton Vale Prison, near Bridge of

Allan in Stirlingshire. She was, in fact, the first prisoner registered at the new facility.

Tevendale had been released in December 1977, but the couple never saw each other again. Sheila's second marriage ended in divorce after eight months.

She now lives in quiet obscurity under another name. Shortly after her imprisonment, a film company wanted to film her life story with Maggie Smith in the main role. She refused, although in 1980 she did publish a book telling her side of the story.

She has never profited from her husband's death. Eighteen months before his death, Max Garvie had taken out two insurance policies worth a total of £50,000. As a convicted murderess, Sheila Garvie could not benefit from the policy and so it was decided that her three children should have the money put in trust until they were twenty-one.

From her cell, Sheila Garvie said she was glad. All she ever wanted was the best for her children.

Chapter Nine

THE COP WHO TURNED KILLER

It was a warm, sunlit day in July 1969 and the three men standing outside the Glasgow bank looked like auditors. They were well dressed and clean shaven. They wore soft hats and sunglasses. They were about to steal £20,000.

It was just before 3.30 p.m. on Wednesday, 18 July, and nineteen-year-old Helga Muirhead was preparing to close the doors of the Williamwood branch of the British Linen Bank for the day when the three men, now wearing stocking masks over their faces, forced their way past her.

One of them waved a gun at the surprised staff while his accomplices brandished plastic bottles containing ammonia. They squirted some of the foul-smelling liquid in the air, just to show they meant business.

'This will only take a few minutes,' said the gunman, his voice muffled slightly by the nylon over his face. 'If no one does anything silly, no one will get hurt.'

He was as good as his word. The raid went off without a hitch and there were no injuries. They bound and gagged the male members of staff but did not touch Miss Muirhead, the bank's only female employee. Then the 'gentlemen raiders', as the press later called them, herded everyone into the small office of manager Len Archibald. After ripping his telephone from the wall, Mr Archibald was marched out of the room and forced to open the safe.

Fifteen minutes after they first entered the premises in Eastwoodmains Road, the three men sauntered calmly out into the sunny streets, casually walked around the corner and into a waiting car. Their briefcases were crammed with banknotes – a total of £20,876. The haul would have been some £4,000 greater if they had not left a briefcase behind in their haste to make a clean getaway.

After they left, Miss Muirhead freed her colleagues and twenty-four-year-old bank clerk Ian Shaw ran to a local newsagent to raise the alarm. Renfrew police were on the scene in minutes. Road blocks were set up throughout the Clarkston and Giffnock areas. Over seventy officers conducted house-to-house enquiries. But the raiders had disappeared into thin air.

It was a perfectly straightforward bank raid. The men had been armed but the weapons had not been used. At that time, police even suspected that the gun had in fact been a child's toy.

But the raid was slightly different from any other: it had been planned and executed by four men, two of whom were ex-policemen and a third a one-time prison officer.

And five months later they would commit another robbery that would ultimately lead to two murders that would set the city's police force reeling in shock and prompt bitter calls for the reintroduction of the death penalty.

Howard Wilson was the victim of debt and an ambition that proved greater than his ability. At one time he had envisioned a glittering career for himself in the police force. When that collapsed he turned his hand to the world of commerce, seeing himself as an entrepreneur. Instead, he slid into a swamp of debt and bitterness. And crime seemed to be his only way out.

Born Howard Charles John Wilson on 21 February 1938, his father was killed in the war in 1941 and the boy was educated at Glasgow Academy. He was smart and popular and described as a reasonable scholar. He had an interest in sports and particularly enjoyed rugby, which he continued to play after he joined the City of Glasgow police in December 1958.

He served with the Force for ten years, gathering three commendations for zeal and efficiency from the chief constable. However, the meteoric rise which he expected proved not to be forthcoming and his initial enthusiasm for the job gave way to bitterness. Promotion proved difficult to attain and he saw his dreams of becoming a top policeman evaporating.

It was during his years on the force that he developed an interest in firearms. Along with an old schoolfriend Donald Anderson* and fellow police officer John Simpson* he joined the Bearsden Shooting Club. Simpson quite legitimately bought a Russian target pistol, a Vistok .22, from the then club president. This gun

* Not their real names: neither of these men had anything to do with subsequent murders and are now free and trying to make new lives for themselves.

would later be put to murderous use in a small flat in the city's south side.

Eventually, Wilson found life 'on the job' unbearable and he resigned in 1967 to set up in business as a fruiterer with partner Archibald McGeachy. They opened their first shop in Mount Florida, and then another in Duke Street.

But Wilson was out of his financial depth – a position he shared with his friends, Simpson and Anderson. The three men talked of committing the perfect crime. At first it was treated as a joke. However, as Wilson's financial problems became more and more acute, he began to think more seriously about it.

Eventually, Simpson, Anderson and McGeachy agreed to take part in the Williamwood robbery. The four of them planned and executed the raid and then split the money between them.

But by December 1969 they were once again in deep financial trouble. A business partnership between Wilson and Simpson had gone sour. Wilson suggested another robbery, just one, that would give them enough to put them all on easy street.

Anderson and McGeachy resisted the idea. Wilson and Simpson worked on Anderson and he eventually weakened and agreed to take part. However, McGeachy remained steadfastly opposed to another raid. He had been more careful with his share of the loot from the first raid than his partners-in-crime so he really didn't need the cash. He wanted no part of the second job.

Then on 23 December 1969, twenty-one-year-old Archibald Ross McGeachy disappeared from his home in Craigie Street. Police found no trace of him, alive or dead. His car, a Triumph 2000 which he had purchased after the July robbery, was still parked near his home. None of his one-time accomplices could explain his disappearance.

Someone had murdered McGeachy, it was said, and had his body buried in the foundations of the Kingston Bridge, then under construction. Rumours of a body under the bridge survive to this day: this is their source.

Officially, McGeachy was pronounced dead by the Court of Session in Edinburgh in 1972. He had left over £9000 behind him and a mystery that will probably never be solved.

At 3.15 p.m. on a cold and damp Tuesday, 30 December, Wilson, Simpson and Anderson called on the manager of the Clydesdale Bank in Bridge Street, Linwood.

The three were expected. The day before, one of them had spoken to the branch accountant about the possibility of opening an account for a plant hire business. He had promised to return with his two partners the following day.

They were not there to open an account. They were there to open the safe. When they arrived, the manager was out and the accountant, Mr Mackin, led them into the back office.

Once inside the office, Mr Mackin was thrown roughly to one side and the door was slammed shut. One of the raiders pressed the barrel of a gun against the accountant's temple.

'Listen,' he said to the terrified bank employee, 'you will hear me release the safety catch.'

Mr Mackin listened and heard the tell-tale click.

Holding a knife to the hapless accountant's throat, one of the other men rasped: 'If we have full co-operation, no members of your staff will come to any harm.'

He did not need to expand on his threat. Mr Mackin knew exactly what he meant.

One of the raiders pulled a pillow case from the bag he was carrying and pulled it over the accountant's head, while another of the men bound his hands.

When Mr Fleming, the bank manager, arrived he found himself similarly treated. The raiders then moved out into the main office where they held the three members of staff and one customer at gunpoint before bundling them into the office. They were all then bound, pillow cases pulled over their heads. The bank doors were closed and locked to allow the gang to go about their business undisturbed.

But they had closed the doors too early and a woman – Mrs Margaret Pirie – was standing outside with her two-year-old son, knocking insistently.

At first the raiders tried to ignore her but she was not going to give up and go away. They realised that her continual knocking might attract attention. They would have to let her in.

When the door swung open, Mrs Pirie must have felt a slight feeling of relief – no one wants to be without money over Hogmanay. Her relief was short-lived though. As she stepped into the bank she was faced with three armed and grim-faced men.

They snarled at her to get into the manager's office but she stammered that her two-year-old son was still sitting outside in his pram. Once again, the bank doors were unlocked and the pram brought inside. Then Mrs Pirie and her son were placed in the office with the staff.

A clerk was untied and forced with a knife at his throat to open the safe and the money drawers. The banknotes were stuffed into the three leather suitcases the men had brought with them. Then one of them noticed the mounds of silver coins and it was decided to take them too.

It was these coins, packed in two canvas bags and a large black metal box, that would cause the deaths of two policemen less than an hour later.

Meanwhile, Mrs Pirie had begun to let the rest of the staff loose and once again found herself at the wrong end of a gun when one of the raiders came back into the office to check on them. He placed the gun first at her head, then turned it on her child. The woman almost fainted with terror.

But the man had no intention of shooting anyone. His actions were meant merely as a warning. He backed out of the room, locking the door behind him. Then he and his accomplices calmly carried their cases and the black box out of the bank and into their car.

No one paid them the slightest bit of attention. The men were purposely casual in their attitude and actions; there was nothing furtive or nervous about their manner. They drove off with £14,212 in banknotes. And heavy silver coins.

Meanwhile, back in the office, Mrs Pirie had freed the staff for the second time and one of the clerks squeezed himself through a window to get help.

But by the time that help arrived, the 'gentleman raiders' were long gone.

Less than an hour later, at 4.25 p.m. Inspector Andrew Hyslop, aged forty-four, and Constable John Sellars, thirty-five, were leaving the then Southern Police Station in Craigie Street on routine patrol. They knew nothing of the bank raid: it had taken place in far-off Linwood – another area and another division entirely.

The two officers sat in their police car at the mouth of a lane behind the station, waiting for a break in the flow of traffic that would allow them to pull out into Allison Street.

As they waited, Inspector Hyslop spotted two men walking across the forecourt of the Melvin Motors Garage on the corner, both carrying what appeared to be very heavy suitcases. Behind them was a third man, hefting a heavy black metal box. The three men disappeared into the close mouth of 51 Allison Street.

The inspector was suspicious. The two men carrying the suit-cases were Howard Wilson and John Simpson – both, he knew, ex-police officers. He also knew that Wilson's two greengrocers shops were far from thriving. Inspector Hyslop's policeman's instincts told him that Wilson was up to something shady. At this time though he had no reason to suspect anything more than the reset of whisky, which he thought was being carried in the black metal box. He at no time expected to meet any violence. He was wrong.

The two police officers parked their car and walked to the close mouth. After Inspector Hyslop had satisfied himself that they had indeed gone into Wilson's flat, he instructed PC Sellars to wait in the street while he went back to the station across the road for assistance.

While he was gone, Wilson came back out of the tenement building and spoke to Sellars. Wilson was affable, greeting the uniformed constable warmly, explaining that he himself had once been 'on the job'. They spoke for a few minutes, then Wilson went into a nearby dairy to buy, he said, a bottle of lemonade.

When Inspector Hyslop returned he was accompanied by three other officers, Detective Constables John Campbell, Angus MacKenzie and Constable Edward Barnett. None of the officers were armed. They did not believe there was any need. No one was going to turn nasty over some stolen whisky.

Wilson came back from the shop carrying his bottle of lemonade. He recognised Inspector Hyslop from his days on the force and greeted him pleasantly. The inspector, just as pleasantly, asked Wilson what he and his friends had been carrying into the flat.

Wilson smiled and invited the police officers in to see for themselves. The six men walked into the close. They were only minutes away from a bout of horrific violence.

In the ground floor flat they found Simpson sitting on one of the suitcases in the living room, drinking beer from a mug. Anderson was also in the room, his face noticeably paling at the sight of the uniforms.

'Do you want a drink, lads?' asked Wilson, playing the polite host. The police officers shook their heads and Inspector Hyslop moved to one of the suitcases. The three bank robbers watched as he stooped to open one up, Anderson growing increasingly nervous. The inspector swung the lid open to reveal the bags of cash with the tell-tale word 'Linwood' stamped on them.

It was then that the policemen realised that they had stumbled on to something far more serious than reset. For two of them it would be too late.

The officers spread out through the flat to search for further evidence. Inspector Hyslop stayed with Wilson, demanding to know where they had put the black box, but Wilson refused to tell him.

At that point, Anderson made the first of two bids to escape, but was brought back into the room by Constable Sellars.

The inspector helped his officers in their search, leaving Wilson and Simpson alone. It was Simpson who had carried the gun in the bank raid earlier and he had hidden it just before the police arrived. Wilson demanded to know where it was. Simpson unthinkingly told him that he had dropped it at the bottom of the wardrobe in the bedroom. Wilson went to fetch it.

Inspector Hyslop was in the hallway when Wilson came back out of the bedroom. The policeman looked up and found himself staring down the barrel of the target pistol.

The two men looked at each other for a split second, the police officer numb with fear. Then Wilson's finger tightened on the trigger. There was a click but no sound of a shot. Hyslop, a firearms expert, realised that the gun had jammed. Wilson jerked at the sliding mechanism and cleared the obstruction.

Then he took aim again. By this time the initial shock had worn off and the inspector realised that Wilson really meant to kill him. He leaped at the man, attempting to knock the gun from his hand.

But he was too late.

Wilson squeezed the trigger again. And this time the gun worked. The bullet hit the police officer on the left side of his face, burrowing itself down into his neck. He was spun around by the impact and he slumped to the floor, blood pumping from his wound. He could not move but was still conscious. All he could do was helplessly watch the bloodbath that followed.

Constable Sellars came out of the bathroom as soon as he heard the shot. Wilson, his eyes flaring, whirled round and levelled the gun at him, just as Constable MacKenzie appeared at the living-room door and Constable Barnett came out of the kitchen.

Wilson was distracted by their appearance, but there was no stopping him now. He was an expert marksman. He knew how to handle the pistol. He was prepared to kill.

He spun around again, bringing the pistol to bear first on DC MacKenzie, shooting him in the head, then swinging round 180 degrees to fire at Barnett, seriously wounding him with another shot, also in the head. Barnett fell to the floor and, believing him to be dead, Wilson lost interest in him.

But MacKenzie was also still alive. The bullet had hit him in the forehead and carried on along his scalp. He was unconscious, but still breathing. From where he lay, the paralysed Inspector Hyslop could see his chest rising and falling.

And so could Wilson. Turning from the stricken Barnett, he

calmly and quite cold-bloodedly stepped over to the wounded MacKenzie and placed the barrel of his gun against the man's forehead. Then he pulled the trigger.

It was the action of a stone-cold killer, of a man who no longer cared what happened to him. A psychiatrist would later conclude that Wilson's reasoning powers were 'temporarily suspended', that the only motive for the violence was that he realised his life was in ruins as soon as Hyslop opened that first suitcase. His elation at having pulled off a successful robbery was brought suddenly crashing down around him with the flick of a suitcase lid.

Police officers have a different theory. They say that if a man takes a gun with him on any crime, sooner or later he will use it.

Meanwhile, Constable Sellars had thrown himself back into the bathroom and was barricading the door. All the while he was screaming for help into his radio.

In the hallway, Wilson was pushing at the door, trying to force it open. He was yelling to Simpson, who stood watching the scene, wild eyed with fear. Wilson was appealing to him for help, demanding more ammunition, but Simpson, who had another clip in his pocket, refused to give it to him. Robbery was one thing: murder was another. It was a brave thing for Simpson to do. Wilson, in his frenzy, could quite easily have turned the gun on him and plucked the ammunition from his dead body.

It was then that Constable Campbell appeared at the living-room door. Wilson whirled again and let off a shot, splintering the wood of the door frame beside the police officer. Campbell ducked back into the room, slamming the door shut behind him. Wilson threw himself at the door. The policeman felt the weight of the killer against him but managed to keep him out.

Snarling with rage and frustration, Wilson moved back to the bathroom door.

'We'll need to get this bastard,' he told Simpson, 'he's the one with the radio.'

Simpson had no intentions of 'getting' anyone and Wilson turned from him again and began to push the door as hard as he could. A terrified Constable Sellars, still calling for help, watched helplessly as the door was forced open a crack. Wilson pushed it open further, wide enough to let him force his gun hand in. He waved the pistol wildly, unable to see clearly but determined to get off a shot. Desperately, Sellars threw his own weight against the door, jamming the killer's wrist.

Cursing fluently, Wilson jerked his hand back and the door again closed tightly. Once more, he demanded that Simpson give him more ammunition. Once more, Simpson refused, screaming that they should give themselves up, that it was no use. Wilson ignored him. He had gone too far now and there was no going back. It was all or nothing.

Then Inspector Hyslop moved.

Seeing the movement, Wilson realised that he had not finished the man off. He moved from the bathroom and towered over the paralysed police officer, the gun aimed at his head in a repeat of the MacKenzie slaying.

By this time, DC Campbell was peering round the living-room door once again. He saw Wilson raise the gun to Hyslop's temple and knew what was going to happen. Wilson, intent on his next murder, was unaware of the policeman's reappearance.

Without thinking, DC Campbell threw himself across the hallway at the gunman. Wilson jerked around at the last moment to squeeze off a shot but the police officer's hand closed round the gun barrel, forcing it away from him. The two men struggled for possession of the weapon, Wilson all the while yelling at Simpson to help.

Simpson did not move.

The fierce struggle continued for a few seconds. Campbell was fighting for his life, Wilson with the determination of a man with nothing to lose.

Eventually though, the policeman prised the pistol away from the killer and, covering both men, backed out of the flat and into the close just as Sergeants Kenneth McIvor and Alistair Allan arrived. They were responding to Sellars' desperate pleas for help and in the dim winter light all they could see was an armed man backing his way out of the flat towards them. Their first thought was that this was the gunman but as they moved closer they realised it was Campbell and rushed to his assistance. Wilson and Simpson were promptly arrested; Anderson had climbed out of a window when the shooting began and escaped.

The carnage had lasted only a few minutes. Constable Sellars emerged, badly shaken but unharmed, from the bathroom. Detective Constable MacKenzie lay dead near the living-room door. Inspector Hyslop and Constable Barnett were gravely wounded. DC Campbell, the hero of the hour, had been wounded in the hand.

Crowds began to gather outside the tenement block as swarms of policemen and ambulances converged on Allison Street. Meanwhile, roadblocks were set up to intercept Anderson who was said to be driving a Ford Corsair. He had actually fled in a terrified state to Gleniffer Braes just outside the city. Things had gone wrong: badly, violently, lethally wrong. What had started out as a quick and reasonably easy way to make money had turned into a bloodbath – a bloodbath that none of the participants had wanted. Anderson was scared out of his mind and even contemplated suicide. However, he balked at the prospect of taking his own life and instead returned to his home in Breadilbane Road, Paisley, where police officers were waiting.

Meanwhile, ambulances with police escorts had sped across the short distance from the Allison Street killing ground to the Victoria Infirmary. Inspector Hyslop had a bullet wedged in his neck, while Constable Barnett had one lodged in his head. Inspector Hyslop would recover, although fragments of the bullet remained embedded, but the young constable would succumb to his wound and die in hospital.

News of his death stunned the district of Mount Florida, where he lived with his young wife and the two children on whom he doted. He had been well known and liked in the area which at the time was still a close-knit, village-like community. One local who remembered the dark days after the slayings said that it was 'as if the whole place was in mourning'.

Howard Wilson was also well known in the area, where he owned a fruit shop. After the killings the shop was spurned and not one apple or potato was sold.

Angus MacKenzie also left a wife, an ex-policewoman. The flag outside Craigie Street police station drooped at half mast as a sign of respect to the fallen officers.

DC Campbell was awarded the George Medal for his bravery that day, as was Inspector Hyslop. However, the horror of the events on that dark December day continued to haunt him and, although he returned to duty after a lengthy period of sick leave, he had to resign from the force in June 1971.

Posthumous awards of the Queen's Police Medal for Gallantry were given to both DC MacKenzie and Constable Barnett.

But awards, no matter how appreciatively or sincerely given, cannot bring the dead back to life or erase the memory of those terrible events from the minds of those who lived through them.

Nor could they prevent the roars of outrage that followed the killings, the shots of which still echo in the minds of police officers to this day.

Twelve days before Howard Wilson first aimed the gun at Inspector Hyslop and gunned down his two young colleagues, the House of Lords officially repealed the death penalty. The

Murder (Abolition of the Death Penalty) Act had been introduced as a 'temporary measure' in 1965. But on 19 December 1969, the peers decided that it should continue indefinitely.

Public opinion polls, however, were in favour of the death penalty – a feeling that increased in Glasgow after the Allison Street shootings. Police spokesmen were particularly outraged and called for the return of capital punishment, as they still do when one of their number is killed.

In 1969, Mr Dan Wilson, the secretary of the Scottish Police Federation, was particularly bitter. Speaking to the press shortly after the shootings, he said: 'I hope this is on the conscience tonight of those MPs, particularly the Scottish members, who did not vote for the retention of capital punishment. I am so angry and sick and fed up with the crimes of violence in this country which culminate in murder. How many police officers and members of the public have to be killed before something is done? We cannot go on treating murder victims as no more than statistics. All policemen in Glasgow must be feeling sick tonight. We might not yet be as bad as America, but we are certainly catching up with it in murders.'

The widows of the two murdered officers also joined the protest, as did the wives of 1000 other city police officers who staged a rally calling for the reintroduction of the death penalty.

At the trial in Glasgow's High Court, Nicholas Fairbairn, QC, publicly expressed Howard Wilson's 'profound apologies to Glasgow Police, for having by his appalling actions impugned their good name.' He also expressed his client's 'profound apologies and deepest sympathies to the widows and their families and to Inspector Hyslop and his family'.

Mr Fairbairn outlined the severe financial difficulties that Wilson had found himself in prior to the first robbery. 'Debt is a cruel and relentless master,' he said. 'It creates in its victim the fantasy that if once paid off all will be well. One visit to the Aladdin's Cave and the terrible burden to which there seemed no answer will be gone forever.'

But Wilson and his accomplices found that one visit to that Aladdin's Cave was not enough. And the second proved to be one trip too many, leading to the horrific events in the Allison Street flat.

It was pointed out at the trial that the gun was unloaded during the robberies and that the clip was replaced just prior to the visit by the police. The court also heard that Simpson had a second clip in his pocket throughout the shooting and that he repeatedly refused to give it up to Wilson. By doing so, he may well have saved more lives and quite possibly have placed himself at risk also.

Throughout the shooting, it was claimed, Wilson was 'numb with fear. He was not rational. He was shouting and yelling without meaning. The whites of his eyes alone were showing and he appeared to be completely out of control.'

Howard Wilson pleaded guilty to the charge of double murder, the first man to make such a plea in Scotland. In passing sentence, the judge, Lord Grant, recommended that he serve at least twenty-five years of his life sentence. A twelve-year sentence for the bank raids was to run concurrently. It was at the time the longest sentence ever imposed in a Scottish court: Wilson had made legal history twice.

Simpson and Anderson were each sentenced to twelve years for their part in the robberies.

These sentences were to prove almost as newsworthy as the crimes themselves. It was Mr Dan Wilson of the Police Federation who predictably exploded with anger after the sentencing. Howard Wilson should have been hanged, he said, while both Simpson and Anderson should have been sentenced to life.

'And I mean LIFE,' he stated pointedly.

He went on to claim that money was obviously more important than the lives of police officers, pointing out that the Great Train Robbers were guilty of only assault and robbery and had each received terms of thirty years while the murderer of two policemen had received only twenty-five years. (Cynics might point out that the Train Robbers dared to steal from the British Government. In addition, sentences in England are traditionally stiffer than in Scotland.)

Also speaking after the trial, Bailie James Anderson, then convener of the Glasgow Police Committee, said the sentences were 'simply an invitation to murder because I honestly feel that, heaven forbid, crimes of this nature will be repeated.'

Crimes of that nature have been repeated but the death penalty remains off the statute books. Police officers have been killed in the line of duty and each time their Federation and some Conservative MPs call for the return of hanging. The matter has been voted on twice in the House of Commons. Each time it has been defeated.

The Wilson Affair brought the year and the decade to a gloomy end. It marked the ninth time that year that shots had been fired at British police officers, although it was the first fatal shooting. However, in December, twenty-year-old William Daniels was sentenced to life for the murder of George Gates, a fifty-year-old

Glasgow Special Constable whom he left for dead in a Possilpark Street.

Prior to 1969, the last full-time Scottish police officer to be killed in the line of duty was Constable John McLeod, gunned down in 1952 by twenty-eight-year-old bank clerk-turned-thief Edwin Finlay in Glasgow's west end. Finlay then fled into a nearby lane and turned the gun on himself.

The year before, Robert Dobie Smith was executed in Edinburgh's Saughton Prison for the slaying of a police sergeant in Dumfries. And in 1946, John Caldwell was hung in Barlinnie Prison for the murder of former Detective Sergeant James Stratton in Carntyne, Glasgow.

Eventually, the furore over the Allison Street shootings died down, although serving police officers still remember the case with bitterness. Wilson is in jail, awaiting release, although in 1972 he was involved in a bloody riot in Inverness Prison along with fellow inmate Jimmy Boyle – the now reformed Glasgow gangster for whom he had once lain in wait while a police officer.

It would be a further seven years, in 1976, before the country was rocked once again by the brutal slaying of a police officer during a nightmarish breakout from the State Mental Hospital at Carstairs in Lanarkshire (see Chapter Thirteen).

Chapter Ten

A MAN CALLED JOHN

During the years 1969 and 1970, Glasgow police were to mount the largest manhunt in their history. No other hunt would compare with it. Undercover detectives would fill the city's dance halls. Newspapers, sensing a story that would fill countless column inches, helped to whip up hysteria to fever pitch. Women were fearful of leaving home alone at night.

All this excitement was created by one man: a man whose real name was then, and remains to this day, a mystery. A man known only as Bible John.

Although Bible John's murderous achievements pale with comparison to those of psychotic killers like Peter Sutcliffe and Dennis Neilsen, this nameless, faceless killer has cast a shadow over the city for more than twenty years. He may not merit a mention in any modern studies of murder and murderers but, even now, his identity is debated by people who can remember the fear and hysteria of all those years ago.

Meanwhile, the name Bible John – given to him by a news editor with a flair for the dramatic – slides into legend and every time a new piece of evidence is brought to the police, as it still is on occasion, a weary CID clerk has to laboriously check it against the files stored in a series of boxes housed in the attic of Glasgow's Partick Police Station.

So who was he? What compelled him to strangle three women whose only crime was that they liked to dance? And where is he now?

His first victim was twenty-five-year-old Patricia Docker, a nurse with the city's Victoria Infirmary. She was an attractive girl, about five foot-three inches in height with dark-brown, wavy hair cut in a medium short style, hazel eyes and a snub nose. She was married, but was living apart from her husband, a soldier at the time stationed in England.

On Thursday, 22 February 1968, Pat decided to get dressed up and go with some girlfriends to an over-twenty-five dance in the Majestic Ballroom, Hope Street. When she left her parents and her four-year-old son in their home in Langside Place that night she was wearing a grey coat over a light orange crocheted dress with a lace pattern. She wore brown shoes and carried a brown handbag.

Early in the morning of Friday, 23 February, a man on his way to work found her naked body in a lane behind Carmichael Place, Langside – only yards from her home. Although police did not realise it at the time, Bible John had claimed his first victim.

Detectives interviewed people who had attended the dance at the Majestic the previous night. They spoke to a number of young men who had danced with Pat but none of them could remember – or would admit – who had danced with her last or who had left the dance hall with her. They did discover that at some point in the evening, Pat had left the Majestic to go to the Barrowland Ballroom in the east end, where she met the man who would later kill her.

A newspaper photographer who had a flat overlooking the lane in which the body was discovered had thrown a party that night. The noisy affair had been attended by reporters and photographers as well as nurses from the nearby infirmary, many of whom knew Pat Docker. The revellers were all questioned by police, some at their place of work, causing problems for some of the newsmen – while they were living it up at the party, they should have been out finding stories. After the police left, news editors had some sharp words for these members of staff.

Pat Docker had not been at the party, but police felt that someone may have glanced out of a window and perhaps spotted a man acting suspiciously in the lane. They believed that Pat had been murdered somewhere else and her body merely dumped there. But no one had seen anything remotely suspicious.

Frogmen searched the nearby River Cart hoping to find something, a shred of clothing, a handbag, anything that would give the police a clue. But the trail ran cold and despite many months of investigation the culprit was never caught.

Eighteen months later, on Monday, 18 August 1969, Mrs Margaret O'Brien was anxiously searching the Bridgeton area for her sister, unmarried mother of three, Mima MacDonald.

Thirty-two-year-old Mima had been missing since the previous Saturday night when she went to the Barrowland Ballroom in the city's east end. A frantic Mrs O'Brien combed the area, looking for traces of her missing sister. It wasn't like Mima to just disappear like that, not without any sort of word.

Then quite by chance, she heard some children talking about something they had found in a derelict tenement in MacKeith Street, twenty yards from her home. The children had been running in and out of the close mouth, talking about 'the body'. Mrs O'Brien decided to investigate, fearing the worst.

She found her sister's body on the ground floor of the empty tenement, lying in a bed recess off what was once the kitchen of the flat. At one time this had been where a typical Glasgow family had cooked, eaten, lived and laughed. Now it was a crypt for a woman beaten and strangled by a shadowy maniac.

Police immediately sealed off the close from idle onlookers, a young constable stationed at the close mouth to bar unauthorised entry. Slowly and painstakingly, they began to reconstruct the dead woman's final hours.

They knew she had left home to go to the Barrowland Ballroom, so Detective Chief Inspector Thomas Goodall, the man who had plagued Jimmy Boyle for most of his criminal life and who had been present when Peter Manuel had poured out his soul in Hamilton Police Headquarters, delivered a plea to the 2000-odd dancers who had also been there on Saturday, 16 August. He asked them to come forward and talk to the police, whether or not they had seen the murder victim. The chances were they had seen something and in a murder investigation every little thing counts.

A description of Mima MacDonald was issued, saying she was five foot, seven inches tall, of slim build, with dyed brown shoulder-length hair which showed traces of fair hair at the roots. On the night of her death she was wearing a black pinafore dress, a white frilly blouse, off-white, sling-backed, high-heel shoes and a brown woollen coat with a belt.

Unlike Pat Docker, Mima was fully clothed when her body was found. Like the previous victim though, her black patent-leather handbag was missing, including a small brown purse and the headsquare she had used to hide the fact that she had arrived at the dance hall still wearing her curlers. This was fairly common in those days and Mima had immediately paid a visit to the ladies room to take the curlers out.

Workers from the then Glasgow Corporation cleansing department were drafted in to help police search bin shelters and back courts in the MacKeith Street area for the missing articles, a search that caused considerable excitement among the children who habitually played there. The handbag, purse and headscarf

140

were never found. Police surmised that some of the children had stumbled over them and taken them away as part of a game, although the youthful onlookers all denied this. Of course, the killer may have taken them with him.

There was another similarity to the previous murder: both Pat Docker and Mima MacDonald had been menstruating at the time of their deaths.

On Tuesday, 19 August, dancers attending the Barrowland were met at the doors by a team of twenty detectives carrying photographs of the dead woman. Inside, the music stopped to allow a detective to make an in-person appeal for vital witnesses to come forward. The detectives all asked the same questions: who had seen Mima on Saturday night? Who had been with her? Who had left with her?

Slowly but surely, police reconstructed Mima's movements on the night of the murder. She had been seen leaving the dance hall around midnight in the company of a tall man. He was estimated to be about six foot-two inches tall with short reddish fair hair and aged somewhere between twenty-five and thirty-five years. He was of slim build and was wearing a 'good' blue suit with handstitched lapels and a white shirt. It was the first, albeit sketchy, description of a man whose appearance would later become all-too-familiar to hundreds of Glasgow policemen.

Witnesses saw the couple leave the ballroom and turn right into Bain Street, then left into London Road. They then walked on towards Bridgeton Cross. They had been seen by a number of people in the street and police pieced together the remainder of their journey to MacKeith Street, taking a short-cut along Landressy Street and across James Street. The walk covered less than a mile and would have taken Mima and her mysterious escort about twenty minutes.

It was the last walk Mima would ever make. It would end in a dirty, deserted tenement building where she and the stranger spent some time 'winching' (kissing) before he choked the life out of her and raped her.

Despite gathering a firm body of clues, detectives were still nowhere near identifying the killer. D.C.S. Tom Goodall issued another plea for potential witnesses to come forward.

'Although we have reconstructed Mima's last movements,' he said, 'we are still anxious for public assistance.'

On Saturday, 23 August, a policewoman walked the route from the ballroom to MacKeith Street. She wore clothes similar to Mima's in the hope that it would jog someone's memory. It did prompt more information but not enough. A more radical step had to be taken if they were to catch this man before he killed again.

For the first time in a Scottish murder hunt, the press were given an Identikit picture of the man Mima had been seen with. D.C.S. Goodall was aware that there was the risk of possible legal complications in court over identification should they ever catch the man, but he took this unprecedented step in the hope that more witnesses would come forward. The Identikit was reprinted on thousands of posters and circulated throughout the city and beyond.

It was a long hard slog, complicated by the fact that many witnesses were hesitant to come forward. A number of the dance hall's customers were married people out without their partners and were loath to admit that they were there at all. Vital witnesses may have been missed in the hunt. Perhaps the one person who could have identified the killer did not come forward for fear of recriminations from his or her partner. Perhaps the killer himself was a married man and his wife was shielding him.

Perhaps if they had come forward, the third and final murder could have been averted.

The body of twenty-year-old Helen Puttock was found in a back court in Earl Street, Scotstoun, during the early hours of Friday, 31 October, by a man taking his dog for a walk. It was the dog which first stumbled on the corpse and at first his owner thought the object was a bundle of rags.

The dead woman was lying face down in the back court, still wearing the ocelot fur coat and black woollen dress she had worn the previous evening during a night out at the Barrowland Ballroom with her sister, Mrs Jean Langford.

As in the previous two killings, the victim's body lay only yards from her home. As in the previous two murders the woman had been raped and strangled. And her handbag was missing. And she had been having her period. Inexplicably, the killer had taken her sanitary towel and wedged it under her arm.

This time though, police had a complete and clear description of the man who had taken Mrs Puttock home. This time, the killer had made a mistake – he had shared a taxi with his intended victim and her sister, Mrs Langford, who was still alive to tell the tale. And tell the tale she did, proving to be a very valuable witness indeed.

Mrs Langford said that she and Helen had gone to the Barrowland together. They knew about the murders, of course – the newspapers had been full of them. However, they decided that they couldn't come to any harm as long as they stuck together. Anyway, murder is something that happens to someone else, isn't it?

Helen met the attractive, well-spoken young man at the dance hall's cigarette machine. The machine had developed a fault – it was taking customers' cash but was refusing to give up its cigarettes. Helen had tried to obtain a pack and the machine had promptly jammed. The man had offered his assistance. The two fell into conversation. He bought her a drink. They danced together. They liked each other.

The man told Helen that his name was John and suggested that he see the two women home. After all, you can't be too careful, he might have said. There've been two murders already and he wouldn't feel right if he didn't make sure that two such nice women got home safely. He was a real charmer, this man called John, and the women obviously felt safe in his company.

They left with another man – by coincidence also called John. But this innocent man would leave them soon after. The trio hailed a taxi at Glasgow Cross and began the drive westwards through the city. All the time, the man talked, telling the two women about himself and his background. How much of it is true may never be known but it is from this conversation that the legend of Bible John springs.

He was a good-looking and completely charming individual. He would have had to be to be able to worm his way into the confidence of his three victims so easily. He was a stylish dresser and apparently a more than capable dancer. He did not appear to do any form of manual work. In fact, during the conversation he gave the impression that he filled a position of authority – a suggestion that would later force the police into a considerable amount of soul-searching.

John told the women that his parents had been strictly religious and were fervent teetotallers. They had tried unsuccessfully to bring both he and his sister up in the same way. He could still recite passages from memory, a feat which he demonstrated.

He said he was staying with a relative in Castlemilk and that he liked playing golf, although his skill at the game left something to be desired. He had a cousin, though, who had managed to sink a hole-in-one recently.

The taxi took Mrs Langford to her Knightswood home first. As the cab pulled away, she caught a glimpse of her sister waving to her through the rear window. It was the last time Mrs Langford would ever see Helen alive.

We will probably never know what was said in that taxi during the ten minutes it took to drive from Knightswood to Scotstoun. We will probably never know what charming ruse John used to lure the unsuspecting woman into the back court where her body was found. All we know is that the two were last seen in the area at about 12.30 a.m.

A new description, much fuller than the last, was issued. Detective Chief Superintendent Elphinstone Dalgliesh, who became head of Glasgow's CID following the sudden death of Thomas Goodall in October 1969, issued the following statement to a press ever hungry for Bible John detail:

'He is about twenty-five to twenty-nine years of age, five foot, ten inches to six feet in height, and is of medium build. He has light auburn, reddish hair, brushed to the right. He has blue-grey eyes and nice straight teeth, but one tooth on the upper right overlaps the next.

'He has fine features and is generally of a smart, modern appearance. This man was known to be dressed in a brownish flecked, single-breasted suit with high lapels. His brownish coat – tweed or gaberdine – was worn knee-length.

'His wristwatch has a military style strap – a thick strap with a thinner strap linked through it.

'He may smoke Embassy-tipped cigarettes and goes to the Barrowland Ballroom. He is thought to be called by the Christian name John. He may speak of having a strict upbringing and make references to the Bible.'

It was this tasty tidbit that prompted that imaginative subeditor to anoint the killer 'Bible John', the nickname that has stuck to this day.

Superintendent Dalgliesh concluded: 'This man is quite well spoken, probably with a Glasgow accent, and there may be marks on his face and hands.'

The last statement obviously meant that Helen Puttock had managed to scratch her killer.

Officers investigating the string of murders had no doubt that the same man was responsible for all three. Each of the women had met her killer in the Barrowland Ballroom. The handbags of all three victims were missing. They were all raped and strangled. They were all escorted home by the killer, their bodies found only yards from their own doorsteps. They were all menstruating. Only Patricia Docker's murder broke the pattern – she was the only one found naked, had been killed in one place and her body then dumped in the lane.

The Helen Puttock murder was committed in Scotstoun, in the

west of the city, so a Bible John headquarters was set up in Partick Police Station, known affectionately as the Marine. Enquiries into all three of the slayings would henceforth be based there. In the days immediately following the release of the new description, over seventy people came forward with information and Detective Chief Inspector Edward Woods said police were 'delighted with the response'.

A passenger on a late-night bus recalled a man answering the description boarding at Gardner Street, Partick, on the night of the last murder. His jacket was dirty, the passenger recalled, and he had a livid red mark on his face.

The man got off the bus at Gray Street, just off Dumbarton Road – and was never seen again. Police were in no doubt that this was Bible John. But the trail ended at Gray Street.

Detectives from other divisions were drafted in to help beef up the investigating team. The hunt for Bible John was a mammoth operation, the largest the city had ever seen. In all, over 100 detectives worked on the case, many of them round the clock. More than 50,000 statements were taken from the public in door-to-door enquiries, interviews and voluntary information. Senior CID officers mixed with mourners at Helen Puttock's funeral in Lambhill Cemetery on Thursday, 6 November.

That night, other police officers were in the Barrowland, posing as ordinary customers, their eyes searching the crowded dance floor, desperate to pick out that one face among the many, the face that had become all-too-familiar to them through constant reading of the description.

These officers would become such regular visitors to the city dance halls – and so proficient at dancing – that they would be dubbed the 'Marine Police Formation Dance Team' by colleagues.

No stone was left unturned in their search. Sometimes detectives would discover something unpleasant wriggling in the harsh glare of the sunlight but nothing that would point them in the direction of the killer. They spoke to anyone they felt might be able to help them, even in a minor way. They talked to countless taxi drivers, bus drivers, pub and hotel staff, nurses, religious leaders, reporters. They visited asylums, hospitals, golf clubs and prisons.

The killer's jacket was deemed so unusual that police visited tailors throughout Glasgow to see if anyone had made it for a customer. A photograph of what was thought to be an identical jacket was issued to newspapers.

They drew a blank.

Detective Superintendent Joe Beattie, now spearheading the

hunt, said they had drawn up a list of every barber in the city and surrounding areas. He said that he and his officers fully intended to visit each and every one of them in the hope that John's immaculately groomed auburn hair would be recognised.

Nothing.

Dentists were interviewed at length in the belief that one might be able to identify the killer through his overlapping upper tooth.

Another brick wall.

Meanwhile, a theory that John was a member of the armed forces was mooted. Bases in Britain and abroad were contacted to see if any serviceman's leave corresponded with the dates of the murders and, if they did, whether the man in question answered the description. Detectives even travelled as far away as Hong Kong to interview one suspect.

It proved fruitless.

Back in Glasgow, suspicion and its help-mate hysteria began to set in. Even after the story began to lose its appeal to newspapers, the public were spirited participants in the hunt – in some cases too spirited. Innocent men were badgered, baited, bullied and beaten because they were unfortunate enough to resemble the accepted description of the killer. Some suspects were picked up by police more than once. One man was invited to assist police with their enquiries so often that he eventually insisted that the chief constable give him a letter assuring all and sundry of his innocence.

Members of Glasgow's underworld also lent a hand. As they did in the Peter Manuel case, they steered information towards the police. It was in their interests that this man was caught as the increased police activity throughout the city was bad for business.

Women began to stay at home at night. Some even invested in large dogs to protect them in the streets even during the daylight hours. Dance hall takings dropped. But Bible John was not to be found. It was if he had vanished into thin air.

Around this time, police took part in one of the most unusual chases they would ever undertake. Painter Lennox Paterson of Glasgow School of Art was to produce a painting in oils based on the description furnished by Mrs Langford. One witness pointed out a dog, saying that its hair was almost identical to the suspect's. Uniformed officers chased the dog through the streets, caught it and snipped a sample of its hair before setting it free again.

The portrait was produced and duplicated. Detective Superintendent Joe Beattie asked the public to study it and to come forward if it resembled anyone they knew.

'What they should not do is to put any suspicions out of their minds because so-and-so is a decent, well-mannered sort,' he said. 'Come to the police. Let us be the judges.'

Detective Superintendent James Binnie, the new deputy head of Glasgow CID, went further. He said: 'I feel this man must be known. Someone, somewhere must recognise him. He might be the man next door. The man you danced with. The man you sat next to in church . . . .'

The plea brought results. The public came forward in their hundreds – over 600 in a few days – and each one had to be checked by already hard-pressed detectives. As a result, over 1000 Bible John suspects were questioned and cleared.

More information was needed. It came flooding in after the BBC produced a documentary which recreated the Puttock killing. A one-time suspect played the mysterious killer while policewomen appeared as the murdered woman and her sister. At the end, the murderer was urged to hand himself over to the law in a plea couched in biblical terms.

Bible John paid no attention. Detectives seemed no closer to catching him than at the beginning of their hunt.

They began to grow desperate, turning their search inward, now beginning to suspect that the man they had hunted for so long was one of their own – a policeman, well acquainted with force procedure. After all, the killer had implied that he held a position of authority and the production of a warrant card would go a long way in creating confidence and chasing away suspicion. Who would suspect a cop? Likely suspects 'on the job' were isolated and interviewed. And cleared.

The strain of working for weeks on end without a break began to take its toll on some of the officers. They began to crack. Nerves frayed, tempers flared. One senior officer, his mind filled with suspects, leads, dead ends and the description of the killer, once leaped out of his car while off duty, leaving it idling in a busy street as he chased a likely looking suspect through the crowds.

Information, tip-offs and suspicions flooded into Partick Marine headquarters. Some were made by cranks, others were malicious. Many were well meant but proved groundless.

On 23 November 1969 officers swooped on to a Salvation Army meeting after someone thought they saw a man who looked like Bible John in the second row. It proved to be yet another false alarm.

Almost two years after the first murder, police were still no closer to finding Bible John, who could well have been reading about the search in the newspapers, hearing about it on television and laughing at his pursuers. He may even have been enjoying it. And all the time, police were dreading the call that would tell them there had been another murder.

One Sunday in December 1969, their worst fears apparently became a reality. A young girl had failed to return to her Kirkintilloch home after going into Glasgow's city centre for a night's dancing. Police feared that she had become victim number four. They made enquiries at the Majestic Ballroom, where the girl had been known to go – a chilling re-creation of the investigation into the murder of Patricia Docker almost two years before.

Their fears deepened when they learned that she had left the dance hall in the company of a man who resembled the description of Bible John. However, the girl turned up safe and well, saying that the car had broken down. Relief was evident all round.

Finally, police turned to the supernatural. During the hunt for the killer of the Watt family, a Glasgow citizen had suggested that Lanarkshire police recruit the talents of Peter Hurkos, a Dutch psychometrist (see Chapter Six). The Lanarkshire Chief Constable did not act on the suggestion.

D.S. Beattie decided not to be so picky. He had heard of another Dutch psychic, Gerard Croiset, and his successes in aiding police investigations throughout the world and when he was told in 1970 that the man was in Scotland, helping police in the search for missing Pat McAdam (see Chapter Seven), he put feelers out to see if the psychometrist would come to Glasgow.

Croiset was in the country at the request of the *Daily Record* and it was in their offices that he turned his talents to trying to unmask Bible John.

Without asking any questions other than Helen Puttock's name, age and date of her death, he drew pictures of the area he thought might hide Bible John. He thought the killer was still in Glasgow, probably somewhere in the south-west. On a map, he pointed in the general direction of Govan, on the south side of the river.

He made a sketch of shops, schools, factories and playing fields in the area. He said he saw old cars near a large engine on a street that ran off a main road. He described two shopkeepers and an elderly customer who, he said, knew something about the murders.

And he described Bible John's personality. He even talked about Helen Puttock's final night, the fact that she went dancing and that she had left the dance-hall with friends. But one of those so-called friends turned out to be a killer.

The editor of the *Daily Record* and the police were satisfied that no details of the murder hunt had reached Croiset. They decided to act on the information.

While police conducted door-to-door enquiries in the Govan area, a *Daily Record* reporter toured the streets. He found the old cars Croiset had described on a side street beside a rusting old diesel engine. He also recognised the shops and schools Croiset described.

But that was all. They did not find the two shopkeepers or the elderly customer. Although Croiset remained in the city for two days, the trail he had uncovered petered out.

There was further news coverage in July 1970 when a Glasgow psychiatrist who had made a twenty-year study of serial killers furnished police with what he believed was a psychological profile of the man they were looking for.

Bible John, he said, was cunning and could easily hide his mental aberrations from his family and few friends. He might be introspective and even withdrawn, spending a great deal of time on his own, avoiding group events such as sport or nights out at the pub.

He might be a 'mother's boy': reserved to the point of timidity and easily embarrassed. He could be highly prim and proper, disliking swearing and vulgarity, and be very slow to anger.

These were some of the outward characteristics suggested by the psychiatrist. The workings of his brain were something different, something twisted and perverse. He would be vain, narcissistic and egocentric. The planning of his crimes would make him feel superior, the slow strangulation of his victims giving him a godlike power over life and death.

He may have effeminate mannerisms, even strong homosexual tendencies. His experience of sex may be limited and the carnal nature of his crimes could be interpreted as a show of masculinity.

The killer would be without pity, perhaps even detached from his deeds: he knew it was wrong to kill but he felt that such restrictions did not apply to him. He was better than everyone else. He was different. He could decide who would live and who would die. But he could also become very excited during the murder and so use more force than was necessary.

In his spare time he would perhaps visit the cinema alone or read books, generally on such subjects as Nazism, concentration camps, black magic, anti-semitism, escapology, eroticism, forensic medicine and torture. He may also have a strong interest in weaponry.

He could also harbour a deep hatred of all women and, according to the psychiatrist, possibly find it difficult to talk to females.

However, if that were true, how did he manage to lure three women to their deaths?

Following the release of the psychiatrist's report, Joe Beattie made yet another plea to the public for information, emphasising the very ordinariness of the killer.

'This man walks about, travels on buses, goes into his local newsagents for cigarettes and his paper, eats out, works and does things that any other person will do,' he said.

Sightings of possible suspects and police investigations continued, but there were no more false alarms and, more importantly, no more slayings.

Bible John was never caught. Despite the use of advanced forensic sciences, despite the full description provided by Mrs Langford, despite the Identikit picture, the portrait, the posters, despite the press and television coverage, despite the small army of police on the job and the thousands of man-hours spent sifting through the masses of evidence, the killer's true identity remains a mystery. And even now, whenever there is a sexually motivated murder in the city, Bible John's spectre rises again.

The case is one of Glasgow police's few failures. The city's force had an enviable record in clearing up homicides, although at the time of the Bible John slayings there were thirteen unsolved murders on police books throughout Scotland.

The file is still open and police are unwilling even to discuss the case. A request by an independent television production company for help in a proposed documentary on the hunt was politely but firmly turned down by Strathclyde police.

Who was Bible John? What compelled him to kill those women? And where is he now?

Perhaps we will never know who he was, although Glaswegians old enough to remember the case have their own theories. Many will tell you categorically that they knew the killer. But press them for proof and their theories collapse like a house of cards. They rely solely on circumstantial evidence and gut feelings.

The murders would appear to have been sexually motivated. All three women were raped and all three were menstruating at the time of their death. Perhaps then the killer turned in a frenzy to rape and murder when his sexual advances were stymied. Or perhaps the women just said 'No'.

So where is he now? Once again we are not short of theories. Some believe he died, which is unlikely – he was a young man and apparently healthy. Others say he must have moved away, which is certainly possible. He was, though, a psychopathic killer who could have felt forced to kill again no matter where he was. There would have been similarities in this new slaying that should, eventually, have sent alarm bells jangling in the police network.

Of course, he could have moved out of the country altogether, to Australia perhaps; at the time it was fairly easy to emigrate. He might even have crossed the Atlantic: in America sexual murders are commonplace – fifty per cent of all murders committed in the States are of a sexual nature. In the land of the serial killer, John could quite easily lose himself in the crowd.

Or, quite simply, his mental state could have 'matured'. In other words, he could have grown out of his murderous tendencies.

Another theory suggests that he quite simply stopped killing because life was getting too hot for him. Once again, this is unlikely – he was getting away with it, so why should he stop, even if he was capable of doing so?

The final possibility is one that is given credence by the police themselves. According to rumour within the force, detectives at the time had firm reasons to suspect one particular man but lacked the concrete evidence to gain a conviction. This man, the story goes, was arrested for another crime, something that was easily proved, and received a long prison sentence – or an extended spell in a mental institution.

According to those who adhere to this particular theory, this man is still behind bars and will never get out. But when pressed for a name, they draw back or plead ignorance.

The talk continues. The theories live. Bible John remains unknown.

There are those who may admire his ability to evade capture. On occasion, shadowy killers can become something that they are not. For example, Jack the Ripper has metamorphosised from a vicious sex murderer into the guardian of a royal secret or a campaigner for social reform with a rather bloody way of drawing attention to the moral abyss of London's east end in 1888.

No such claims can be made for Bible John. He callously and needlessly murdered three women whom he first charmed and then conned into dark and deserted places. He shredded the lives of three families, leaving children motherless and husbands confused, bitter and angry.

Whoever he was and wherever he is now, police believe that he was then and is now being shielded by a wife, mother or lover. Someone must know his true identity and of what he is capable.

Bible John may still be out there.

Chapter Eleven

BLOOD WILL OUT

They found the first parcel near Broomhouse just outside Edinburgh on the main railway line between the capital and the Granite City of Aberdeen.

British Rail sub-inspector James Bremner was walking along the track with gangers John Shand and Thomas McGhee, checking the work of a plate-laying gang when he saw the long package, wrapped in what looked like an old blanket.

Mr Bremner picked it up from the line and threw it aside but John Shand was more curious. It was a funny shape, he thought. It could have been anything – perhaps even a dead cat or dog.

Something about the shape.

He retrieved the bundle from the side of the track and cut the string. He ripped away the old blanket – then dropped the parcel as if it was red hot, admitting later that he had 'got one hell of a shock'.

Wrapped inside the blanket was the leg of a woman, bent double and still wearing the remains of a nylon stocking.

It had been hacked from the body and the blood could still be seen encrusted around the raw, ragged ends of flesh.

It was 9.30 a.m. on Monday, 24 March 1969.

The discovery was the first link in a chain of horror that would join two Scottish police forces with colleagues all over Britain in their desperate efforts to trace the identity of a murdered woman – and find her killer.

The torso murder hunt had begun.

Reasoning that the parcel could have either been thrown from a passing train or from the road bridge across the track, police from the Edinburgh City force and British Transport Police converged on the railway line, fanning out in all directions to check the debris at the side of the rails for any other human remains.

Forensics experts studied the ground, officers conducted door-to-door enquiries in the new housing estate on one side of the track, asking if the locals had seen anyone acting suspiciously near the railway track or on the bridge. Dog owners were urged to keep their pets on a lead for fear of the animals running off with a vital piece of evidence.

Throughout the day, the search gradually widened and officers from the neighbouring Fife and Lothian forces were recruited to comb their sections of the track and its immediate environs. Ultimately, the entire 130-mile length of railway line between Edinburgh and Aberdeen would be searched.

They had no way of knowing at the time, but they were looking in the wrong direction.

It was at 6 p.m. that evening that an officer from Lothian and Peebles police stumbled over the second parcel in the Waters of Leith in the Midlothian village of Balerno. It was wedged between some rocks, once again near a road bridge. It contained another leg.

The investigation now involved officers of two forces. Supervising the search was Detective Chief Superintendent Ronald Clancy from Edinburgh, aided by Detective Superintendent Andrew Brown of Lothian and Peebles.

Police issued a statement to the press the following day, quoting D.C.S. Clancy as saying, in the stiff and formal style of all police statements: 'We are anxious to hear of any female member of a family unaccounted for, or from neighbours who have knowledge of a missing female.'

On discovery of the first leg, ganger Thomas McGhee had commented that it looked to be the leg of a teenage girl. Police pathologists were now able to determine that the dead woman was 'well nourished' and aged between twenty and forty years and was between five foot and five foot, two inches in height.

As the investigation progressed they discovered that the woman 'had connections with children'. This, however, did not mean that she was a mother – she could have been a nanny or even a teacher. Routine checks were then made on foreign au pairs.

Meanwhile, over 100 officers from the two forces were continuing the search, some with tracker dogs, following up all of the reports from members of the public answering Mr Clancy's appeal.

At one point, following a tip-off, they used grappling hooks to dredge part of the Union Canal at Calder Road near Sighthill – again near a road bridge – but found nothing.

Balerno had a population of about 3000 people and uniformed

constables visited each and every home in an effort to uncover any tiny bit of information.

Every police force in Britain was alerted and reports of missing women from all over the country were followed up with increased vigour.

D.C.S. Clancy and his men were of the opinion that the killer was lying about the whereabouts of the murdered woman, telling friends and neighbours that she had gone on holiday, was visiting relatives or, if she was a foreigner, had gone back to her own country.

'Someone, somewhere may know that someone is unaccounted for and may not yet appreciate the significance of that fact,' said the detective.

'There was a couple somewhere – a man and a woman – and that woman is no longer about. Someone else knows this but may be reluctant to come across with what may seem to be a small bit of information.'

He also warned the public to report any suspicious parcels to the police. Walkers, fishermen and families on outings were asked to be on the lookout for further packages that may contain human remains. They were instructed not to open them but to report directly to the police.

As a result, they received hundreds of tip-offs and found themselves gingerly opening up parcels which contained discarded fish suppers, clothes and rubbish.

Every scrap of a clue, every fragment of evidence was carefully studied and considered by murder squad detectives in Edinburgh. They had to discover who the dead woman was before they could even hope to make an arrest.

It was one of the most difficult cases ever tackled by police in the east of Scotland: the woman could have come from anywhere in Britain and the rest of her body dumped in any number of lonely spots.

The search moved from the railway tracks and the banks of the Waters of Leith to tracts of lonely moorland banking the A70 Lanark road west of Balerno and the shores of the Firth of Forth where the Waters of Leith flooded out towards the North Sea. Every stolen and recovered car in Scotland was examined minutely by forensic scientists.

Meanwhile, the nationwide search turned up dozens of runaway wives who wanted to stay hidden. Their wishes were respected and they were crossed off the list of possible victims.

Police intimated that they knew more about the woman than they were willing to make public – including the colour of her hair. But they felt that making that known would be of little use – there were too many dyes and wigs in use throughout the country.

Anyway, detectives like to keep some details back in any murder enquiry.

'It's like playing poker,' said D.C.S. Clancy. 'We don't want to show our hand.'

Then on Sunday, 13 April, the squad were alerted by an Edinburgh angler about a brown paper parcel on the banks of the River Clyde, near Symington Old Ford in Lanarkshire. Officers searched the river banks for a mile and finally found the parcel but all it contained were the remains of seagulls and pigeons.

They were still no closer to discovering the dead woman's identity, let alone find her killer.

On Wednesday, 16 April, four weeks after the legs were found, D.C.S. Clancy appeared on Scottish Television's *Police Call*, appealing for more information.

'Some members of the public must know this person,' he emphasised. 'We are trying to reach every section of the community throughout Scotland, and the British Isles, if necessary.'

Detectives continued to work around the clock, still sifting through mountains of reports, suspicions and accusations.

Then, suddenly, the inquiry seemed to focus on the disappearance of housewife Mrs Elizabeth Keenan, aged twenty-nine, who had gone missing from her Lanark home four days before the legs were discovered.

However, the police insisted that they were not treating her case any differently from the other missing women being seen as potential victims.

But on Thursday, 24 April, D.C.S. William Muncie, head of Lanarkshire CID – now involved in the case – appealed for the first time for information relating directly to one missing woman – Mrs Keenan.

According to her husband James, aged thirty-four, a driver's mate with a road haulage company, they had had a row on 19 March and his wife had walked out of their council house at about 8.45 p.m. while he was putting their fifteen-month-old daughter to bed. She had apparently told him that she would like to visit relatives.

Police appealed to her to contact any police station and have her picture taken, just to assure them that she was safe and well. She did not need to inform anybody of her exact whereabouts.

'We must find this woman,' said D.C.S. Muncie.

He continued: 'This woman conforms in age, height and colour of hair with the description of the murdered woman.

'I appeal to her to go to the nearest police station immediately. We don't want to pry into her business but we want to know that she is safe so we can eliminate her from our enquiries.'

But there was no word from Mrs Keenan – and enquiries in Lanark and London failed to shed any light on the mystery.

On Sunday, 27 April, a tearful James Keenan spoke to reporters, pleading with his wife to give them some sign that she was still alive.

'We're all praying she's safe,' he said, 'but until she gets in touch we cannot be sure.'

She did not get in touch.

James Keenan first met Elizabeth in 1956, at a dance in Lanark. They seemed the perfect couple and friends began to call them 'the lovebirds'.

He was a small man, only five foot, one inch, who desperately wanted to be seen as a big man, both physically and socially. He exercised regularly, being dubbed 'Tarzan' by his friends for his body-building habits. He helped locals in trouble, taking neighbours to and from work in his car. He also took a retarded girl and her father from a nearby village for regular drives. Gradually, he became known as 'Mr Kindness'.

In 1958 he and Elizabeth were married. They both wanted children but were unsuccessful until 1968, when their daughter was born. After that, their idyllic life seemed to darken. According to Mr Keenan, his wife resented the child.

'Everything was fine until the baby arrived,' James Keenan told reporters, 'then she became jealous of the attention I gave [the child].

'I blame it on the fact that I spoiled Betty before the baby arrived. I gave her too good a time.'

Five days after giving that interview, he would be arrested for murder.

In the early hours of Friday, 1 May 1969, tinker William Townsley, aged thirty-five, decided to take a stroll through Thankerton woods, on the A73 Biggar to Lanark road.

He and his family of twelve had made overnight camp in a lay-by near the area of woodland on Thankerton Moor. They were only yards from the busy main road, but at that time of the morning there were very few cars speeding by.

The family travelled the country, collecting scrap where they could, living out of their caravan and lorry, making camp where they were able. More often than not they would be moved on by the police after locals complained of their presence.

On this morning they would again be a focus for police attention. But they would not be moved on. Not for a few days anyway.

Mr Townsley had only been walking for a few minutes when he saw the parcel, two feet square and wrapped in a blanket. As soon as he saw it he thought about the murder hunt – it had been in all the newspapers, on radio and TV for thirty-nine days.

Without touching his find, he ran back to the caravan and aroused his cousin Matthew and Uncle John. Then the three men returned to the parcel and cut the string. Inside was the body of a woman. The legs were missing. And so was the head.

Once again leaving their bloodcurdling discovery unattended, they ran back to the lay-by and drove to the nearby village of Symington where they alerted the local policeman on his beat.

Murder squad detectives rushed to the scene while other officers prepared Mrs Keenan's mother for the worst. The woman had to be placed under sedation. James Keenan was informed at work.

The area, not far from the site of an old POW camp, was immediately sealed off and teams of police officers conducted a painstaking search of the wood and moor, searching for clues. And the head.

But that would not be found until the following day – after police arrested James Keenan for the murder of his wife. On his way back from his first appearance at Lanark Sheriff Court he told police: 'I would like to show you where I put the head.'

He told the detectives to take him to a wood known as Lang Whang, near the Lanarkshire village of Carnwath. Once there, he took them immediately to the spot where he had hidden his wife's head. It was still in good condition and was easily recognised as Mrs Keenan.

Police had suspected James Keenan for some time. While the search for the remainder of the body was continuing, detectives were slowly building up a solid body of circumstantial evidence against the man. Once the torso was found, their evidence was complete.

Keenan's big mistake was in not reporting his wife's 'disappearance' until after the murder hunt had begun. Had he reported Elizabeth missing before the legs were found, he may well have got lost in the shuffle – at the time there were 668 women missing throughout the United Kingdom. His wife had gone missing on

19 March, he said, while the legs were discovered on 24 March. Keenan did not contact the police until five days after their discovery.

During the course of their enquiries, detectives took a pair of Mrs Keenan's shoes from the family's second-floor council flat. The shoes fitted the feet perfectly. They found traces of fibres on Keenan's clothes which matched fibres taken from the blankets in which the legs were found. They showed one of the blankets to the missing woman's mother, who recognised it immediately – and even showed them an identical one in her possession.

Most damning of all was the blood. The murder had been particularly vicious. A frenzied attack with an axe and then dismemberment with a hacksaw leaves a great deal of blood at the scene of the crime. Keenan had made strenuous efforts to remove all traces of blood from the flat. He scrubbed and cleaned and hoovered. He used the strongest cleaners on the market to bleach the bath in which he had sawn his wife up. But no matter what, blood will out.

Disposing of a body is difficult enough. Over the centuries, murderers have found many ways of getting rid of or hiding the so-called corpus delicti. Keenan's method was dismemberment, but others have tried acid, boiling, burning and burying. The human body is surprisingly resilient and throughout criminal history men and women have been caught out by a piece of the corpse which refuses to stay hidden.

But it is still possible to completely dispose of a body: the Hosein Brothers, for instance, were said to have fed the corpse of their victim Mrs Muriel McKay to the pigs of Rook's Farm, Hertfordshire, in 1968.

However, as many a killer has found to his cost, it is virtually impossible to remove all traces of blood from the scene of a crime. There is always a residue somewhere – between tiles, in cracks, under carpets, soaked into floorboards.

Forensic scientists patiently inspected the Keenans' bathroom, looking for any traces of blood. A substance found in the U-Bend of the bath's drain was tested to see if it was in fact blood – and if it was, was it Mrs Keenan's?

Certain substances and chemicals can resemble dried blood and so it is necessary to scientifically test suspect specimens to confirm that they are firstly blood and secondly, human.

The first question is answered through the application of processes like the Kastle-Meyer test, which utilises a solution which turns pink when it detects the peroxidase enzyme in even the most minute traces of blood. Other processes are also used to confirm the findings of the Kastle-Meyer test.

After that, the scientist must then determine if the blood is human or animal, this time using the precipitin, or Uhlenhuth, test. Serum made up from rabbit's blood which has produced antibodies to fight small amounts of human blood, is brought into contact with the suspect specimen. If there is a reaction the blood is human.

The blood found in the drain and on the side panel of the bath was, in fact, Mrs Keenan's. And when the torso was finally found, and the fingerprints on the decomposing hands matched those lifted from the Keenan home, James Keenan's fate was sealed.

On 27 May 1969, James Joseph Keenan was escorted for the third time since his arrest into Lanark Sheriff Court by two police officers. He was accused of striking his wife repeatedly on the head with an axe or other instrument and murdering her.

His father was in the public gallery and he heard his son plead guilty to the charge before being remitted to the High Court in Edinburgh for sentencing.

On Tuesday, 3 June, Keenan appeared in Edinburgh before Lord Justice Clerk Lord Grant and for the first time the full story of that dark and bloody night in the Lanark flat was made public.

Keenan and his wife had been arguing. He had earlier claimed that the row began after she had dropped the baby's spoon during feeding and had merely picked it up and started to use it again without washing it.

Whatever happened, their argument soon became bitter and vicious. Elizabeth Keenan eventually threatened to leave him – and take the child with her.

'She kept repeating that I would never see the baby again,' his confession read. 'I must've just lifted this axe and hit her.

'The next thing I remembered she was on the chair with a tie around her neck. I don't know how many times I hit her. I can't remember anything about hitting her and then finding her lying in the chair.

'I realised I was standing over her with the tie around her neck. I realised what I had done and must have panicked. I drank a bottle of whisky and remembered being violently sick in the bathroom. My wife was lying in the bathroom cut up.

'I remembered that I had a hacksaw in my hand and that I was sick. I wrapped up the legs, the torso and the head in blankets and papers and I must have fallen asleep.'

Also at some time, with the curtains drawn, he feverishly scrubbed and cleaned the house, including the bath and washbasin as well as the axe and hacksaw.

Meanwhile, his fifteen-month-old child slept peacefully in the next room.

'I woke up in the morning and took the parcels to my car . . .'.

That day, he took his child to stay with his mother and then drove his wife's sister to an appointment at Law Hospital. And all the while, the dismembered body of his wife was lying in four bloodstained packages in the boot of the car.

His confession continued: 'I then went to my wife's mother and told her my wife had left me.

'Then that night I got rid of the parcels . . .'

He made the eighty-mile round trip in the rapidly gathering darkness. First the legs were thrown from the bridges at Balerno and Broomhouse, then the head at Lang Whang and finally the torso in Thankerton wood. After the deed was done, Keenan went back to his mother's house and played with his child.

Throughout the following few days he carried on as normal. He took care of the baby, he returned to the family flat every morning to uplift the two bottles of milk still being delivered; he went to work – even beginning a new job with the road haulage company – and went out at night to the pub, drinking with his friends as if nothing had happened.

And when reports of the search for the dead woman hit the newspapers and television screens, he said to them: 'I hope that isn't Elizabeth' – knowing full well that it was.

It is a grisly and disturbing tale of a man whose mind had obviously snapped, if only momentarily – although he was judged to be sane and fit to plead in court.

Finally, he felt he had to report his wife's so-called disappearance to the police, and started the countdown to his eventual arrest.

After hearing the confession read in court, Lord Grant turned to the short, stocky figure who stood before him in the dock dwarfed by the two tall policemen on either side, and said: 'As you know there is only one sentence I can pass and that is one of imprisonment for life.'

And so 'Mr Kindness' began his new life behind bars. And a child, not yet two years old, began her life without a mother or father.

Chapter Twelve

TWO HOURS OF TERROR

On Thursday, 31 July 1969, the body of a Lancashire man who had arrived in Glasgow only a few months before was slowly lowered into a pauper's grave in a city cemetery.

There were no mourners. No clergy. No relatives of the deceased paying their last respects. There were only two undertakers and four gravediggers, the latter leaning on their shovels, eyeing the proceedings with bored, disinterested expressions.

From a distance, a knot of reporters watched the brief ceremony. Notes were taken, photographers' flashbulbs popped brightly, preserving for posterity the final laying to rest of a small-time crook who had brought wild-west-style violence and terror to Glasgow before finally being gunned down by a fluke shot fired through a letterbox.

Like that other Glasgow gunman, Peter Manuel, James Griffiths lived most of his thirty-four years in a fantasy world of his own creation.

Born in Rochdale in 1935, he found himself in trouble with the law as early as six years of age. At first he indulged in small thefts from his parents and friends, before graduating at the age of thirteen to full-blown breaking and entering.

Spells in an approved school and borstal succeeded only in toughening him up and deepening an already strong resentment against the world. He was sullen and prone to dark moods. He did not make friends easily, the fantasies he weaved about himself tending to keep him apart from his contemporaries.

Griffiths did find popularity with women though. They seemed to like his boyish good looks, his muscular physique, his unruly mop of hair. When he married in the mid-1950s, his family hoped that he would settle down and put his crimes behind him. He joined the Army Ordnance Corps. His wife gave birth to two sons.

However, his criminal compulsions were not to be denied and he was soon arrested for breaking into his own brother's home. He also stole from his army base and received a twelve-month suspended sentence. Before his unit left for a tour of duty in Cyprus, Griffiths indulged his deep-seated desire to steal fast cars. When he returned from overseas he was promptly arrested and sentenced to six months in prison.

A divorce from his wife followed soon after his release and Griffiths stepped up from car theft to forgery and burglary. He also began to go out on jobs armed with a gun or a knife, often boasting that if anyone caught him while in the act of committing a crime he would use them.

He did just that in Blackpool in 1963 when he stabbed two men with a bayonet during a break-in that went wrong. He hacked at one across the side of the head and chopped at the other's hand, almost completely severing his fingers. Surprisingly, he then tried to give his victims first-aid before making his getaway.

When police arrested him later in his flat they found him with two guns in his possession. Had they not surprised him, he might have been tempted to shoot it out.

It was in Parkhurst Prison on the Isle of Wight that he would meet Glasgow safeblower Paddy Meehan for the first time. The meeting would have fateful consequences for both of them.

While in Parkhurst, Griffiths staged a quite audacious escape, literally walking away from a working party. He even managed to reach the mainland on the regular ferry and shared a train compartment with a prison officer and his wife. Throughout it all he still wore his prison clothes.

He managed to evade capture for some weeks, but was eventually caught and returned to Parkhurst where he and Meehan shared a cell with another Glaswegian, Archibald Hall, a con-man who would later achieve notoriety as 'The Demon Butler' after killing five people, one his own brother (see Chapter Fourteen).

Griffiths tried to ingratiate himself with the two Glasgow men, and Hall particularly impressed him with his carefully cultured manners. Meehan was also someone Griffiths looked up to. The Glaswegian had been living a life of crime since adolescence and was a 'respected' safeblower.

From his cellmates, Griffiths heard a great deal about Glasgow and what the city had to offer a bright, good-looking lad who wasn't afraid to break a few laws. On his release he decided to head north of the border.

Once in the second city he rented an attic flat at 14 Holyrood Crescent in Kelvinbridge, part of the city's fashionable west end.

He called himself Mr Douglas, telling his landlady he was an antique dealer.

He did, in fact, deal in antiques, although he stole them first. His passion for stealing fast cars also continued unabated. He would take them from the forecourts of fashionable hotels and drive them around the highlands, before dumping some of them in one of the many lochs in the Scottish hills. Others he kept and resold.

On one such thieving spree he found two rifles, a shotgun and a variety of ammunition. And on a bright sunny day in July 1969 he would use them to wound twelve innocent people and murder a nervous old man.

It was in Glasgow that Griffiths renewed his friendship with Paddy Meehan, turning up one night with some stolen goods to reset.

All the time, Griffiths was desperate to pull off a big job and he saw Meehan as his ticket to the big time. In the early hours of the morning of Sunday, 6 July 1969, Meehan and Griffiths were 'casing' a motor taxation office in Stranraer with a view to robbery.

At the same time, fifty-two miles away in Ayr, two masked men were robbing and viciously beating sixty-seven-year-old bingo hall owner, Abraham Ross and his seventy-two-year-old wife, Rachel. Mrs Ross would later die from her injuries, sparking off a full-scale murder hunt and generating mass public disgust.

Meehan was eventually arrested for the crime even though the case against him, based on the evidence of the badly beaten Mr Ross and a rather shaky identification parade, was tenuous at best. Police also received a tip-off that Meehan had been in Ayrshire on the night of the murder.

Meehan claims that this tip-off came from Special Branch who were keeping him under observation. His story is a complex tale of covert action and conspiracy which reads like a John Le Carré novel. Quite simply, he alleges he was framed by Britain's security services.

The story really begins in 1963 when Meehan escaped from jail and made his way to Eastern Europe where he claims he was arrested by the KGB who questioned him for many months about conditions inside Britain's prisons. They were particularly interested in information about the layout and procedures within Wormwood Scrubs.

Meehan knew that Soviet spy George Blake was being held in the Scrubs and suspected that the Russians were going to stage an escape. When he was returned home, he tried to warn British security about the plan but, he said, he was either not believed or deliberately ignored.

In 1966, George Blake staged a dramatic escape from Wormwood Scrubs. Meehan believes the spy was deliberately allowed to escape for reasons best known to the security services – but from that moment the Glasgow safecracker was a marked man. He feels he was a man who knew too much and had to be silenced somehow.

On that fateful night in July 1969 Meehan made a phone call from Ayrshire to his wife, completely unaware that M15 were tapping his phone. This placed him in the area on the night of the murder and gave his watchers the ideal opportunity to silence him.

Other circumstantial evidence also worked against him. Mr Ross told police that the raiders had called each other Pat and Jim and spoke with Glasgow accents. He also picked Meehan out in an identification parade.

Meehan insists that the ID parade was rigged and points out that he has never been called Pat, always Paddy. As for the Glasgow accents, Griffiths was from Lancashire.

On the day that Griffiths was careering across north Glasgow armed to the teeth, Meehan was being kicked and spat at on the steps of Ayr Sheriff Court by an angry public. Despite attempts by his solicitor, Joseph Beltrami, to prove his innocence – including obtaining a court order to prevent Scottish Television from screening a *World in Action* special on the James Griffiths affair – Meehan was found guilty of the murder and sentenced to life imprisonment.

He would serve seven years in self-imposed solitary confinement – his only means of protest, he has said – before new evidence came to light.

In 1976, Glasgow thug William 'Tank' McGuinness died in hospital after being beaten up in Parkhead. His death freed his lawyer – the aforementioned Joseph Beltrami – from his code of client confidentiality and he was then able to tell the Lord Advocate of the confession McGuinness made to him years before.

It was McGuinness and, it was alleged, Ian Waddell who had in fact forced their way into the Ross's Ayr home that night, beat Mr Ross with an iron bar and tied both he and his elderly wife up. They then made off with £7000 in cash.

McGuinness was, in fact, picked up by two Ayrshire police constables as he left the Ross house to fetch their getaway car, parked some distance from the house.

The two policemen pulled up in their car and asked McGuinness what he was doing in the area. He told them he was from Glasgow and had been in Ayr on Saturday for a 'piss-up' but had missed his bus home.

His story was believed and the two officers gave McGuinness a lift to the bus station. Once they were out of sight, the Glasgow crook hot-footed it to the getaway car.

Mr and Mrs Ross lay undiscovered until the early hours of Monday morning. The old woman suffered from a respiratory illness and subsequently died.

On 19 May 1976, Paddy Meehan was given a Royal Pardon and was set free. In November, Waddell would be tried for murder – and cleared.

Later, the controversy would blow up again when, in 1989, Meehan published his book, *Framed by MI5*. The book was critical of Mr Beltrami's handling of the case and the lawyer threatened to sue for defamation. No action was taken, although he did succeed in having the book removed from bookstore shelves for a period. Determined not to let his story die, Meehan moved out into the city streets and sold his book direct to the public.

Back in 1969, Meehan's arrest put Griffiths in an uncomfortable position. He knew that Meehan was innocent and that his evidence could perhaps clear him. However, that could only be accomplished by giving himself up – and explaining exactly what they were doing in Ayrshire. He was unwilling to do that, even for his only friend.

Meehan, for his part, was also hesitant about implicating Griffiths. Even in his straightened circumstances his deeply held scruples about informing held him back.

It must be said that Griffiths did everything short of turning himself in to clear his friend's name. He tried to tell reporters about the man's innocence and even contacted Detective Chief Superintendent Thomas Goodall about the affair. D.C.S. Goodall urged him to hand himself over. Eventually, Meehan had no choice but to give the police Griffiths' address.

Shortly before 9 a.m. on Tuesday, 15 July, two detectives called on Mrs Theresa Austin, the caretaker of the terraced flats in which Griffiths lived. They asked her about Mr Douglas in Number twenty-nine. She told them he was a dealer in antique silver, that he was a quiet, polite Englishman who liked to keep himself to himself.

The two detectives thanked her and left, but returned just before 11 a.m. with three colleagues. The posse of policemen climbed the stairs to the attic flat and rapped firmly on the door, identifying themselves and demanding that Griffiths open up. Inside, a radio was switched quickly off but otherwise there was no response to their demand.

They were not expecting any trouble. Griffiths had a history of violence but they were used to tough customers. A brief struggle was the most they expected.

What they did not expect, when they broke the door down, was to be faced with the barrels of a shotgun and a deranged James Griffiths spitting obscenities at them.

The five detectives backed swiftly out of the doorway and back downstairs, closely followed by the still screaming Griffiths. From the landing he fired the shotgun, the round punching a hole in the back of Detective Constable William Walker. With a cry, the plainclothes officer stumbled down the rest of the stairs where he was picked up by his colleagues and carried to the home of a retired doctor nearby.

The officers called for assistance while Griffiths barricaded himself back into his flat and began a barrage of shotgun fire into the street below, sending police and startled passers-by alike scurrying for cover.

It was the beginning of what would later be called The Siege of Holyrood Crescent. It would end 105 minutes later and five miles away in a cul-de-sac in Springburn.

Before reinforcements could arrive, Griffiths decided to arm himself further. He burst out of the building, firing the shotgun wildly. He ran down Holyrood Crescent to the busy Great Western Road, still blasting from the hip at anyone who moved.

Stopping at his car, he took a high-velocity rifle, complete with telescopic sight, and a cartridge belt from the boot. Slinging the light-coloured bandolier over his shoulder Griffiths then began to blast his way back to the safety of his flat.

'You won't take me!' he cried as he fired all around him.

Once back in his attic, he resumed his position at the window, shooting at any and all available targets in the street below. From here he could see any frontal assault made by the police.

A police land-rover pulled into the crescent and was brought to a screeching halt, its occupants diving out of the doors as shotgun pellets shattered the windshield. A detective, pinned down behind a police car, was wounded in the neck as he peered round the bonnet.

Bullets whined through the air, burying themselves in the body-work of parked cars, ricocheting off walls and fragmenting windows. This once quiet street now looked and sounded like a war zone.

Even ambulances rushing in to help the wounded had to run through the gauntlet of fire.

D.C.S. Thomas Goodall arrived and took personal charge of the siege. He brought with him reinforcements armed with bullet-proof shields and vests. A police marksman with a .22 high-velocity rifle – similar to the type used by American snipers in Vietnam – took up position and squinted down the barrel, waiting for a target to present itself. But Griffiths was too sly to allow that to happen and for his part, D.C.S. Goodall wanted him taken alive. If possible.

Over 100 officers converged on the area, halting traffic and closing off the street. The army was contacted and asked to send more men to allow the authorities to sew the area up even tighter. D.C.S. Goodall contemplated using tear gas to incapacitate Griffiths.

Then an eerie hush fell over the street. There were no more shots from the attic window, no more screams of abuse.

Suddenly, D.C.S. Goodall realised that Griffiths may have escaped and gave the order to rush the building. Dozens of armed policemen stormed up the stairs and kicked open the door. But Griffiths had gone. At some point he had climbed through a skylight and had clambered across roofs and down the rear of the building to a lane. He could have gone in any direction and an immediate bulletin was issued to all officers to be on the lookout for him.

Meanwhile, in nearby Henderson Street, Mr James Kerr, a travelling salesman with Tennent Caledonian Brewers, had just left the Grapes Bar and climbed into his car, a dark blue Anglia. As he sat in the driver's seat, he suddenly became aware of a figure standing next to his window.

It was Griffiths, his face streaked with dirt, the ammunition belt crossed over his chest, the rifle aimed at the salesman through the window.

Before Mr Kerr could do anything, Griffiths pulled the trigger and, wrenching the car door open, hauled the wounded man from the seat. Then he leaped in and drove off, leaving his latest victim lying alone in the street, blood streaming from the wound on his arm.

Griffiths sped through the streets of North Woodside to the Round Toll, Possil, where he crashed his car in Carnbrae Street. Abandoning the wrecked Anglia, the crazed gunman looked around for somewhere to hide. In the distance, he could hear the wail of police sirens and he knew it would only be a matter of time before they swooped down on the crossroads. He had to find somewhere to hole up.

His gaze fell on the Round Toll Bar in Possil Road. He sprinted across the street and burst through the doors. There were only a few customers at that time of the morning and every one of them turned round to see this short, stocky and wild-eyed man framed in the sunlight, an ammunition belt draped across his body, a shotgun hanging from one shoulder and a rifle in his hands. He looked like a Mexican bandit in a film.

But this was no film.

Griffiths fired twice into the ceiling to show that he meant business, showering plaster on to the customers and bar staff.

'If anyone moves, I'll shoot you!' he yelled. 'I've shot two policemen already!'

No one was about to argue the point with him. There wasn't a sound as he swaggered up to the bar and demanded a drink. Watched by the increasingly nervous clientèle, Griffiths reached out and grabbed a bottle of brandy from the gantry. His rifle still aimed at the customers, he put the bottle to his lips and poured some of the fiery liquid down his throat. Some of it spilled from the corner of his mouth and dripped down on to his shirt. Griffiths didn't seem to mind. Dry cleaning was the least of his problems.

A slight movement caught the corner of his eye and he whirled round, expecting some sort of attack. He fired twice without thinking, both bullets finding their mark. Local newsvendor, William Hughes, slumped to the floor, blood seeping from his wounds.

Five days later, this sixty-five-year-old man would die in the Western Infirmary. And all because his hand had twitched involuntarily towards his glass.

The shooting was enough for bar manager, James Connolly. He had been in the trade for many years and had seen and dealt with trouble in various guises. He grabbed Griffiths roughly by the shoulders and threw him bodily out of the bar. It was a very courageous thing to do and a greatly surprised James Griffiths found himself sprawling in the street.

Angrily, he leapt to his feet and kicked open the bar doors, firing his rifle blindly. The bullet buried itself harmlessly into a wall as Mr Connolly, who had been making for the phone to call the police, threw himself to the floor.

But the police already knew where Griffiths was and cars were closing in on the Round Toll. Griffiths could hear the insistent scream of their sirens coming closer. He knew he did not have the time to punish the bar manager. He had to move – and he had to move now.

John Craig had been passing by the bar in his lorry when Griffiths pushed his way back into the bar for the second time.

Knowing nothing of what was going on, the lorry driver mistook the rifle fire for some kind of explosion. He pulled his vehicle to a halt and opened the cab door to investigate. He heard another explosion and something whined past him and screamed off a wall. He looked around and saw Griffiths running towards him, the rifle aimed straight at him.

The driver leaped out of the cab and ducked behind a lamp-post for cover as Griffiths pulled himself up into the driver's seat and once again drove off just as police cars came screeching into Possil Road.

Griffiths headed north-east, towards Springburn, pursued hotly by police cars. He drove wildly through the streets, bringing traffic skidding to a halt as he tilted round corners and sped through stop lights. As he drove, he perched the rifle on his lap, every now and then firing it one-handed out of the window.

The convoy of vehicles drove at breakneck speed for two and a half miles before Griffiths swung into Kay Street, not realising it was a dead end. Leaping out of the cab, he ran up the short street towards the corporation baths at the far end before ducking into the close mouth at number twenty-six.

Behind him, police cars sealed off the street and officers quickly cleared the area of screaming people. Members of the public were politely but forcefully ushered into shops and close mouths, the suspicion being that Griffiths would soon be firing into the street again. They were right – in a few minutes these people would be lying on the floor of the shops as smashed glass and spent bullets rained down around them.

Meanwhile, Griffiths had pounded his way up to the top landing of the tenement building. He battered on the door of one of the three flats but the occupant inside refused to open up, having heard the sirens and suspecting – rightly – that something was wrong. Cursing fluently, Griffiths moved away from the door and kicked at the next one. There was no answer from inside so he blew the lock off and ducked inside quickly.

From that moment, he had ten minutes to live.

The flat was the home of a woman and her three sons. Luckily for them they were out at the time.

After blocking the door behind him, Griffiths moved swiftly through the flat to the living-room window which looked down on to the street below. Police had cleared Kay Street as best they could. Passers-by had been shepherded to safety, women and children in the public baths had been locked in.

However, they had missed one small person – a tiny child sitting in a pram only yards away from the mouth of close number twenty-six. His parents had to be restrained by police from rushing out to save him. Had Griffiths seen them, he would have had no compunction in shooting them. He delighted in picking off easy targets.

As usual, it fell to a volunteer to bring the child to safety. An armed detective crept along the pavement, his back flat against the wall of the tenements. All it would take was for Griffiths to glance down and it would be all over for the detective – and the youngster.

However, luck was with them, for a few tense seconds later the child was snatched out of the pram and handed to waiting hands through a ground-floor window. The detective made a hasty retreat back to cover.

Meanwhile, Griffiths had been doing some creeping of his own. He had fired a few rounds from his window but the police had the area tightly sealed. There was no fun in shooting at an empty street. He retraced his steps down the stairs to the first-floor landing and found himself a new vantage point at a window on a back landing. The rear of the red sandstone building overlooked a children's playground – and police had not yet been able to clear it.

Clouds of dust spurted upwards as his bullets buried themselves in the soft earth of the playground. Mothers ran out and clasped their children to their chests before darting for what cover they could. One eight-year-old child was wounded and had to be dragged to safety, leaving behind a smear of blood on the ground where, only a few minutes before, he had been playing happily.

An eighteen-year-old girl was hit in the thigh. Her husband of only two weeks rushed to her side and helped pull her to shelter behind a car. When he saw the blood flowing from the hideous wound on her leg, his temper exploded. He leaped to his feet and started to rush towards the building, screaming abuse at the unknown gunman sitting at the first-floor window. Two men jumped on him and dragged him to the ground, holding him down. If he had managed to get away, he would have been killed.

Another man injured at this time had only been released from hospital two weeks before after being stabbed by thugs in the city centre. He was rushed back to hospital again, this time with a bullet in his neck.

Griffiths decided that he had left the front of the building unattended for too long, so he moved back up to the top floor flat and sent another blistering volley of gunfire storming down on to Kay Street. From where he sat he could hear the anguished screams of terrified women and children drifting up from below. Somewhere, someone was sobbing with fear.

Sunlight streamed through the open window as he looked out. For a few moments, there was silence. It had been almost one and three-quarter hours since the first siege began. During that time he had loosed off over 100 rounds of ammunition and had wounded nine men, two women and a child. And now he was trapped in a small flat on the top floor of a tenement in Springburn.

It is doubtful if he realised the hopelessness of his situation. It is probable that he was enjoying it.

At that moment, Griffiths was fulfilling all the boasts of his youth. In borstal and prison, fellow inmates had scoffed when he said that if he was ever caught with a gun in his hand he would use it. They had sneered when he said that he would take as many of 'them' with him as he could when he went. They would know different now. They would know he had meant what he said. He had proved himself.

Perhaps, at that moment he saw himself as a Hollywood gangster, just like James Cagney, screaming defiance at the lousy coppers, finally on top of the world.

A slight creak made him whirl from the window, rifle raised to fire. He would have just had time to see two pairs of eyes peering at him through the gap. Bellowing with rage, he launched himself at the door, rifle in one hand, shotgun in the other. One of the police officers outside quickly poked the barrel of his revolver through the letterbox and fired.

The bullet slammed into Griffiths' shoulder, spinning him round, the shotgun slipping from his nerveless fingers. The two policemen forced the door open and rushed towards him just as he turned to face them again and triggered the rifle for the last time. This time, he missed.

The two policemen grabbed him as he slumped to the floor and pulled his guns away from him. He groaned as they wrenched the ammunition belts over his head. Then they hoisted him to his feet and carried him to the street.

By the time they reached the bottom of the stairs, James Griffiths was dead. The police superintendent who had fired his pistol through the letterbox had meant only to wound his target, but the bullet had travelled down through his body, glancing off his ribs and tearing through vital organs. It was a freak shot, fired under difficult and dangerous circumstances. The two officers would later receive bravery awards.

Griffiths' body was stretchered into an ambulance, hidden from prying eyes by a coarse blanket. A priest accompanied the corpse to

Glasgow Mortuary. With his death, the gunman had gained himself a dubious place in legal history as the first wanted person to be shot down by Scottish police.

His family, whom he had alienated years before through his criminal behaviour, refused to come north to identify the body. His father, the caretaker of a school in Northamptonshire, said he would not be attending any funeral.

'Our son died fifteen years ago,' he said.

It was left to what was then Glasgow Corporation to bury the man who was, for two hours, the most wanted man in Britain. A rumour that he was to be buried alongside his victim, William Hughes, was quickly scotched.

Griffiths' grave lies in Linn Park Cemetery on the south side of the city. There were no wreaths, no sympathy cards. And no stone marks his grave.

Chapter Thirteen

BREAKOUT

There was madness in the young man's eyes as he burst into the classroom of Dundee's St John's Roman Catholic secondary school. Dressed in a khaki army-style shirt, pullover and trousers, his blond hair shaved uncommonly short for 1967 fashion, the youth waved his shotgun menacingly at the eleven-year-old girls and their teacher, ordering them to barricade the door behind him.

It was 2.30 p.m. on Wednesday, 1 November 1967. Two hours later everything would come to a sudden, insane end after the young man had sexually assaulted two of the schoolgirls, put a pretty young student nurse through forty-five minutes of sheer hell and finally, for no reason, shot one person to death. It was also the first episode in a story that would climax almost ten years later in a night of bloody horror.

The noise coming from Mrs Nanette Hanson's needlework class was bound to attract attention and at just after 2.30 p.m., teacher Miss Margaret Christie poked her head out of her own classroom to see what was going on. She could hear the girls screaming and the sound of classroom furniture being pushed roughly around. It was unusual for Mrs Hanson's class to be so unruly – needlework was not the type of subject to provoke such an uproar. However, clearly something was happening in the room to generate the excitement.

The woman walked down the corridor towards the classroom door, the sound inside growing in intensity as she moved closer. Through the glass she could see the figure of a man yelling at the young pupils, and twenty-six-year-old Mrs Nanette Hanson trying desperately to calm him down.

Then Miss Christie saw the shotgun in his hands. She must have made some sort of noise because the young man whirled round, hefted the weapon and fired at the door.

Glass shattered around the terrified teacher as she jerked away.

173

Ignoring the sharp pain from the shards that had embedded into her flesh, she fled down the corridor to get help.

Police converged on the Dundee secondary school but were forced back from the door of the classroom as nineteen-year-old Robert Mone, a private in the Gordon Highlanders, screamed and blasted at them, threatening to turn the shotgun on his hostages if they came any closer.

They tried to negotiate the girls' release, but Mone was not interested in their promises. They wanted to send someone in to talk to him. Mone refused, then recalled the name of a girl he had met four years before in a youth club. He had liked her. She had always listened to him, understood his problems. He would speak to her, and only her.

The girl, Marian Young, was now eighteen and a student nurse. When police officers found her and asked her if she would be willing to help she agreed immediately, even volunteering to go into the classroom and talk to the crazed gunman face-to-face.

At first police were unwilling to offer Mone another hostage on a plate, but the young girl was convinced it was the only way. Eventually they agreed.

At 3.30 p.m., one hour after the siege began, Marian was allowed into the room. Behind her, the door was closed swiftly, locked and rebarricaded by the teacher under Mone's instructions. Most of the eleven girls in the class cowered in terror behind a partition at the end of the room. One girl sat at a desk, her face chalk white, fear tumbling from her eyes.

According to Marian, Mone himself had one leg draped over the corner of a sink at the rear of the classroom, his shotgun held loosely over his knee. He smiled at the student nurse as she entered and said: 'You thought you were being a brave little girl? How did you know I wouldn't blow your head off?'

Calling him 'Bobby', Marian said she didn't think he would do that and proceeded to coax him into letting the children go. She must have been very persuasive: at 3.40 p.m., only ten minutes after she first walked into the room, all eleven girls were allowed to leave.

'Thank God,' breathed Mrs Hanson as the last girl ran down the corridor to safety.

Mone could afford to be generous. He still had two hostages, Marian and the Yorkshire-born teacher.

After the girls were gone and the door was blocked again, Mone pulled out some sandwiches he had brought with him. Obviously, he had come prepared for a lengthy stay. Offering one to Marian, he asked Mrs Hanson if she had any cigarettes. She gave him one and asked if she could start to tidy up the room. He nodded, saying: 'Make sure I can see you. Don't try any funny stuff with scissors.'

The two women tried to reason with him, tried to talk him down from the heights of insanity he had scaled for who-knew-what reason. At one point, he even put the shotgun down. Casually, Marian picked it up and started to examine it. Mone launched himself at her with a scream, pushing her to the floor and snatching it back off her.

Then he aimed the weapon at the nurse and asked if she thought he could kill anyone. She said she thought not. Swivelling the gun round to point it at Mrs Hanson, he asked the same question. The teacher admitted that she didn't know.

He smiled, pointed the barrels away from both women and pulled the trigger.

The shotgun did not go off.

Mone trained the gun on Mrs Hanson and jerked the trigger again. Again there was no gunshot.

Furiously, he whirled round and aimed it at Marian. Still it did not fire.

Cursing, Mone jerked the shotgun open and reloaded – just as there was a movement from the corridor outside. Mone spun round and fired at the door. This time, the weapon worked, the round punching its way through the wood.

His behaviour more frenzied than ever, he filled the classroom sink with water and dipped his head in. Shaking the water from his hair and face, he told Mrs Hanson to close a curtain at the end of the room. The other curtains had been closed earlier and only this one remained opened to allow him to see the activity outside.

Mrs Hanson moved down the room to do as she was told.

Mone watched her.

The teacher reached up to close the curtains.

And then Mone shot her.

Marian later said the woman just stood there frozen for a second before slumping to the floor. The student nurse rushed to her side, found a weak pulse, begged Mone to allow her to call an ambulance.

Mone was laughing now, looking down at the seriously wounded teacher. He told Marian to do what she wanted.

Ten minutes later, at 4.15 p.m., the ambulance men were allowed into the room. They were accompanied by two of the Marist brothers who ran the school, Brother John and Brother Bede, who had refused to let the the ambulance men enter the classroom alone.

The brave monks rushed into the room, praying quietly under their breath.

The stricken teacher was lifted gingerly on to the stretcher and someone hissed into Marian's ear that she should leave now. Mone did not seem to care.

As Marian scurried down the corridor to safety, her hands covered with Mrs Hanson's blood, she could still hear Mone laughing, the sound echoing and echoing off the painted walls.

At 4.30 p.m., armed police forced their way into the classroom to arrest the gunman. He was sitting in the room singing pop songs as they cuffed him and led him away.

When they inspected the shotgun they found that it had a faulty firing pin, which explained the misfires.

Half an hour later, word reached them that Mrs Hanson, a bride of only seven months, had died in hospital. She was later buried in Ilkley, Yorkshire, where she had been married. The school authorities, paying tribute to her bravery, announced that every year a cup for needlework would be presented in her name and a commemorative plaque was to be erected in the school. And every 1 November, there would be a special Mass held in her memory.

Born on 25 June 1948, Robert Francis Mone's unhappy childhood had been further marred by a history of delinquency. He had joined the army after being released from an approved school and at the time of the St John's siege he was on leave from his post at Minden, Germany.

However, he soon found that the regimented military life was not for him and looked for ways to engineer his release. One thought was that by committing some sort of crime he may be discharged, and it was later suggested that this was the motivation for taking over the classroom.

But just after his arrest, Mone claimed that a few months before he had joined a Nazi devil cult which called on its members to spill blood before they were twenty-one years of age. However, the army's special investigation branch could find no trace of such a cult.

He was an admirer of tattoos and his muscular arms were decorated with a skull and crossbones, a picture of a woman's breasts and two hearts bearing the words 'Helen' and 'True Love'.

On 23 January 1968, Mone appeared briefly in Dundee High Court. After only an eighteen-minute trial, during which two doctors testified that he was schizophrenic, Lord Thomson ruled that Mone was insane and ordered him to be detained in a mental institution under Section 63 of the Mental Health (Scotland) Act 1960.

When he heard the ruling, Mone laughed and said to the judge: 'Good for you.'

Then this laughing killer was taken away to begin his treatment in the State Mental Hospital at Carstairs.

His name slid from the public memory to be replaced by those of new monsters like Bible John in Glasgow, Donald Neilsen – The Black Panther – in England, Ted Bundy in Washington.

But eight years later, after a night of unprecedented savagery and horror, Mone would again hack his way into the headlines.

Only this time he would not be alone.

It was a miracle that no one was killed the night Thomas McCulloch went on the rampage in a hotel near Glasgow.

Thomas Neil McCulloch was born on 7 March 1950 and during his youth was addicted to both drink and drugs, while his strong homosexual tendencies forced him to seek and obtain psychiatric help in 1969 and 1970. His violent nature eventually led to his psychiatrist declaring that he had a personality disorder of a psychopathic type.

He made the diagnosis on Friday, 15 May 1970. The following night, McCulloch showed just how dangerous he was.

He had been drinking heavily by the time he reached the Erskine Bridge Hotel on the outskirts of Glasgow. He ordered more drinks and a round of sandwiches. When he bit into one of his sandwiches he realised that there was no butter on them, which provoked an argument between him and the chef.

Seething with anger, he went home, tape recorded his plans to kill the chef and then went back to the hotel. This time he was armed with a shotgun, a .45 revolver and a bandolier of ammunition draped across his shoulders. It was as if the ghost of James Griffiths had returned to plague the city.

Bursting through the hotel doors at about 11 p.m., McCulloch darted up the stairs, finding chef John Thomson (thirty-nine) in the kitchen. He fired once, luckily only wounding the man in the cheek.

Then the crazed gunman ran through the hotel, at one point firing through the closed door of a staff bedroom, hitting manageress Mrs Lilias Rodger (forty-nine) on the shoulder.

From there he pushed his way into the function suite where fifty members of the Milngavie and Bearsden Round Table were holding a social evening. The very proper gentlemen and ladies must have been very surprised indeed to see this heavily-armed, wild-eyed, panting madman standing in the doorway of their hired room.

But his violent energy was all but spent. After threatening the business people for a few minutes, he was disarmed and led away by police.

When police visited his home they found an arsenal of weapons, and a senior police officer later said that McCulloch had at one time expressed an interest in going to Vietnam so he could shoot the North Vietnamese.

On 20 July 1970, McCulloch was deemed unfit to plead and remitted to be detained under Sections 55 and 60 of the Mental Health (Scotland) Act of 1960 and sent to Carstairs State Mental Hospital . . .

. . . where he met Robert Mone.

Carstairs was then, and is now, not a prison but a hospital with heavy security. Opened in 1948, it was a detention and treatment centre for those patients who required, in the wording of the 1960 Mental Health (Scotland) Act, 'treatment under conditions of special security on account of their dangerous, violent or criminal propensities'.

At the time of the 1976 escape, there were 341 patients and 245 staff members. Not all of the inmates were dangerous mental patients: the hospital also catered for mentally handicapped persons.

Carstairs operated a progressive regime of treatment, in which patients could slowly progress from being under strict supervision as their mental condition improved, to wards where that supervision was more relaxed and they were granted more privileges.

Such was the case with Mone and McCulloch.

Mone was deemed to be of above average intelligence and was the planner of the escape attempt in 1976. While in Carstairs he not only studied for and obtained three Higher Certificates of Education but also just narrowly missed passing the exams for an Open University law degree. He did, however, finish a correspondence course in playwriting in 1974 and in October 1976, less than two months before the escape he masterminded, became editor of the hospital magazine.

To do this job he was given full parole, which allowed him to move freely around the hospital during daylight. At night, he was locked in his own room just like all the other patients.

However, he was described in the public report on the escape as being 'arrogant, supercilious and argumentative and, although his attitude and demeanour improved during his stay in the hospital, his potentiality for aggression was always evident'.

178

The report goes on to say that Dr Loweg, his Responsible Medical Officer, described him as having 'a sadistic, schizoid psychopathic personality' and that there was never any suggestion of him being transferred to a psychiatric hospital.

McCulloch, on the other hand, seemed to be making progress in Carstairs. He showed no sign of the violent behaviour which led to his arrest in 1970, co-operating fully with the doctors and nurses and apparently 'maturing' – basically, growing out of his psychopathic personality.

He was a time-served painter and decorator who showed a proficiency for other trades. From 1971 his skills were put to good use in the paint shop's woodworking department and in 1976 he was allowed full parole. However, he was still considered too dangerous to be transferred to a psychiatric hospital.

In 1973 he had struck up a friendship with Robert Mone. In the closing weeks of 1975 the two men began to talk about an escape, but it was not until the autumn of 1976 that they started to make serious plans and preparations.

On Tuesday, 30 November 1976, they put their plan into action.

Nursing Officer Neil MacLellan made his way to Clyde Ward at about 5.45 p.m. to collect Robert Mone from the charge nurse. That night, he was to supervise Mone and McCulloch, who were members of the hospital's drama group, in the recording of books and plays for illiterate patients.

As the nurse and his two charges walked from Tweed Ward, which housed McCulloch's room, to the social club where the recordings were to take place, Mone held a brown folder while McCulloch carried two boxes, ostensibly containing toy-making equipment and an extension cable. On this occasion though, they contained a frightening array of other, more dangerous, items.

When the group reached the social club, the patients were surprised to find Nurse Mary Hamilton waiting for them. They had expected only Mr MacLellan to supervise them that night.

Her presence may have complicated matters. However, Mrs Hamilton was to escape the blood-letting to come. She had taken a message from the ward of patient Ian Simpson, who wished to come to the social club to talk to Mr MacLellan.

Simpson was a double murderer who had thumbed a lift in the Highlands in 1962 from thirty-year-old George Green of Leeds. He then shot the man dead near Newtonmore in Inverness-shire and buried him in a shallow grave beside a lay-by on the A9. Stealing the dead man's car, Simpson then drove south.

179

Seven weeks later, the corpse of twenty-four-year-old Hansreudi Gimmi was found in a forest at Eskdalemuir, Dumfriesshire. The Swiss student had been making his way home to be the best man at his sister's wedding.

The following day, Simpson was arrested in Manchester. At his trial he was declared insane and unfit to plead and so sent to Carstairs.

Like many psychopaths, including Mone and McCulloch, Simpson was a highly intelligent, if dangerous, man. His years in Carstairs were spent in study, teaching himself to play a number of musical instruments and in 1975 he gained a Bachelor of Arts degree through the Open University.

Mrs Hamilton, who did not like Simpson, had another duty to fulfil that night. She was due to compile a list of patients who wanted to attend the hospital's Christmas party and so she asked Mr MacLellan if she could retire to her office in the recreation hall to do the work in peace.

As she left, she noticed a garden fork and spade resting against the wall of Mr MacLellan's office. They had been borrowed two weeks earlier to allow some work to be done on flower beds near the social club.

While Mr MacLellan spoke to Simpson in an office, McCulloch opened the boxes he had carried from his ward, revealing a lethal arsenal of home-made weapons, including an axe, various knives, and garrottes.

Three of the knives had been fashioned from the flat steel used as runners on sledges made in the woodwork department. One of the garrottes was made out of a violin string with handles made of brass-covered rod. Thick wire stolen from the occupational therapy department was used in the manufacture of the other garrotte, the weapon completed by two wooden handles made in the woodworking shop.

All of the weapons had been carefully and painstakingly made and concealed by McCulloch, his desire to kill rising steadily as each lethal object was completed. He had also made a sword and a crossbow but neither were used during the escape, the latter being broken up because he had difficulty in hiding it.

The boxes also contained the men's disguises – false beards and moustaches, faked identity cards, obsolete nurses' caps and a makeshift rope ladder.

McCulloch had also fashioned a belt with sheaths for knives and a holder for the axe and he strapped this round his waist. Then he and Mone, armed with bottles of Nitromors, a strong, caustic paint stripper which was used in the paint shop where McCulloch worked, went into the office where Nursing Officer MacLellan was talking to Simpson.

Mone's plan was that they would first disable any nurses with Nitromors, throwing it into their face like ammonia, and then force them into a large safe in the social work office. They would then be free to make their escape undetected. Unfortunately, he seemed to know nothing about his partner's growing need to kill.

MacLellan turned as the men entered and Mone squirted some of the Nitromors into his face before launching himself at him. McCulloch sprayed his at Simpson and then attacked him.

The bloodbath had begun.

McCulloch had drawn one of his knives and hacked at Simpson, who was attempting to defend himself. Both Mone and MacLellan saw the savage attack, saw the knife swinging round towards the patient's head. Mone was surprised at the ferocity of his companion's attack – he had always felt that they could escape without any bloodshed – and MacLellan managed to struggle free and leap to Simpson's aid.

But Simpson was not finished yet. He managed to wrest the knife from McCulloch's grasp and prepared to give as good as he got.

The fight moved out into the hallway, with McCulloch now closing in on Nurse MacLellan, who was trying to lock the door of the office and trap the escapees inside.

But McCulloch closed in on him, now brandishing the axe he had made out of a sharpened piece of metal and a hammer handle. The two men grappled fiercely for possession of the weapon until the nurse managed to twist it out of McCulloch's hand. They faced each other for a second before McCulloch drew yet another knife from his belt and once again attacked the nursing officer.

Meanwhile, Simpson had thrown himself at Mone and the men were fighting nearby. McCulloch managed to get his axe back but was still struggling with Mr MacLellan and calling to Mone for help. But Mone was busy holding off Simpson and could not come to McCulloch's aid. At one point the furious McCulloch hit his partner in crime across the back of the head with the flat of the axe blade.

By this time, Mone had picked up the garden fork and jabbed and lunged until Simpson collapsed, blood flowing freely from his various wounds.

Mone then tried to disable Mr MacLellan by squirting the paint stripper in his face. The liquid had very little effect but by this time the nurse had been severely wounded by McCulloch, including a

181

deep gash on his throat, and he fell. McCulloch dropped down on top of him in a frenzied attack, still stabbing and cutting and slashing.

Neither Mr MacLellan nor Ian Simpson were in any condition to resist any further and so the two men left them alone. For the moment.

Mone cut the wires of both the internal and external phones while McCulloch gathered up their equipment. Pushing the items they needed into Mone's arms, McCulloch told him to wait outside the door and keep watch.

Then he went back into the office and finished the job he had started on Mr MacLellan and Ian Simpson. Siezing the axe, he beat them continuously on the back of the head until they were both dead. Simpson's ears were completely separated from his body.

Then he cut Mr MacLellan's keys from his belt, opened the safe and took out a large fire axe before he went back outside to Mone's side.

The two men then put on the obsolete nurse's caps which they had stolen from the drama group's prop box, checked their false beards and moustaches were in place and walked across the brightly lit area near west wing to a dark section of open ground near the perimeter fence.

Using the rope ladder, they climbed over the fence, managing to get over the barbed wire without using the canvas sheet they had brought with them. Then they crossed the railway line and ran across some fields towards Carstairs Junction, slipping into the icy blackness of the November night.

It was approximately 6.30 p.m.

Mone and McCulloch were free for almost half an hour before the first body was discovered. But it would be closer to an hour before the siren would be sounded.

At about 6.45 p.m., while further violence was taking place on the road outside the hospital, Mrs Hamilton telephoned one of the wards to see who among the patients had expressed a desire to attend the Christmas festivities. The ward in question was the one which normally housed Ian Simpson and the charge nurse there did not know if the patient wanted to go to the party so he tried phoning the social club office. But there was no reply.

The charge nurse phoned Mrs Hamilton back and asked her to keep ringing the social club on an outside line while he continued on the internal system.

There was still no answer.

Sensing that something was wrong, he sent a pupil nurse to the social club. The young man found Mr MacLellan's mutilated body lying in a pool of blood in the corridor. There was more blood smeared up the walls. Assuming that the three patients known to have been with the murdered nurse had all escaped, he ran back to his ward and told his superior.

The charge nurse then made a serious mistake. Instead of informing the central office and the gatehouse of the escape he alerted all the other wards, telling staff to lock their patients in. He also sent staff to the social club.

It was left to the two nurses sent to the social club to call the gate-house to ask for a doctor and also report to the officer in charge of central office, telling him that Mr MacLellan had been killed and that Simpson, Mone and McCulloch had escaped.

A few minutes later they found Simpson's body behind the office door. By that time, police were in the gatehouse, investigating a third murder.

The escapees had decided to make their escape bid between 6.00 p.m. and 6.30 p.m. because Mone had earlier determined that that was when traffic was at its heaviest on the road which runs through the hospital.

It was about 6.40 p.m. when they saw the twin beams of a car's headlights piercing the darkness up ahead. Mone lay down on the road and McCulloch, wearing his false beard, moustache and nurse's cap, flagged the car down with a torch. He told the driver, Mr Robert McCallum, that there had been an accident.

Mr McCallum climbed out of his car to see if he could help. The heavily armed McCulloch, who had already killed two men, stood beside the driver, the darkness broken only by the car's headlights and McCulloch's lamp. Mr McCallum was in danger of becoming victim number three . . . but then a police car on routine patrol appeared on the road.

The panda car pulled up a few yards away from the group and Constables George Taylor and John Gillies climbed out to see what was wrong.

McCulloch was exceedingly nervous now and demanded that Mr McCallum give him and the 'injured' man a lift.

The police officers were walking towards them.

Mr McCallum ignored the so-called nurse's demands, calling out to the approaching policemen that there had been an accident.

P.C. Taylor shone his torch on McCulloch's face . . .

That was when both patients went for him.

Mr McCallum immediately leaped into his car and drove off for help.

Meanwhile, McCulloch had seriously injured P.C. Taylor and Mone had threatened, and probably stabbed, P.C. Gillies. As the first policeman lay bleeding on the road, McCulloch, again wielding his home-made axe, turned on the second. Although badly wounded, Gillies managed to get away from the two men and jumped over the embankment at the side of the road, landing in a boggy ditch. The policeman sank into the thick mud and was unable to pull himself out for another four or five minutes.

However, by that time, everyone had gone – Mone and McCulloch in the police car, the dying P.C. Taylor staggering along the road. He later stumbled into the path of an approaching bus, was taken to a doctor's house nearby and then rushed to Law Hospital.

But it was too late. The policeman would later die from the savage wounds inflicted by both McCulloch and Mone.

Meanwhile, the terrified Mr McCallum had reached the gate-house and told the gatekeeper there that two nurses appeared to be fighting with policemen in the road. The gatekeeper did not completely believe the story but telephoned the police station at Carnwath all the same. The report was passed on to Lanark Headquarters. Just as P.C. Gillies was screaming into his radio that he and P.C. Taylor had been attacked. It was 6.45 p.m.

Still no alarm had been raised at the hospital, and when the gatekeeper saw a panda car speeding by his window a few minutes later he assumed that any trouble had been taken care of and thought nothing more if it. But that police car was being driven by McCulloch and Mone, who were speeding away from the scene of the third killing.

Ten minutes later, Detective Sergeant Mortimer, who was investigating the attack on the two police officers and who still knew nothing of the murders in the social club, telephoned Carstairs from Lanark to ask if any patients had escaped. A check was made on all beds, a process that took about ten minutes.

Meanwhile, the pupil nurse was on his way to the social club where he would make his gory discovery.

By 6.55 p.m., P.C. MacKillop from Carnwath had visited the scene of the attack and found a knife, the two nurse's hats and an NHS card bearing the name of a patient who was still in the hospital's Ochil Ward. Why this card was found at the scene of the policeman's murder was never discovered.

Just before 7.10 p.m., D.S. Mortimer and the wounded P.C. Gillies had arrived at the gatehouse. The report of the escape was a few minutes away yet and so the hospital siren had still not been sounded.

Surprisingly, none of the police officers in the gatehouse at the time were informed of the murders in the social club. D.S. Mortimer eventually heard the news from another police officer, who had been told by a member of the nursing staff and had in fact taken it upon himself to go to the social club to investigate.

Finally, at 7.25 p.m. – after the principal nursing officer had been phoned by both *The Scotsman* and the BBC looking for information about the attack on the police officers and possible links to the hospital – the siren was sounded.

And all the while, Mone and McCulloch were getting further away.

Being the only one of the two who could drive, McCulloch took the wheel of the stolen police car. However, he did not have a licence and his driving skills were rough to say the least.

The inexperienced driver managed to speed through the village of Carnwath to the Melbourne Junction of the A721 and A702, about ten miles away. The road was icy and McCulloch was having great difficulty in steering the car. Finally, he lost control altogether and the vehicle skidded and careered off the road into an embankment.

The accident was witnessed by William Lennon and Thomas McIlroy who were travelling along the same road in a Motherwell Bridge Steelworks van. They stopped and got out to see if they could help what they thought were two policemen in trouble.

The two men were attacked by Mone and McCulloch. One was struck on the back of the head and the other stabbed. Both men were thrown unceremoniously into the back of the van and McCulloch again climbed into the driver's seat.

He drove at breakneck speed down the A702, passing through the town of Biggar and the village of Lamington until he once again left the road near Roberton. He had taken fright when he saw what he believed was a police light up ahead, stopped and, when trying to reverse, backed into a boggy field. The van's wheels spun uselessly in the thick mud and the men were again forced to abandon their vehicle, leaving the two injured men in the back. They would later be found by police and would recover from their wounds. The light that had panicked him turned out to be a railway signal.

The River Clyde is little more than a stream as it runs through Roberton and the two men waded across the cold waters to Townhead Farm.

Farmer Rennie Craig opened his door to find the two desperate and dangerous men, brandishing a knife and an axe, on his doorstep. They pushed their way into the house, ripping the telephone out of its connection on the wall.

As his wife Catherine and three of their children huddled together in terror, Mr Craig was forced to hand over the keys of his gold-coloured Austin Maxi.

But the phone they had disabled was only an extension and, unknown to the murderous duo, the farmer's twelve-year-old daughter had slipped into a back room and phoned the police.

It was 7.25 p.m. At Carstairs, over twenty-five miles away, the siren had just been sounded. The men sped off south towards Carlisle. This time, thanks to the young girl's telephone call, police were in hot pursuit.

The Maxi was spotted on the A74 near Dumfries and again at Beattock Summit. Two van loads of armed police chased them at high speed until the men crossed the border at Gretna. Here the Scottish officers had to stop – but the pursuit was taken up by similarly armed police from the Cumbrian force.

Finally, three hours after their escape and ninety miles away from the scene of their murders, the fleeing mental patients were forced off the road by a police car which rammed them at Roundabout 43, near Carlisle.

McCulloch and Mone were no doubt tempted to fight it out. Amazingly, they even tried to hijack another car but this time the odds were too great. After a brief struggle, the two killers were back in custody. Police found the fire axe and a knife in their possession and Mone claimed McCulloch had gone 'berserk'. McCulloch admitted using the axe.

It was 9.14 p.m. The long, bloody night was over.

Almost immediately after the escape, the 245-strong staff at Carstairs demanded that internal security at the hospital be tightened. They also called for a public enquiry into the affair, threatening to take strike action if their demands were not met.

Sheriff Principal R. Reid headed the enquiry and made a number of recommendations in his report, published in October 1977, that would help tighten security in the hospital. Early in 1978 the

Secretary of State for Scotland announced that almost £2 million was to be spent in upgrading security, including a new internal perimeter fence and a floodlighting system which would bathe the entire hospital in light at night. But the changes came too late to help the three men who had been hacked to death.

More than 1000 officers from prisons, police forces and state mental institutions attended the funeral of Nursing Officer McLellan in Carnwath Parish Church on Friday, 3 December 1976. The church building itself was not big enough to hold the crowd and so hundreds stood outside during the service.

As pipers played a plaintive lament, the mourners walked the mile or so to the cemetery where the coffin was lowered into the ground.

Mr McLellan left a widow and a twenty-year-old son.

Many of the mourners then travelled by coach to Glasgow where P.C. George Taylor was to be cremated in Daldowie Crematorium. He also left a wife and had four children.

Ian Simpson was buried in Coatbridge on Saturday, 4 December.

McCulloch and Mone were tried in Edinburgh High Court in February 1977. McCulloch had pled guilty to three charges of murder and three charges of attempted murder, while Mone pled guilty to the murder of P.C. Taylor. His plea of Not Guilty to the murders of both Mr McLellan and Ian Simpson were accepted by the Crown.

Psychiatrists had testified that the two men were fully responsible for their actions, were sane and fit to plead. It was pointed out though that McCulloch had a severe psychopathic disorder and, although being deemed untreatable by doctors, he appeared to be making satisfactory progress. The sheriff's report determined that the actual process of making the weapons had either 'aroused or renewed in McCulloch a homicidal intention' that may well have led to murder even if he had met no resistance during the escape attempt.

Mone, who was the self-confessed mastermind of the escape but who believed that they could break out without resorting to violence, also suffered from a psychopathic disorder but was making very slow progress.

On Friday, 28 February 1977, both Mone and McCulloch were sentenced to spend the rest of their lives in prison.

On passing sentence, Lord Dunpark said: 'I will recommend that you are not to be released from prison unless and until the authorities are satisfied, if ever, that you have ceased to be a danger to the public.

'It is plainly no obvious case of mindless murder. You hatched a plot to leave Carstairs and you were determined to succeed even if you had to kill to do it.'

It is doubtful if either of them will ever be released from prison.

Chapter Fourteen

THE DEMON BUTLER

The manager of the North Berwick hotel did not like the look of the two men. They had arrived in the town, perched on the mouth of the Firth of Forth, on Monday, 16 January 1978, and registered under the name Ponton at the Blenheim House Hotel.

But there was something suspicious about them. Something not quite right. Manager Norman Wight felt the 'two characters did not seem to be ordinary travellers'. At best he felt they might be conmen, intending to stay the night and skip without paying their bill; their habit of charging drinks to their bill only heightened his suspicions.

At worst . . . well, there had been a great deal of publicity about the murders of Christine Eadie and Helen Scott near Edinburgh. The bodies had been discovered in October the previous year but the killer – or killers – had not been caught. He did not know it but his second, more sinister, fear was closer to the truth.

That night, as the two men sat down to dinner, Mr Wight phoned the police and told them of his suspicions. They sent a police car to the hotel and a young P.C. checked the registration number of their Ford Granada, parked in the hotel car park. It turned out that it was in fact registered to a Ford Escort. The tax disc was also faked. Clearly, the two men were far from innocent.

The men were approached as they enjoyed an after-dinner brandy and were invited politely to the police station for questioning. Meanwhile, Mr Wight was searching their rooms at the request of the police. He found an envelope containing seventy-six silver Edwardian coins, which the police soon realised was part of the loot stolen from the London home of a former Labour MP in December. Neither the eighty-two-year-old ex-MP nor his wife had been seen since the robbery. Their butler had told neighbours that they were on holiday in Italy.

Meanwhile, a police officer had made a more frightening discovery in the boot of the car . . . the body of a man, his thumbs tied together behind his back. And he had drowned.

Obviously, there were questions that needed answering by the two men. But by that time, one of them had escaped.

The man who made his bid for freedom on that snowy winter's night in 1978 was fifty-four-year-old Archibald Hall, thief, conman and, ultimately, murderer.

Born on 17 June 1924 in McLean Street, Partick in Glasgow, Hall early on in life displayed the two characteristics which would later help him in his criminal career: as a boy he was fastidiously clean, and he showed a taste for the high life. The former was exemplified by his near-pathological need to wash his hands several times a day, the latter by his fondness for eating and staying in the best hotels. He was introduced to this luxury by an older woman to whom he lost his virginity at sixteen years of age. The woman would treat him to meals in expensive hotels and he saw that there was more to life than dirty city streets and tenements.

He began his criminal career in his teens. He befriended, then robbed, an old lady who obviously did not believe in banks and who kept thousands of pounds in suitcases in her home; and he defrauded the Red Cross by making collections in two areas of the city, one wealthy, one a slum district. He used two tins for these collections, keeping the contents of the one filled by the well-off folk to himself.

He went to prison – on a theft charge – for the first time when he was seventeen and again, for housebreaking, when he was nineteen. In 1944, he received another two years for housebreaking and in 1947 wound up in London, but was soon in court on a forgery charge. For that he was given another two years.

In addition to his criminal apprenticeship, he became an admirer of the writings and teachings of Aleister Crowley, the occultist who claimed to be the Devil's emissary on earth and styled himself as the Great Beast 666.

Meanwhile, he carefully cultivated his appearance and poise until he was able to pass himself off in the highest society. He was suave, polite and even engaging, his quick wit and obvious talent for play-acting coming in handy when he decided to turn from the coarse and vulgar world of the small-time criminal to the glittering stage of the confidence trickster.

In 1951 he talked his way into a job as a butler with a wealthy Stirlingshire family. At one point, when they were on holiday, Hall opened their mail and found an invitation to a garden party at Holyrood Palace in Edinburgh. This was too good an opportunity to miss. Wearing a hired dress suit and driving the family Bentley he attended the party in his owner's stead. On the way home he browsed through an antique shop, talking to the owner. Then he robbed her.

Ultimately though, his past caught up with him and the local police informed his employer of his criminal activities. Hall tried to pretend that he was endeavouring to go straight but eventually had to tender his resignation.

He showed an audaciousness in some of his crimes that is almost admirable. Once he posed as a wealthy Arab prince, staining his skin with walnut juice. Arriving in a borrowed Rolls Royce, he booked a suite of rooms in a plush London hotel and ordered that a number of top jewellers come to see him with their finest products.

While the jewellers stood in the living-room, Hall hid in the bathroom, occasionally stretching one hand out to snatch what he could from the nearest displays.

Eventually the jewellers grew tired of waiting for him and knocked on the bathroom door. When there was no answer they opened it themselves to see a pile of discarded Arab robes on the floor and a door leading to the hallway lying wide open. Naturally, there was no sign of their gems.

But, in 1956, the law caught up with him and Hall was sent to Parkhurst on sentences totalling thirty years. It was during his seven years in the Isle of Wight prison that he shared a cell with fellow Glaswegian Paddy Meehan and the impressionable Lancashire-born James Griffiths. The latter was so in awe of Hall's impeccable manners and his airs-and-graces that he would try desperately to emulate him. Griffiths was also impressed by the stories the two Scots told of their native city and decided to move his base of operations to Glasgow, culminating in the shoot-out in the city streets in July, 1969 (see Chapter Twelve).

Between then and 1977, Hall's life followed a regular pattern of prison, theft and back to prison. In the mid-sixties he escaped from a jail near Lowestoft in Norfolk and when caught was sentenced to a further five years on top of the ten he had already received for jewel robbery.

In 1972, just after being paroled, he met and married Ruth Holmes in London. After a few weeks he decided that married life was not for him and packed his bags. He could not accept the responsibility of sharing his life with someone else and disliked the feeling of being tied down. He was not long without female company however: he immediately rekindled a somewhat passionate affair with widow Hazel Paterson.

Finally, it was his friendship with another ex-convict which led him to commit his first murder.

David Wright came to stay with Hall, who was then a butler for Lady Mary Hudson on her Kirkleton estate near Waterbeck in Dumfriesshire. He used the name Roy Fontaine, his favourite alias. Telling her that Wright was his nephew, Hall asked his employer, the widow of former Tory MP Sir Anthony Hudson, if she would give Wright a job on the estate. Lady Hudson did not offer the man employment, although she did give him a place to stay on the grounds and a few odd jobs to do.

At long last Hall appeared to be settling down. He had spent many long years behind bars and, even when he was free, he was often just one step away from the law. Of course, he could just have been pausing for a breath – later evidence suggested that he was in fact planning 'a job' – but to all intents and purposes he really seemed to be making a fair attempt at going straight.

Wright, a petty thief, had other plans. He felt that it would be foolhardy to pass up the chance of lifting some of the loot in the big house. Hall refused and so Wright decided to strike out on his own, stealing a silver tray and a ring.

Hall was furious when the theft was discovered and confronted his so-called friend, who promptly denied that he was responsible. Hall did not believe him and made enquiries, talking to a girlfriend of Wright's to whom the thief had given the ring. Hall returned the item to Lady's Hudson's jewel box.

Wright was none too pleased at Hall's interference and one night when Lady Hudson was away from home, he broke into her wine cellar, drank himself some courage and threatened the butler with a rifle. The silver-tongued conman talked the drunken petty thief into giving up the weapon, promising that the two of them would indeed rob Her Ladyship. Wright was suitably mollified and agreed to go to bed – but not before he had fired one shot into Hall's headboard and split the butler's face open with the barrel of the rifle.

But Hall had no intention of being forced into stealing from Lady Hudson. The following day, he and Wright went rabbit shooting on the grounds of the estate. When he was sure that the younger man was out of ammunition, Hall shot him three times in the head and buried him in a shallow grave in Pokeskinesike Burn, half a mile from Kirkleton House.

He would return to the grave site many times during the next week, constantly improving the makeshift tomb. He would often take Lady Hudson's gundog, Tessa, who had formed an attachment to Wright. If the dog was able to lead him to the grave then Hall knew it was incomplete. He did not give up until he had approached the grave from all directions and Tessa could not find it.

When Lady Hudson returned from her trip, Hall told her that Wright had found himself a job in Cornwall and had left. She had no reason to disbelieve her butler and thought nothing more of the man.

However, Hall's days in her employment were numbered. In September 1977 Lady Hudson received a telephone call from a man who claimed to be a detective, telling her of the man's criminal record. The information only confirmed her suspicions – on a number of occasions she had overheard Hall on the phone talking about 'a job'. The phone call was not from a detective. It was, in fact, the eighteen-year-old son of one of Hall's jilted girlfriends.

Hall was dismissed immediately and he returned to London. A few months later he took up employment with Captain Walter Scott-Elliott and his wife Dorothy in their Knightsbridge flat.

Captain Scott-Elliott was a former Labour MP whose family had been lairds of a Dumfriesshire estate near the home of Lady Hudson for 400 years. However, he had upset many of the local landowners during an election campaign when he rallied support from among the land workers who complained of threats of reprisals from their employees if they did not vote Conservative. Scott-Elliott promised to raise the matter in parliament – thus outraging his neighbours.

The captain had received his commission during the First World War while serving with the Coldstream Guards. He retired from military service in 1919 and before going into politics was the managing director of East India Merchants.

During World War Two he served in the Ministry of Labour, while in the years 1946–47 he was parliamentary private secretary to the Secretary of State for War. However, it was just before the Second World War that he hit the nation's headlines following a love affair with Austrian Baroness Marie Alice Von Groeller, working in her country's embassy as a secretary.

Following the *anschluss* of 1938, when Germany invaded and annexed Austria, the Baroness found herself in danger. Her new masters knew of her anti-Nazi sympathies and viewed her romantic entanglement with an influential British ex-army officer with some suspicion. When she refused to return to Austria, they threatened to drug the woman and smuggle her out of the country in a diplomatic bag. Captain Scott-Elliott saved the woman's life by visiting her at all hours of the day and night to ensure that she was well.

The couple were married in May 1939 but the marriage failed eight years later, ending in divorce. It may well have been only a marriage of convenience to save the Baroness's life and allow her to remain in Britain during the war.

In 1948, the captain married his second wife, Dorothy. Over the years he built on his family fortune quite considerably. In addition to the houses in Dumfriesshire and Knightsbridge, the Scott-Elliotts had property in Rome and Nice.

In November 1977 he hired Archibald Hall as his butler. By the end of the year, both he and his wife would be dead, their bodies dumped in lonely spots in the Scottish Highlands. But, before that, another principal character would enter this 'strange and sombre tale'.

Michael Kitto was introduced to Hall in a London pub by 'Irish Mary' Coggle, a lover of the suave conman who also worked part-time for the Scott-Elliotts. At the time, thirty-nine-year-old Kitto was on the run from the police, having made off with £1000 from a pub in which he had worked as a barman. He had been staying in a variety of hotels and had very soon ran out of cash. As their friendship developed, the two began to discuss potential criminal enterprises – particularly robbing the Sloane Street home of Walter Scott-Elliott and his wife.

Hall was of the opinion that it was a two-man job: Kitto was to break in and take what he could while the butler stayed in the owner's employ, laying the groundwork for a more subtle fraud.

On 8 December 1977, Hall took his new partner back to the flat to study the lay-out of the various rooms. They did not expect to be disturbed: Mrs Scott-Elliott was in a nursing home and the eighty-two-year-old captain would be sound asleep, having taken his customary dose of sleeping pills.

But the sixty-year-old Dorothy Scott-Elliott was not in the nursing home and she surprised the two would-be thieves as they cased the house's bedrooms. She immediately guessed what was going on and would have raised the alarm if Hall had not roughly thrown her to the floor and, while Kitto held her, pushed a pillow over her face, pressing down hard. Eventually, the woman's jerking body became still. Hall removed the pillow and felt for a pulse. There was no pulse: he had claimed his second victim.

Mrs Scott-Elliott's body was hastily placed in her bed, the covers pulled up over her to make it look as if she were asleep should her husband awaken. The captain did indeed get up, and asked his butler what was the cause of the noise he had heard. Hall told him that Mrs Scott-Elliott had been having a nightmare but was all right now. The elderly man, heavily drugged from his sleeping pills, accepted the story and went back to his own room.

The following day, while Mr Walter Scott-Elliott was out, Mary Coggle was recruited to pose as the murdered woman and accept delivery of a hired car and that night, after they had doped the captain with his own sleeping pills, they wrapped the corpse in a blanket and threw it into the boot. Then the four of them – Hall, Kitto, the drugged Captain Scott-Elliott and Mary Coggle, still posing as the old man's wife – drove north.

They stayed that night in a cottage in Newton Arlosh, fifteen miles from Carlisle, before heading into Scotland, where they threw Mrs Scott-Elliot's body into a ditch near Comrie in Perthshire.

They also stayed at the Tilt Hotel in Blair Atholl, posing as 'The Scott Party'. Then they carried on to Inverness-shire where Hall and Kitto left the old man, who was so doped up that he really did not know what was happening, and his 'wife' in a hotel while they returned to London to dispose of some of the stolen goods.

When they finally returned to Inverness-shire, having stayed again at the rented cottage in Cumberland and the Tilt Hotel, Hall and Kitto had come to a decision regarding the poor confused ex-MP.

'This time we finally decided that the old man had to go,' said Kitto later.

It was in Glen Affric, one of the loneliest glens in Inverness-shire, that the old man was allowed out of the car to urinate. He walked unsteadily into a clump of trees, followed by both Hall and Kitto. 'We strangled him,' said Kitto. 'We took him into the bushes and strangled him.'

But the old man showed surprising strength and fought back fiercely. At one point, Hall held the old man down in the heather by pressing the sole of his foot on to his windpipe and ordered Kitto to beat him to death with the shovel they were going to use to dig a grave. Kitto did as he was told.

They hid the body in a clump of rhododendron bushes thirty feet below an old stone bridge, just west of Guisachan House on the Tomich to Cougie road.

Mary Coggle sat in the car throughout the murder. She knew what they were doing, but did not care.

As they made their way back to the car, Hall and Kitto were seen by a couple out walking. The woman, quite properly, described them as 'evil looking creatures' to her husband. She did not know then just how evil they were.

The three stayed that night in Inverness and then headed for Edinburgh. But all was not well between them. Mary Coggle was tiring of the fresh Scottish Highlands and wanted to go back to London. There was, however, a problem – she wanted to keep the £3000 mink coat and jewellery that Hall had given to her to complete her disguise as Mrs Scott-Elliott.

Neither Hall nor Kitto thought this was a good idea. Irish Mary was hardly the type of woman to own such an expensive item. They felt she would attract undue attention. Coggle, however, was adamant.

They stayed overnight in Hall's rented cottage in Newton Arlosh on 17 December, where Hall suggested that the coat be burnt. Coggle would hear nothing of it and so Hall picked up a heavy poker and battered his lover on the back of the head. In a replay of the murder of Mrs Scott-Elliott, Kitto held the woman down while Hall attacked her, beating her with the poker and finally tying a plastic bag over her head and suffocating her to death. After tying her hands and feet together, the two men went off to the local pub for a drink.

The following day, they left the body in the Black Burn near Middlebie in Dumfriesshire, not far from the A74 Glasgow to Carlisle road and only a few miles from the country estate where Hall had first murdered and then buried David Wright.

And then there were two.

Returning again to London over the Christmas and New Year period, Hall and Kitto cleared the Scott-Elliott's Sloane Street home of all the antiques, porcelain, jewellery and cash they could. In January 1978 they met Hall's younger brother Donald, a petty thief who had just been released from Perth Prison for sexually assaulting litle girls.

Donald was the complete opposite of his older brother. Where Archibald was cultured, intelligent and strong-willed, Donald was coarse, stupid and weak. Gradually, he began to wonder where his brother and Kitto had raised the money they were spending so freely. He questioned the two men constantly, accompanying them back to the Newton Arlosh cottage, collecting new number plates for their car on the way.

Gradually, Donald became something of an irritation, if not a danger. He would have to go.

In the cottage, Donald rather stupidly showed the men the best way to tie someone up with six inches of string. He asked them to tie his thumbs together behind his back. As he lay face down on the floor, he then instructed them to push his feet between his wrists, to show them that he was unable to move from the position.

Hall was not one to ignore such a golden opportunity. While his brother lay on the floor, his back arched, his hands and feet immobile, Hall thrust a wedge of padding impregnated with chloroform over Donald's face. Struggling violently against the two men, Donald managed to do what he claimed he could not – free his legs. However, they were too strong for him and he soon slumped into unconsciousness.

The two killers then carried his comatose body to the bathroom and placed him into a bathful of water, holding him down until he drowned.

Once again they were two.

The body tucked away in the boot of the car, Hall and Kitto again returned to Scotland. They had already used the country as their own personal cemetery and saw no reason why they should not dispose of Donald's corpse in the same way. However, they had not reckoned on the ferocity of a Scottish winter and found themselves in the middle of a blizzard, with the ground so frozen that they could not sink their spade into the earth.

They decided to spend the night in a hotel, booking in at the Blenheim House Hotel where, thanks to the suspicious owner, the law caught up with them.

At the time, of course, the police thought they were dealing with nothing more than a pair of car thieves. It was not until Mr Wight uncovered the stolen coins in Kitto's room and the constable made his own startling discovery in the car boot that they realised that they had stumbled into something a great deal more sinister.

Kitto, who had given the name Blackmore to the police, proved to be an ideal prisoner, telling them everything they wanted to know, even voicing his fear that he would have been next on Hall's hit list as the man fully covered his murderous tracks. Hall, however, proved a bit more troublesome. To start with, he managed to escape from the police station.

Early on in the questioning – before Donald's body was found – he had asked to go to the toilet. The police allowed him to go unaccompanied and the enterprising conman-turned-killer squeezed out of the small window, cheekily leaving a one pound note on the cistern.

Once outside, he flagged down the car of a female gym teacher. The charm with which he captivated females all his life did not fail him under pressure. He convinced her his car had broken down and talked her into driving him to the nearest taxi rank. The teacher did more than that – she drove him to the home of a local taxi driver.

Hall told the man that he was trying to get to Dunbar where his wife had been taken into hospital after being involved in an accident. The taxi driver drove him to the east coast town where Hall actually went into the hospital and then returned, saying that his wife had been transferred to Edinburgh Royal Infirmary.

It was on the way to the capital that Hall's luck finally ran out for good: the taxi was stopped by a police roadblock at Wallyford Roundabout on the A1.

Back in North Berwick, Kitto was pouring his heart out to police officers. While being interviewed by Detective Inspector Thomas Maclean of Lothian and Borders police, he said: 'You might not believe it, but there is another three bodies I want to tell you about.'

He then went on to tell them all about the murders of Mr and Mrs Scott-Elliott and Mary Coggle – and where the bodies were buried. The police already knew about Mary Coggle. Her corpse had been found just before Christmas and, although unidentified, buried in Annan Cemetery.

However, Kitto's directions to the makeshift graves of Hall's erstwhile employers were sketchy. Attempts to find the bodies were further hampered by heavy snows and deep snowdrifts.

It was the largest murder hunt in Scotland for twenty years. Hundreds of police searched Glen Affric and the area around Braco and Comrie in Perthshire. Cumbrian officers also converged on the cottage at Newton Arlosh.

They found Walter Scott-Elliott's body on Wednesday, 18 January. It was badly decomposed and had been savaged by wild animals. However, his wife's burial site was proving more difficult to pinpoint. Kitto had told police that it was on a small, little-used road near a power station close by Comrie or Braco. Police officers had dug up the snow-covered ground in the area and searched alongside the dry-stane walls which bordered various roads but had found nothing.

Lisa and Dorie, tracker dogs specially trained to find people lost in snow drifts, were brought in from Lancashire to help in the search. The dogs had helped in the massive search for the missing Mrs Renee Macrae and her son who had disappeared in 1976 – a mystery that remains unsolved to this day.

Finally, at lunchtime on Sunday, 22 January, the corpse was found in a stream at the side of a small road between Comrie and

Dalchonzie power station. Mrs Scott-Elliott was lying face up in the shallow water, half covered with leaves and twigs.

Meanwhile, Hall had also been talking to the police, surprising detectives with news of the killing they knew nothing about.

'For starters,' he said, 'you had better phone Dumfries about one that no one knows about. A guy called David Wright is buried in the forest near Lady Hudson's place. I shot him in the head.'

So while police were searching the Highlands, the Dumfriesshire constabulary sent fifty men and tracker dogs to comb the Kirkleton Estate, finally coming across a man's bare foot protruding from the snow in a freshly planted wood.

Hall may have been co-operating but he was still determined to avoid another spell in prison. He had managed to hide a bottle of tranquillisers from the police and on Wednesday, 18 January, he attempted suicide. He was rushed from the Lothian and Borders police headquarters in Edinburgh's Fettes Avenue to the Royal Infirmary where his stomach was pumped.

The media, meanwhile, were told that he had taken ill with a 'stomach complaint'.

While Hall and Kitto awaited trial, the *Daily Mail* published a report of the murders that Hall's solicitor claimed was prejudicial to his case. He wanted the newspaper to be cited for contempt while also hoping that the charges would be dropped against his client.

There was a precedent for this tactic. In November 1977, the day before the trial of an Edinburgh nursing sister accused of serious assault, London Weekend's *Weekend World* programme broadcast a report on the case. Defence counsel argued that this broadcast prevented their client from receiving a fair and unprejudiced hearing and the trial was abandoned, the charges against the woman withdrawn by the Crown. In January 1978, LWT and three staff members were fined a total of £61,000 for contempt.

The charges against Archibald Hall and Michael Kitto were not dropped and, in Edinburgh's High Court on 2 May 1978, Hall and Kitto were both sentenced to life imprisonment.

Although he had been certified as insane when he was younger, Hall was deemed sane and fit to plead. He did, however, suffer from a psychopathic personality disorder and showed no shame or concern for his victims.

Hall and Kitto had pled guilty to the various Scottish charges and the judge, Lord Wylie, told the court that he had been urged not to fix a minimum sentence on either of them, pending their appearance in England on the charges of murdering Mrs Scott-Elliott, Mary Coggle and Donald Hall.

'Certainly in the case of you, Hall, the circumstances seem to me to indicate that it would be appropriate to make a recommendation and I propose to exercise it,' Lord Wylie said. He then ruled that Hall should serve at least fifteen years. He made no recommendation in the case of Michael Kitto.

As the sentences were announced, Hall and Kitto attempted to put on brave faces. Hall plastered a smile across his fleshy features while Kitto nodded to the scribble of reporters in the press box.

After the trial, Hazel Paterson, the widow with whom he had enjoyed a torrid affair in London, proclaimed undying love for the multiple killer.

'I still love him and I will wait for him no matter how long it is,' she told the press. 'Anything I can do to ease his pain I will. He must be punished for what he did but if he realises someone is prepared to forgive then it might help him.'

Ruth Holmes, his ex-wife, visited him in Edinburgh's Saughton Prison before his trial. She was shocked at how much he had changed.

'Gone was the charmer of yesterday,' she said. In his place was a haggard and washed-out individual, 'a finished man', she said.

On Wednesday, 1 November 1978, an Old Bailey judge sentenced Hall to another term of life imprisonment for the murders committed on English soil, with the recommendation that he not be released unless in the case of serious infirmity.

The judge said he was satisfied that Kitto had merely followed Hall's lead. Nevertheless, he had played his part without demur and so he was sentenced to a minimum fifteen-year life sentence for the murder of Mary Coggle and the manslaughter of Donald Hall and Mrs Scott-Elliott.

As Hall took up residence in Wandsworth Prison, Aberdeen police announced that they were investigating his alleged involvement in the death of an unnamed American helicopter pilot working on the north-east coast.

The suspicion of murder was apparently raised by Hall himself in a letter to BBC Scotland. However, after exhaustive enquiries, police could find no report of a missing pilot, let alone another body.

And so the bizarre career of Archibald Hall, alias Roy Fontaine, had come to an end. Had it not been for his criminal leanings, this polished, intelligent Glaswegian might have made a highly successful businessman. At the very least, he could have been a damned fine butler.

Chapter Fifteen

THE CASANOVA
CONMAN

The far north coast of Scotland is an area of fiercely stunning beauty. Craggy hillsides sweep down to heather-covered moorland which in turn give way to bright golden sandy beaches, fringed with rocks and dunes. On a sunny day, with the sea sparkling a bright, clear blue you would be forgiven for believing you are on a tropical island.

It is a peaceful area totally devoid of the hustle and noise of Scotland's more popular coastal resorts. Even at the height of summer the beaches are never crowded and it is still possible to discover an empty, unspoiled stretch of sand.

In August 1989 that peace was rudely shattered when dozens of uniformed police supported by helicopters and tracker dogs converged on the Sutherland village of Tongue searching for a Glasgow woman who had vanished shortly after announcing her engagement to a charming Englishman called David Kerr.

On 25 August, after a two-day hunt, the brutally battered body of widow Margaret McOnie was found under a bush on a desolate stretch of moorland on the west side of the Kyle of Tongue. She had been dead for nine days.

But of David Kerr, the man who had proposed marriage to her after a whirlwind holiday romance, there was no sign.

David Kerr was also David Rodgers, Richard Grieves, Phil Kerr and Dr Stephen Barbour. In reality, they were all fifty-one-year-old Brian Newcombe, an unemployed motor mechanic from Huthwaite in Nottinghamshire who, in July and August 1989, left a trail of theft, fraud and murder stretching from Nottinghamshire to Tongue.

Newcombe was described by one of his neighbours in the Nottinghamshire village as a 'Billy Liar loner'. His life was filled with fantasy; he claimed that he was an ex-racing driver who was now a mechanic with Ferrari in Italy, or the personal assistant to Lotus chief Colin Chapman.

'He always had a flash car,' one neighbour recalled to reporters. 'You could've eaten your dinner off his engines, they were so clean.'

He was a smooth talker who believed he was God's gift to women. Telling them that he was wealthy and professing undying love, he conned them into parting with their cash and jewellery. And what he could not charm out of them, he stole.

On two occasions he turned to murder.

His final spree began in July 1989 when he slipped out of his ground-floor flat in Springwell Street, Huthwaite, just ahead of the police who wished to question him regarding the theft of several thousands of pounds from a number of heart-broken females. His wife, Penny, had left him only a few weeks before and was staying with relatives.

Between 18 and 25 July, Newcombe, using the alias Phil Kerr and claiming to be a wealthy New Zealander, stayed in a guest house in Salen, Isle of Mull, owned by sixty-six-year-old Eileen Samler, whose husband was off on a trip at the time. At first she did not want to let this unannounced stranger in, but he proved so charming and polite that she felt she could not refuse.

But she slept with a poker beside her bed just the same.

Mrs Samler introduced him to her friend Anne Wood, a thirty-eight-year-old divorcee. 'Phil' worked his magic on her, proposing marriage within hours, presenting her with a diamond ring stolen, unknown to Anne, from her best friend Mrs Samler.

After promising to take Anne and her thirteen-year-old daughter back with him to a new life in New Zealand, he disappeared, leaving the mother and daughter in the lurch in Oban. He took with him £35,000 worth of his landlady's jewels.

Newcombe fled back to England, staying in a number of boarding houses and hotels on the way and walking out without paying his bills.

On 3 August he was in the picturesque village of Ingleton in North Yorkshire, booking in at a local guest house. During his stay in the village Newcombe talked his way into the home of retired bus driver and ex-boxer Jack Shuttleworth, aged eighty-eight. The silver tongue that worked so well with women served him less well with another man and so Newcombe was forced to turn to more violent means to relieve the pensioner of his cash. He beat the old man to death and made off with £200 out of his wallet.

The bloodily battered body would lie undiscovered in a garden shed for a further two days, giving the killer time to escape back to Scotland.

And his second murder.

Widow Margaret McOnie had left her home in Sinclair Street, Milngavie, just north of Glasgow, on 6 August for a relaxing walking holiday in the north of Scotland. Her husband had died five years before and although she was an active member of the local Liberal Democrat party she was described as a slightly shy, lonely woman.

An ideal target for Brian Newcombe. They met between 6 and 10 August. He swept her off her feet, proposing marriage within days. On 11 August, Mrs McOnie phoned her daughter Sandra at home and told her that she had met this wonderful man called David Kerr and that they planned to get married.

Although delighted to hear her mother sounding so happy, Sandra tried to discourage her from leaping into marriage. But Mrs McOnie was bowled over by 'David', who, she said, was so like her first husband, Alex. She told her daughter that they were going to spend a few days on the Orkney Isles.

On 13 August, the couple booked into the Castle View guest house, Loyal Terrace, Tongue. Three days later, Mrs McOnie left the house with 'David' to go for a walk. She was never seen alive again.

At some point during the day of 16 August, 'David' crept up behind the unsuspecting woman and beat her to death, possibly with a rock. He then hid her body under some bracken near the old road that runs around the Kyle of Tongue to the village of Melness and not far from the more modern causeway that links the two shores.

Newcombe returned to the boarding house alone that night, telling the owner that Mrs McOnie had met some friends. He disappeared himself the following morning, as usual without paying his bill.

Four days later, Mrs McOnie's worried daughter reported her disappearance and the search was launched. A further four days after that, the widow's body was found.

By that time, Newcombe had scurried back down to England, leaving a stream of unpaid bills behind him.

Newcombe was now the most wanted man in Britain. Detectives had early on connected the two murders and officers from both the

Yorkshire and northern forces were working hand-in-hand to catch the killer before he struck again. As detectives travelled to the far north coast of Scotland to link up with colleagues investigating the murder of Mrs McOnie, they probably passed the killer on the road travelling in the other direction.

The man leading the hunt for the killer of Mr Shuttleworth, Detective Superintendent Ian Peacock, told the press that there was no doubt that the killer of Mrs McOnie was the same man 'we seek to eliminate in our enquiries'.

He continued: 'We wish to trace him and speak to him urgently.'

A description of the man was issued, saying that 'Evans' had black curling hair, greying at the temples. He also sometimes wore glasses to help correct a defect of the left eye.

However, as the search went on, detectives told pressmen that the suspect could probably change his appearance, simply by growing a beard or moustache and changing his hairstyle. Two photographs were eventually issued and printed in newspapers the length of the country.

Scottish police set up an incident room in Tongue's village hall, installing computer equipment, filing cabinets, desks and telephone lines. All activities planned for the hall were cancelled for the duration of the investigation, including a wedding reception booked for Saturday, 26 August. Police drove bride Helen Burr and her new husband Jeffrey Thompson, plus 106 guests, the fourteen miles to Bettyhill village hall, where the reception was now to be held.

The reception went off without a hitch, thanks to local hotels providing dishes and Farr primary school donating the tables. Superintendent Sandy MacGillivray, in charge of the Scottish inquiry, said that it was typical of the tremendous co-operation he and his team had received since they arrived in Tongue.

But the man they were looking for was long gone.

Newcombe himself had been in Bettyhill soon after the murder but had moved on after one night, leaving his bill unpaid as was his custom. He also left some old clothes in his room, and on the post bus which ran from Tongue to Lairg he left clothes belonging to Mrs McOnie.

On his way out of Bettyhill – having proposed to yet another woman in Tongue, sealing the bargain with a ring stolen from Margaret McOnie – Newcombe hitched a lift from a French couple touring the Highlands. The couple spoke very little English and witnesses later said that they did not seem to understand what Newcombe was saying most of the time. The trio booked into the

Smoo Cave Hotel in Durness, twenty-eight miles to the west of Tongue.

A compulsive talker, Newcombe found himself unable to maintain a low profile. He claimed to the owners that he was in the yachting business, buying and selling vessels throughout the world. He claimed that his own £65,000 yacht was moored off either the Isle of Skye or Mull.

Noticing that the hotel was up for sale – it had, in fact, only recently been sold – he insisted on leaving a cheque for £40,000 as a deposit on its purchase, telling the owner that his agent, Mrs McOnie, would be along later with the balance.

When he left with his new-found but totally unsuspecting French friends, Newcombe left a rucksack belonging to Mrs McOnie behind in his room.

A few days later, the news of Mrs McOnie's murder hit the front pages. Suspecting that Newcombe would attempt to leave the country with the couple, police placed every port, ferry terminal and airport in Britain on the alert. Photographs were issued to newspapers in the hope that the public would spot the man being dubbed 'the Casanova Conman' and help bring him to justice.

They were not disappointed. Newcombe was spotted in a variety of places between Yorkshire and the far north.

They also took the opportunity to warn the public that the man was dangerous, urging lorry drivers and motorists not to pick up any hitchhikers until he was caught. Detective Superintendent Peacock also urged Newcombe to bring the chase to an end.

'Give yourself up now,' he advised. 'Ring me personally. You have my word you will be treated fairly.'

But Newcombe paid no attention. He had left the French couple in Inverness, where he proposed to yet another woman, a tourist, continuing south alone, finally turning up in Morecambe on 21 August. Spending three days in the coastal resort, the cool, confident killer then travelled to Ambleside in the Lake District, where he booked himself into yet another guest house.

Landlady Helen Ireland of the village's Melrose Guest House said that the man turned up on her doorstep, looking for lodgings for four nights. However, she could only offer him two nights.

Mrs Ireland had not seen any of the photographs of the wanted man and described Newcombe as being 'nothing out of the ordinary'.

'He wasn't dishevelled,' she told reporters, 'he looked tidy and responsible. He was very pleasant and quite natural but he didn't have much to say for himself.'

It was a very different Newcombe from the loudmouthed braggart who had held court in the bar of the Smoo Cave Hotel in Durness a few days before.

When he left the Melrose Guest House he still owed £20 and left behind the clothes he had been wearing when he arrived. Mrs Ireland immediately informed the police, who now had another link in the chain.

On 26 August Newcombe stole a brown Colt Gallant in Bolton and was spotted in Derbyshire on his way back to Morecambe for another two days. While in the Lancashire resort he stole a cheque book issued by the Royal Bank of Scotland to a company called Utilidata Ltd. Hotel and guest house owners throughout the country were promptly warned to be on the lookout for a man trying to pass the cheques.

The theft of the car was a mistake.

From Morecambe he drove to Mansfield, only two miles from his home in Huthwaite. On the night of 29 August a passing police patrol car spotted the stolen car outside the town's Parkhurst Guest House.

Shortly after midnight, a cadre of police officers surrounded the hotel. Detectives crept stealthily up the stairs and then burst unexpectedly into his room. Newcombe was alone and he meekly allowed the officers to handcuff him.

'Thank God it's over,' he said as he was led away.

Newcombe confessed his crimes to his estranged wife while he was being held in Leeds' Armley Prison awaiting trial. Penny Newcombe said that he was bright and cheerful as he talked about the murders. He knew he was facing a thirty-year prison sentence and said that he planned to enrol in an Open University course.

A few weeks later he was dead. On 13 November, the double killer fashioned a rope out of his bedclothes and hung himself from the bars of his cell. His body was found a few minutes after midnight by a prison officer making a routine check.

Newcombe had left three notes, one to his wife, one to his mother and another to his solicitor. In the solicitor's letter, read out at the inquest on 13 December, he absolved the authorities from any blame, saying that they had treated him with kindness and consideration.

'They are blameless,' he wrote.

He also said: 'I take this decision to end my life with a clear and well-balanced mind. In fact, it has never been more clear.'

The Inquest jury finally decided that Newcombe killed himself because he could not face the guilt of being convicted of murder.

Detective Superintendent Peacock said later that Newcombe had not once shown any remorse for his actions.

'In twelve hours of interviews not once did he say he was sorry,' he said. 'They were matter-of-fact conversations in which he admitted killing two people.'

He added that he was not surprised that the man had killed himself.

Meanwhile, the residents of Huthwaite had objected strongly to the decision to bury the killer in their village. However, the local vicar pointed out that the wishes of the man's relatives had to be respected and the ceremony was allowed to proceed.

Finally, the daughter of murdered Margaret McOnie showed an understandable bitterness in an interview with the *Daily Record*, pointing out that Newcombe could choose the way he died but her mother, perhaps killed because she had learned too much about the man she knew as David Kerr, was not given such a choice.

'I hope that worm rots in hell,' she said.

Hell.

Newcombe is not alone there. We see their faces dimly through the smoke and the noxious fumes. They sit together in that one small corner that is forever Scotland – Manuel, Higgins, Merrett, Burke, Hare and the others.

It is getting crowded now but it is never full. There is always room for one more, always space for new recruits. And no shortage of volunteers . . .

BIBLIOGRAPHY

Bailey, Brian, *Hangmen of England* (W. H. Allen) 1989.

Boyle, Jimmy, *A Sense of Freedom* (Pan) 1977.

Fido, Martin, *Bodysnatchers: A History Of The Resurrectionists* (Weidenfeld & Nicolson) 1988.

Forbes, George, and Meehan, Paddy, *Such Bad Company* (Paul Harris) 1982.

Garvie, Sheila *Married To Murder* (Chambers) 1980.

Gaute, J. H. H., and Odell, Robin, *Murder Whatdunnit* (Pan) 1982.

Gaute, J. H. H., and Odell, Robin, *Murder Wheredunnit* (Harrap) 1986.

Gaute, J. H. H., and Odell, Robin, *Murderer Who's Who* (Harrap) 1989.

Glaister, Professor John, *Final Diagnosis* (1964).

Hall, Angus, *The Crimebusters* (ed) (Treasure Press) 1976.

Hodge, Harry and James, *Famous Trials* (eds) selected by John Mortimer (Penguin) 1984.

Horan, Martin, *Scottish Executions, Assassinations and Murders* (Chambers) 1990.

Rumbelow, Donald, *The Complete Jack The Ripper* (W. H. Allen) 1975.

Simpson, Keith, *Forty Years Of Murder* (Harrap) 1978.

Smith, Sir Sydney, *Mostly Murder* (Harrap) 1959.

Wilson, Colin, *The Psychic Detectives* (Pan) 1984.

Wilson, Colin, and Seaman, Donald, *The Encyclopaedia Of Modern Murder* (Arthur Barker) 1983.

Winn, Dilys, *Murder Ink* (Westbridge Books) 1977.